ELEMENTARY READING TODAY

ELEMENTARY READING TODAY
Selected Articles

WILMA H. MILLER ILLINOIS STATE UNIVERSITY

HOLT, RINEHART AND WINSTON, INC.

New York Chicago San Francisco Atlanta Dallas
Montreal Toronto London Sydney

Copyright © 1972 by Holt, Rinehart and Winston, Inc.
All rights reserved
Library of Congress Catalog Card Number: 70–160669
ISBN: 0–03–085031–2
Printed in the United States of America
2 3 4 5   090   9 8 7 6 5 4 3 2 1

To my mother, RUTH KARIN MILLER

Preface

It is imperative that both prospective and in-service elementary teachers receive the best possible instruction in the teaching of reading. Good reading ability is the cornerstone of school achievement, and elementary reading must be presented so that each student may experience his maximum possible success. Countless cases of reading disability may be effectively prevented if elementary teachers possess the knowledge and attitudes necessary to teach reading effectively.

This book of readings was compiled to meet the needs of both preservice and in-service elementary teachers of reading. It was designed to supplement the author's textbook, *The First R: Elementary Reading Today*. This book of readings contains the same major divisions that are presented in the textbook. This enables the reader to easily locate additional material on any of the topics presented in the text. Therefore, the reader is able to gain a depth of understanding about any of the topics that he might not otherwise be able to obtain. Often it is difficult for a reader to locate periodical articles to reinforce or to clarify the ideas he has gained from other reading material.

This book of readings also can serve as a valuable supplement for preservice teachers who are using some other textbook in an elementary reading methods course. The book of readings can be of special value to in-service teachers who want to learn more about the recent trends in research in elementary reading.

Current periodical articles, most of which have been published in the last five years, are contained in this book. Several older articles are included because they are considered classics in the area. The articles also are readable and offer practical suggestions. They reflect a wide range of views in the field of elementary reading instruction.

Part I contains articles which should help to clarify the many facets of the complex reading process. Reading readiness development at home and at school is treated in Part II. In this part two articles are presented that illustrate aspects of the home environment which best help prepare children to achieve success in beginning reading instruction. One article also is presented that illustrates facets of reading readiness development in kindergarten.

Part III contains a number of articles which help to clarify the various modern elementary reading approaches. The methodology of the language-experience and basal reader approaches is illustrated in five articles. Five other articles describe individualized reading and show the reader how individualized reading can be used in combination with other reading approaches to utilize optimally its best features. A few articles clarify the complex linguistic approaches and illustrate how current linguistic research can be applied to the teaching of elementary reading. The initial teaching alphabet, words in color, programmed reading, and an approach emphasizing neurological dominance also are described in several articles in this part.

Two articles in Part IV describe the very important word recognition skill of phonetic analysis. In this part articles on the use of context clues and structural analysis also are included. Three articles describe some ways to develop a meaning and conceptual vocabulary in the elementary school. A number of articles illustrate the lower- and higher-type comprehension skills, including those of critical reading. Two of the articles illustrate some methods of developing the reading-study skills in the various content fields. Three articles are included on different methods of grouping for reading instruction with special emphasis on the Joplin Plan.

Part V is devoted to articles on the diagnosis and remediation of reading difficulties in the elementary school and to articles on teaching culturally disadvantaged children and disabled readers. The values and limitations of using standardized reading tests are described in two selections, and one article describes the very useful informal reading inventory. Two articles are presented which give suggestions for teaching culturally disadvantaged children to read more effectively in the elementary classroom. One article illustrates some principles for initiating and conducting a corrective reading program in the elementary classroom.

The author sincerely hopes that this book of readings will be a valuable source of information for each reader. She wishes to express her appreciation to all of the publishers and authors who gave permission to reprint the articles contained in it and to express special thanks to her mother for her help and encouragement in its compilation.

Normal, Illinois   WILMA H. MILLER
June 1971

Contents

ELEMENTARY
READING
TODAY

PART

I

THE
READING
PROCESS

The first part of this book concentrates on the factors which comprise the complex process of reading. The reading process is thought to consist of the following interrelated and cumulative factors: the visual aspect, which consists both of the role of eye movements and word recognition; the association of symbols with the experiences they represent; interpretation, critical reading, and creative (integrative) reading, which is the application of reading to problem solving.

Buswell (Selection 1) describes the reading process and stresses its physiological aspects, for he has made his principal contribution in this area. The reading process also is described by Kingston (Selection 2) who emphasizes the contributions that psychological theories have made to reading. Hildreth (Selection 3) describes the reading process in a comprehensive manner, emphasizing both the physiological and the thought processes that are involved.

The following questions may serve to guide the reading of the articles in Part I:

Do the various aspects of the reading process operate singly or simultaneously?

What is the role of eye movements in the reading process?

Is reading considered to be a perceptual process or a thought-gathering process?

1 | The Process of Reading*

Guy T. Buswell

When children first enter school they have already learned to communicate through speech. The process of learning to read can best be understood by relating it to the nature of speech and to the experiences which children have had in learning to speak. Psychologically, the processes of speech and reading are quite similar, the difference being mainly in the sense avenue through which the verbal stimuli are received.

When children enter school they have an oral vocabulary of several thousand words. They have learned to distinguish very small differences in word sounds. They have learned that the ideas expressed in speech depend on the serial order in which the words are spoken. And they have attained a degree of skill in listening that enables them to understand speech at the usual rate of adult conversation.

The essential difference between knowing how to read and how to understand oral speech is the substitution of visual perception of printed verbal symbols for the auditory impression of the same symbols when spoken. The thoughts expressed are the same, the vocabulary is the same, and the word order is the same. The new problem in reading is to learn to recognize the visual symbols with accuracy and reasonable speed.

*From *The Reading Teacher,* vol. 13, December 1959, pp. 108–114. Reprinted in *Education Digest,* vol. 25, March 1960, pp. 48–51. Reprinted with permission of Guy T. Buswell, the *Education Digest,* and the International Reading Association.

The unit in reading material is the same as the unit in speech, namely, the word. The first problem in learning to read is to recognize these printed symbols and to relate them to the corresponding speech symbols. The early American schools failed to see this essential relationship and instead introduced reading by teaching first the letters of the alphabet, then syllables, regardless of whether or not they were meaningful, and finally whole words and phrases. However, studies using a tachistoscope have shown that familiar words can be recognized about as quickly as individual letters or syllables, and that short phrases of familiar words can be recognized almost as readily as single words.

Word Patterns

The effect of the extensive research of this type has been to emphasize that reading deals with word patterns rather than with individual letters or syllables. To be sure, in initial learning of new words, attention may need to be given to the sequence of certain letters and syllables, but when the child has learned thoroughly to recognize a word, the relationship of length of word and difficulty disappears. Learning a word is not a matter of getting the meaning from the sum of the letters or syllables, but rather from learning to recognize it as a whole much as one learns to recognize a person. The appearance of words should be learned so thoroughly that, during the process of reading, only a minimum of attention needs to be given to these details.

Tachistoscopic research has shown that it is easily possible to recognize a familiar word in one-hundredth of a second. But it does not follow that a person can recognize 100 words in one second. Reading is not a process of rapid recognition of one word after another. Rather, it is a process of fusing the meaning of single words into a sequence of meaning. The total act of reading is, therefore, a combination of the visual recognition and the central thought processes that are stimulated by them.

This complex act is sometimes separated into the mechanics of reading and comprehension. This may be a convenient way to analyze the total reading process provided one understands clearly that both are necessary for the complete act of reading. Several studies of oral reading in the first grade have shown that pupils sometimes carry on the process of word-calling without any apparent comprehension of the fused thought content.

Rate of Reading

During the past 30 years there has been wide interest in reading. And today the fact that an increasing number of young people continue their education beyond high school is focusing new attention on *rate* of reading. However, in spite of interest and research into mechanics and methods there is little evidence of the application of these in such a way as to increase the rate of reading among students. Yet, the demands of college programs continue to put an even greater strain on the slow reader. The usual rate of reading nontechnical material at the end of the elementary school is about 250 words per minute, while for college students the average rate is about 300 words. This smallness of the increase beyond the rate of the elementary school is a cause of much concern, particularly in view of the selective character of the college population.

Research on Rate

There has been a great deal of research on methods of increasing rate of reading. One method has been to use flash cards or tachistoscopes to induce quicker perception of printed words. By and large, the results have been disappointing. In an attempt to deal with rate of reading in a more functional situation, various methods have been devised to stimulate and control rate. Of the different methods used to present successive parts of a line at controlled rates, the Harvard reading films are perhaps the best known.

More recently, attention has shifted to methods of exposing, or covering, successive lines of a printed page by mechanical devices which make possible the exposure of material to be read at whatever rate is desired. The results from these methods have indicated that rate, without loss of comprehension, can be increased far beyond the rates usually obtained in school classes. Evidence from eye-movement records taken at the end of such training shows that the principal change has been in span of recognition rather than in duration of fixations. A gain of 50 percent in span of recognition is usually accompanied by gains of not more than 10 percent in speed of recognition.

There have been extreme claims for gains in rate of reading that go quite beyond the credulity of serious researchers, but there is well substantiated evidence from research on rate of reading that leaves little room for doubt that a sizeable increase in rate without loss in comprehension could be achieved if schools were to attempt it seriously. There is no support in research for the popular notion that the slow reader is superior in comprehension.

An increase in rate by even 25 percent by the end of high school would be of incalculable value to those who go on to college and would make possible increased breadth of information and ideas for those who leave school. More serious research on rate is needed, but studies now available indicate that, at the college level, rate of reading may be forced from 100 to 300 words per minute above the reader's present rate without a break in the level of tested comprehension.

The Basic Problem

In the writer's view, the teaching of reading is basically a problem of visual perception. The first goal is to enable the child to derive meaning from printed verbal symbols at the same level of functional efficiency that he has already attained in getting meanings from spoken words. The child has learned to interpret speech at a functional level before entering school. The first obligation of the reading class is to produce this same efficiency with respect to the visual perception of print. There is no substitute for this ability; this is a first obligation. The process of learning to read is the process of doing just this.

Other aspects of reading are less important until basic reading ability is achieved. The school has so often cluttered its program of reading with secondary objectives, some of them of admitted value, that the primary objective of teaching reading is not achieved. The writer has had in his college classes students of unquestioned intelligence who were slow, clumsy readers because their basic reading ability was permitted to level off too soon. On tests of basic reading they scored below sixth-grade norms.

Learning to read a foreign language is a parallel case of perceptual learning. If I want to learn to read the Russian language, my first task is to learn the words when they are printed in Russian and to associate them with their meanings. My goal is to learn these words in their various forms so well that I can read them at the same rate as I read my vernacular. I do not need to be taught how to think, or how to solve problems, or how to spell, or how to improve my personality by reading Russian, or what the great classics of Russian literature are. These may be good, but they do not teach me to read Russian. I already know how to read, but not in the Russian language.

The reading process is basically this kind of perceptual learning. The school needs to know how to accomplish it more effectively. The present intellectual climate is more favorable to basic research on methods of teaching reading than has been the case for three decades. Reading would be served by some singleness of purpose.

2 | The Psychology of Reading*

Albert J. Kingston

Reading is a complex act performed by humans. Within the traditional meaning of the word, humans seem to be the only fauna which read. Although it is possible, perhaps, to argue that other types of animals read signs while seeking food or searching for mates, most of us likely will stipulate that reading is something that only humans do. Psychology is commonly regarded as the study of behavior. And because reading is one type of behavior, and an extremely important one to modern man, it might be assumed that psychologists have devoted considerable time and effort to studying it systematically. Unfortunately such is not the case. While many psychologists have on occasion studied some aspect of reading which momentarily interested them, few, if any, have devoted their entire professional careers to the study of the reading process. There are perhaps a number of reasons for a lack of interest manifested by psychologists in reading. One reason may be the ascendancy which behaviorism has held in American psychology during the present century, and the reluctance of the behavioral psychologist to deal with covert behavior. Another reason, undoubtedly, is the obvious difficulties encountered in attempting to explicate and to study under controlled conditions many of the more

*From *Forging Ahead in Reading,* IRA Conference Proceedings, 1968, pp. 425–432. Reprinted with permission of Albert J. Kingston and the International Reading Association.

significant aspects of reading behavior. Regardless of the reasons, however, there has not emerged and does not exist at present a systematic, well-formulated psychology of reading.

Yet many aspects of reading as it is taught and discussed today have been influenced by psychology. The familiar concepts of readiness, developmental reading, vocabulary control, drill and repetition, emphasis on meaning and interpretation, and evaluating pupil progress, to mention but a few, have been influenced by psychological findings. Unfortunately, the applications of psychological findings have been piecemeal and sometimes even seem to serve merely as "garnishes," rather than to function as basic or fundamental principles underlying reading pedagogy. At present only one current text uses the word *psychology* in its title. This text entitled *Psychology in Teaching Reading* has three major goals according to the authors. First, it seeks to select data that are most relevant to the teacher's understanding of the reading process; secondly, it seeks to interpret these data in terms of the problems that the teacher will encounter; and finally, it seeks to apply the interpretations to the specific classroom problems that teachers meet (20). Although these objectives are laudatory, it is questionable whether a psychology of reading is sufficiently structured to be of much value to the classroom reading teacher. The text seems to select a number of different aspects of educational psychology which appear to bear upon reading behavior and instruction. As such it falls short of presenting a systematic psychology of reading.

There is, however, no systematic psychology of reading, nor is there an adequate theory of reading, a situation which complicates the task of this author. In attempting to deal effectively with this assignment, the writer deliberately has not attempted to report research bearing upon such familiar reading topics as readiness, perception, sensation, intellectual abilities, etc. Nor has any attempt been made to discuss in detail the research of persons having special interest in reading. Rather, the strategy has been to discuss the work of certain psychologists that may have bearing upon the field of reading and to suggest possible areas where psychology can make significant contributions to reading.

Basically, one major contribution which psychology can make to reading is to provide the impetus needed to develop a more adequate theory of reading. The term *reading* has been applied to such a wide range of behaviors that it has ceased to have a single identifiable meaning. If a science of reading behavior is to be developed it must draw heavily on what has been learned regarding the behavior of humans in a related field such as psychology. Although at present many psychological theories, i.e., personality, learning, psychometrics, growth, and development, have been developed largely in special and limited contexts, there is no reason to suspect that the successful theory building found in social services cannot also be achieved in reading. Much of science has had its great impetus from the discovery of principles that apply to merely a limited range of events. Thus, it might be expected that a psychology of reading may evolve not from a comprehensive treatment, but rather from the discovery of principles or the development of theories which apply to limited segments of reading behaviors. In fact, one difficulty the reading specialist faces is the limited degree to which many current psychological theories appear to be related to any aspect of classroom behavior. However, it is important that the present body of knowledge in the field of reading become so organized that generalizations and laws be applied to a wider range of problems and be testable under a number of conditions.

A major difficulty in achieving this end stems from the very complexity of the human organism. Modern psychologists recognize that the organism functions in a holistic fashion, and that in any given situation behavior is a function of both the attributes of the individual and the situation in which the individual operates at that moment. Both Raygor (18) and Weaver (23) have suggested that the task is difficult because much reading behavior is covert, and the researcher must infer what goes on within the organism by studying how an individual reacts to various stimuli. Chomsky (5), in an excellent review of Skinner's *Verbal Behavior,* states

> . . . that insights that have been achieved in the laboratories of the reinforcement theorist, though quite genuine, can be applied to complex human behavior only in the most gross and superficial way, and that speculative attempts to discuss linguistic behavior in these terms alone omit from consideration factors of fundamental importance that are, no doubt, amenable to scientific study although their specific character cannot at present be precisely formulated.

It seems likely, however, that because of its adherence to the methods of science, psychology offers the promise of providing the means for explicating the current confusions concerning reading. To date, though, psychology offers the promise rather than the fruits of the scientific method. The writer believes, however, that the major contributions of psychology will result from the theoretical considerations and carefully controlled experimentations of psychologists, which may serve as models for reading research.

Despite the present lack of an adequate psychology of reading, the work of certain scientists seems to bear on the interests of reading specialists or those concerned with reading behavior. Probably one of the most significant areas of congruence is the work of linguists, psycholinguists, information-theorists, and psychologists concerned with language. Carroll (4), for example, notes three points at which linguists and psychologists have common interests. These are the possibility of universals in grammar and in language structure, the possibility of significant differences between languages in the kinds of relationship they exhibit between their expression and content systems and the possible implications such differences may have for the cognitive behavior of the speakers of those languages, and the possibility of making a psychological interpretation of grammatical structure. Carroll also suggests that language may be viewed as a communication system. As such, language has two major aspects: one, a physical and biological system in which communication takes place, and, two, a sign system in which messages are formulated. Weaver(23), who has attempted to apply the rubric of information theory to language and reading, points out the shortcomings of communication theory, but believes that it probably fits as well or better than S-R psychology. He argues that in communication theory neural action (covert though it may be) is considered whereas behaviorism excludes such physiological considerations from its theoretical structures. Today, however, there is a group of neo-behaviorists who attempt to deal with mediating processes.

Most reading specialists would agree that the reading process involves some sort of interaction between writer and reader and that some sort of language system is employed. A genuine problem that must be faced in finding similarities between the interests of language specialists and reading specialists lies in the tendency of linguists to talk mainly about oral language. Auding and reading obviously do involve the two aspects of communication which Carroll stresses, yet there also are certain significant differences between the two modes of behavior. Buswell(2) notes that the major difference in reading and speech is the difference in the sense avenues through which stimuli are received. According to Buswell, the essential difference between knowing how to read and how to understand oral speech is the substitution of visual perception of visual symbols for auditory impressions of the same symbols when spoken. The thoughts expressed are the same, the vocabulary is the same, and the word order is the same. The problem in reading is thought to be one of learning to recognize the visual symbols with accuracy and reasonable speed. Buswell's thesis has more accuracy in describing reading at the earliest stages of development than it does for the reading behavior of more sophisticated scholars. Many of us, for example, have first discovered words in print long before we have heard them presented orally. Textbooks and published reports in the academic disciplines are filled with specialized vocabulary that has not been previously encountered in oral form by the typical scholar. Carroll, furthermore, even suggests that an individual might learn to read a foreign language fluently without much acquaintance with its spoken form(3). Deaf children also learn to read without previously having heard language in its oral form. It may be that beginning readers rely on some sort of implicit speech to a greater degree than do more proficient or mature readers. At present it only seems safe to say that auding and reading are somehow related, yet the exact nature of the relationship is obscure. The relationships obviously grow out of the mediating processes generally associated with cognition.

Reading, typically, is regarded as a thought process. The relationship of reading to thought was noted by Thorndike(21) fifty years ago. Gray (10), speaking for the Yearbook Committee of the National Society for the Study of Education, stressed the viewpoint that reading and thinking are inseparable as shown by the following quotation:

> The Yearbook Committee believes that any conception of reading that fails to include reflection, critical evaluation, and the classification of meaning is inadequate. It recognizes that reading includes much that psychologists and educators have commonly called thinking.

Unfortunately for reading specialists many psychologists shunned research in thinking and cognition in the years that followed Watson's attacks on Wundt's introspection experiments. Even today many behaviorists avoid research in this area because such covert activities are not thought to be subject to adequate experimentation. Those interested in reading found a greater affinity with psychologists of the Gestalt school who stressed perception and meaning. Unfortunately, the experiments of the classical Gestaltists, although interesting, have yielded little of permanent value concerning the nature of cognition. On the other hand, their experiments in perception have been of more value yet do not answer many important questions concerning reading(19).

Perceptual learning is part of the skill of reading. Particularly significant is the acquisition of the directional scanning habit. Also necessary is letter differentiation and, as with learning the Morse code, there is a second stage of perceptual learning in reading—wherein the letter units now discriminable, are organized into higher-order units so that more is perceived at a glance(9).

During the last decade there has been a resurgence of interest in the psychology of cognition, perhaps because it is becoming more apparent that any psychology of human behavior must deal with this important human attribute. Unfortunately for the reading specialist, there seems to be a number of different positions which are identifiable among those psychologists who work in the area of cognitive investigation. Ausubel, for example, identifies one group as neo-behaviorists as typified by Hebb, Osgood, Hull, Berlyne, and Staats; another group as cognitive theorists including Bruner, Ausubel, and Gagné; a group of developmentalists typified by Piaget and Vygotsky; and finally, a group interested primarily in cognitive organization and functioning. A cogent review of these various positions can be found in Ausubel's introduction to a book of readings edited by Anderson and Ausubel(1).

Educators, of course, have been interested in cognition for many years. Evidence of this interest is obvious from even a casual scanning of the current educational literature on curriculum materials in any academic discipline, ranging from reading and language arts to science and mathematics. The keen interest of educators sometimes has caused them to accept the theories and experimental findings of cognitive theories prematurely. Currently there seems to be a rather prevalent belief among educators that mediational responses are primarily verbal in nature and that they can be taught by the careful exposure of pupils to various teaching procedures and materials. Unfortunately, the truth is that although some teachers talk blithely about such words as concepts, concept attainment, concept formation, and learning by inquiry or discovery, these terms usually represent merely hypothetical constructs or psychological inferences. Cognition theorists tend to be more reserved concerning the nature of these constructs and their function in mediation and learning. Although the work of cognitive theorists holds promise, the extent to which these terms are misused, overgeneralized, and employed as new labels to describe old behaviors may cause eventual difficulty. Reading, for example, does not necessarily need new terms but rather needs operational statements which more adequately serve to define the behaviors we think we observe.

A number of experimental studies by researchers interested in cognition seem to hold promise for persons interested in reading. Kendler, Kendler, and Leanard[15], for example, studied the mediating responses of children of various chronological ages. They found that children below age six tended to behave predominately on a single S–R basis and that with increasing chronological age an increasing proportion behaved in a mediating manner. The experimenters suggest that since there is a relationship between learning and choice behavior mediators learned more rapidly than did nonmediators. An analysis of the verbalizations of the children after they had completed the presented tasks suggests that there is a relationship between the ability to connect words with actions and the tendency toward mediated choices. This study seems to verify the emphasis placed by reading teachers on the relationship of language and reading and also indicates the need for further research to ascertain the nature of the factors which lead to cognitive differences among children at an early age.

A number of researchers have conceptualized cognitive functioning in terms of principles of control or cognitive styles[24,25]. Such control principles, styles, or strategies as leveling-sharpening, tolerance for unrealistic experience, focusing-scanning, equivalence range, constructed-flexible control, and field dependence-independence have been studied. Holzman and Klein[11] relate leveling and sharpening to modes of organizing stimuli. Leveling implies a low level of articulation in a sequence of stimuli, while sharpening implies a high level of articulation. Tolerance for unrealistic experience has been described by Gardner (6) as acceptance of experiences that do not agree with what one knows to be true. Equivalence range relates to organizing ability as related to the awareness of differences. Focusing-scanning deals with the tendency to narrow awareness, to keep experiences discrete, and a tendency to separate affect from idea and thus to maintain objectivity. Field dependence-independence is employed to describe the ability to abstract an item from the field in which it appears or is embedded (6). In essence, the theory of cognitive principles implies that an individual develops certain characteristic modes of cognitive control as he matures. These styles, then, are employed in coping with various situations which the organism faces. At present most of the research in this area seems to be focused upon the personality, yet the consistency with which these modes of control appear to be manifested in various individuals makes it reasonable to assume that the same controls may function in reading. The work of Kagan (13,14) bears on this possibility.

Kagan postulates two stable dimensions upon which children and adults are distributed. The first is called reflection-impulsivity and describes the degree to which a child reflects upon alternative classifications of a stimulus or alternative solution hypotheses in situations in which many response possibilities are available simultaneously. In such situations some children have a fast conceptual tempo; they impulsively report the first classification that occurs to them or carry out the first solution that appears appropriate. On the other hand, reflective children or adults characteristically delay before carrying out a solution hypothesis or reporting a classification. They actively consider the alternatives available and compare their validity. The reflective individual behaves as if he cared that his first response is as close to correct as possible. A second dimension, called visual analysis, describes the child's tendency to analyze complex stimuli into their component parts. Some children fractionate a stimulus into small subunits, others label and react to a larger stimulus chunk. According to Kagan, analysis is relatively independent of the reflection-impulsivity dimension and each contributes variance to a variety of cognitive products. Kagan and his associates have conducted a number of interesting and thought provoking experiments to verify these hypotheses. Their findings appear to have important implications for reading specialists.

Reading teachers who have observed how some children will guess at unfamiliar words—even though they have little likelihood of success, while others appear reluctant to guess, even though they probably know the word—should study the work of Kogan and Wallach. Kogan and Wallach have studied the process of decision making in individuals and the types of judgments and the manipulations of alternative solutions which lead toward judgments. Presumably some individuals constantly are more willing to take risks than are others(16).

If reading behavior involves thinking, and apparently it does, cognition and cognitive styles must play some part in the manner in which the reader comprehends and interprets what has been read. Cognitive styles, for example, imply various modes of conception, categorizing of ideas, and organizing significant facts and details. Reading is one mode by which "signs" and cues are inputted to some sort of a categorizing system by the organism. The nature of these categories is not known at present, but apparently the syllogistic or reflective patterns of reasoning long described by philosophers are not satisfactory descriptions of the process. It seems likely that in some types of reading the individual already has many concepts and that reading is a simple task of recognition and association. In another type of reading, the individual has merely a limited number of concepts and is able to organize just a few related associations so that considerable effort is required to either retrieve concepts or search for relationships associated with the inputted cues. In a third case, the reader may have little or no familiarity with the information being processed and must rely mainly upon the information contained in the reading selection for processing. Obviously, the latter type of reading is most difficult and frustrating. Presumably, cognitive styles and previously developed modes of control play a role in the degree of persistence the reader brings to the reading task.

Educators long have recognized maturational influences in the life cycle of the child. Significantly, the previously mentioned research also recognized developmental patterns, perhaps of a type not generally observed by the classroom teacher. It has been said that

> Development is the complex product resulting from the cyclical actions that occur between physiological growth and learning. And because all development, whether it applies to one structure, one skill, a series of behaviors, or an entire personality, follows certain natural laws and consists of universal characteristics, it can best be defined as a rhythmic flow of qualitative changes proceeding in specific directions in a predictable sequence(7).

It is apparent, however, that we have considerable difficulty in identifying many of the important attributes and characteristics of the organism for systematic study. The traditionally employed concepts of intelligence, physical development, psychomotor abilities, personality, and social-emotional adjustment represent extremely broad traits. Maturation and learning are difficult to measure and predict under the best conditions and do not take place in segmented, piecemeal fashion. Rather, development and learning are continuous and constantly interrelated and integrated. In the

United States the acquisition of reading behavior generally is regarded as taking place in some developmental fashion that is typically regarded as being akin to and correlated with the process of physical and intellectual development. Much has been made of the concepts of readiness and the apparent relationship between the age of the child and the acquisition of various skills and their integration in subsequent stages. While the research of Piaget (17), Vygotsky (22), Gesell (8), and Ilg and Ames (12) has indicated that development proceeds in certain patterns, two other truths also are apparent. First, there are wide individual differences in developmental rates and, secondly, much significant development takes place prior to the age the child typically enters school. The typical research study, which stresses correlations between reading achievement and other characteristics related to development, has tended to ignore the lack of relationships and variance among traits and/or patterns of development. Such studies have emphasized uniformities and commonalities and ignored differences.

Despite the difficulties of measuring stages of development, it seems safe to assume that the process of maturation, coupled with learning at each stage, is related to reading. As yet, just how the reading process is related is not clear. Typically, one factor is the increasing capacity of the individual to acquire more complex abilities with age. Measurable differences in language, intellectual abilities, and formal social behavior obviously are other facets of the developmental cycles. Many areas of growth and development need some precise study. There seem to be certain "pre-reading" stages, other than those now employed to assess readiness, that should be considered by reading specialists. One example is the development of visual and auditory discrimination abilities related to letters, syllables, words. With skillful readers these abilities appear to be less important by the intermediate and upper elementary grades. At this stage somewhat different response modes and "sign" and language manipulation seem to be more important. In addition to the literal language needed during the primary grades, ability to handle figurative language and more complex structures seems to be necessary for reading success. The reasons why some children have less difficulty in acquiring these abilities is not so simple as many teachers think. It also should be noted that recently there has been a shift in emphasis from the biological concept of maturation to an emphasis on the effects that environment, particularly a stimulating and nurturing one, have on the course of development.

In summary, it has been suggested that, at present, a well formulated psychology of reading has not been developed. Reading specialists have tended to select various psychological positions to support certain of their own practices and beliefs. These are fragmentary and piecemeal. The major help that reading will gain from psychology is the assistance that any science with a more rigorous methodology can offer to any nonscience. The work of current psychologists working in fields which appear to have bearing on the reading process were discussed as examples.

REFERENCES

1. Anderson, Richard C., and David P. Ausubel. *Readings in the Psychology of Cognition.* New York: Holt, Rinehart and Winston, 1965.
2. Buswell, Guy T. "The Process of Reading." *The Reading Teacher, 13,* 1959, 14–21.
3. Carroll, John B. "Wanted: A Research Basis for Educational Policy on Foreign Language Teaching." *Harvard Education Review, 30,* 1960, 128–140.
4. Carroll, John B. *Language and Thought.* Englewood Cliffs: Prentice-Hall, 1964.
5. Chomsky, Noam. "Review of Skinner's *Verbal Behavior." Language, 35,* 1959, 26–58.
6. Gardner, R. W., *et al.* "Cognitive Control: A Study of Individual Consistencies in Cognitive Behavior" in G. S. Klein (Ed.), *Psychological Issues.* New York: International Universities Press, 1959.
7. Garrison, K. C., A. J. Kingston, and H. W. Bernard. *The Psychology of Childhood.* New York: Scribner, 1967.
8. Gesell, A., and F. L. Ilg. *Child Development.* New York: Harper & Row, 1949.
9. Gibson, Eleanor J. "Perceptual Learning." *Annual Review of Psychology, 14,* 1963, 29–56.
10. Gray, William S. "The Nature and Types of Reading," Guy N. Whipple (Ed.), *The Teaching of Reading: A Second Report. Thirty-sixth Yearbook of the National Society for the Study of Education, Pt. I.* Bloomington: Public School Publishing Co., 1937, 23–28.
11. Holzman, P. S., and G. S. Klein. "Motive and Style in Reality Contact." *Bulletin of the Menninger Clinic, 20,* 1956, 181–191.
12. Ilg, F. L., and L. B. Ames. *School Readiness.* New York: Harper & Row, 1965.
13. Kagan, J. "Developmental Studies in Reflection and Analysis." A. H. Kidd, and J. L. Rivoise (Eds.), *Perceptual Development in Children.* New York: International Universities Press, 1966, 487–522.
14. Kagan, J., H. A. Moss, and I. E. Siegel. "Psychological Significance of Styles in the Basic Cognitive Processes in Children." *Monographs of the Society for Research in Child Development,* No. 28, 1963.
15. Kendler, Tracy S., H. H. Kendler, and Beulah Leanard. "Mediating Responses to Size and Brightness as a Function of Age." *American Journal of Psychology, 75,* 1962, 571–586.
16. Kogan, N., and M. A. Wallach. *Risk Taking: A Study in Cognition and Personality.* New York: Holt, Rinehart and Winston, 1964.
17. Piaget, J. *The Origins of Intelligence in Children.* New York: International Universities Press, 1952.
18. Raygor, Alton E. Behavioral Research in Reading: What Does It Offer? J. Allen Figurel (Ed.), *Improvement of Reading through Classroom Practice,*

Proceedings of Ninth Annual Conference International Reading Association, 1964, 235–238.

19. Spache, George D. "The Perceptual Bases of Reading." Delivered at the World Congress in Reading, Paris, 1966.

20. Smith, Henry P., and Emerald V. Dechant. *Psychology in Teaching Reading.* Englewood Cliffs: Prentice-Hall, 1961.

21. Thorndike, Edward L. "The Understanding of Sentences: A Study of Errors in Reading," *The Elementary School Journal, 18,* 1917, 98–114.

22. Vygotsky, L. S. *Thought and Language.* Cambridge: MIT Press, 1962.

23. Weaver, Wendell W. "On the Psychology of Reading." E. Thurston and L. E. Hafner (Eds.), *New Concepts in College-Adult Reading.* Thirteenth Yearbook of the National Reading Conference, 1964, 67–74.

24. Witkin, H. A., *et al. Personality through Perception.* New York: Harper & Row, 1954.

25. Witkin, H. A., *et al. Psychological Differentiation: Studies of Development.* New York: Wiley, 1962.

3 | Understanding the Reading Process*

Gertrude Hildreth

What is reading? What are the characteristic features of efficient reading? The nature of the reading process is no longer a "dark continent" because of the information research has furnished on this subject. In recent years new insights have also been gained from studies in linguistics, visual and auditory perception, and the nature of learning processes in childhood. Facts about the nature of the reading process and skills involved in reading will be summarized in this chapter.

The Reading Process

The psychological processes involved in reading are highly complex. Reading in any language involves the interpretation of graphic symbols that stand for spoken words. The central process is the same regardless of the form and inscription of the symbols, whether stone carvings, inscriptions on wax tablets, handwritten text, symbols in a stenographer's notebook, or imprinting with ink on paper; and the mental process is the

*From *Teaching Reading,* pp. 64–83, by Gertrude Hildreth. Copyright © 1958 by Holt, Rinehart and Winston, Inc. Reprinted by permission of Holt, Rinehart and Winston, Inc.

same regardless of the particular sensory organs through which the messages from the inscriptions reach the brain.

Reading is a twofold process: First, there is the mechanical aspect, the physiological responses to the print consisting of certain oculomotor skills, the eye movements, through which sensations are conveyed to the brain; and second, the mental process through which the meaning of the sense impressions is perceived and interpreted, involving thinking with swift inferences. As the eyes move rhythmically across the lines of print, sensations are received which are interpreted almost instantly by the mind as ideas expressed in language.

Which is the more important, the mechanics of eye movements or the mental process of interpreting? Neither, since the latter is always dependent on the former. However, in the case of visual reading, the role of the eyes is so impressive that the inner mental process may be overlooked. A moron might have perfect visual equipment and be able to perceive all the words on the page yet be unable to read because of inability to grasp meanings. On the other hand a person with a brilliant mind might be unable to interpret print because of serious defects in visual accommodation.

Although the eye movements in reading furnish evidence concerning the reader's perceptual habits and, indirectly, the mental processes taking place during reading, they do not establish these habits, control the mental processes, nor explain the reasons for habitual patterns of performance or inadequacies in performance.

Eye Movements in Reading

During reading, the eyes, like a motion picture camera, take a series of rapid snapshots. The eyes of the mature reader move rhythmically and involuntarily across the lines from left to right. Pauses following each successive jerk of the eyes across the lines serve to bring small blocks of print into clear foveal vision. The image that is focused on the retina is transferred to the brain by the optic nerve. These sensory signals become meaningful percepts when they are interpreted by the mind of the reader.

Sighted reading requires sustained, intensive work at near-point vision, with continual accommodation of the eyes in focusing on the print from one fixation point to the next. The eye-movement habits rather than mere visual efficiency determine the degree of reading efficiency.

The essential facts about the performance of the eyes in reading have been determined through photographic studies of the eyes working at the reading task. Cinematographic records of eye movements made with the modern eye-movement cameras furnish the most accurate picture of eye behavior during reading. Photographic studies of the eye movements in reading originated with the psychologists B. Erdmann and Raymond Dodge at the University of Halle, in Germany in 1898. Dr. Guy Buswell of the University of Chicago was among the first to demonstrate the improvement in the eye movements of children as they matured in reading habits, and to chart the progressive changes in the direction of greater speed, regularity, and reduction in the number of fixations with improved comprehension(3).

Nomenclature of the Eye Movements

The technical terms for the eye movements are: fixation pauses, interfixation movements, regressive movements, return sweep, and refixations. The fixations are the pauses during which the eyes view the print, the interfixation movement is the movement from one fixation to the next. Regressions are the movements backward along the line of print to correct any misreading.

Here is the reader about to begin at the top of a new page of interesting material. As the eyes strike the line of print they focus slightly within the line and then march steadily across the line in a series of rapid stop-and-go movements, sweeping back from the end of the line to the beginning of the next. The return sweep is as rhythmical from line to line as the movements of the eyes within the lines. These jerky movements of the eyes, first detected by Javel at the University of Paris, were called *saccades* from the powerful sets of muscles that move the eyes horizontally from one fixation point to another. Hence the term *saccadic* movements.

Children will be observed turning their heads to make the successive pauses to focus the eyes, the fixation pauses; but mature readers can move the eyes to get a new focus without obvious head movements.

The smooth beat of the eye movements is the most characteristic feature of the motor habits of reading. The skilled reader proceeds across the lines with the regularity of the typewriter carriage. The number of fixation pauses in a line of print becomes quite uniform, but the split-second focusing on the print during these pauses will vary with the difficulty of the material, new items, line length, and other factors.

What happens during these eye jerks or interfixation movements in terms of reading? Nothing, because the eyes catch clear images only when they pause, never when in motion. During these jerks from one fixation point to the next, clear vision of the print is impossible. Perception takes place only during the pauses at the end of each jerk.

The jerks or interfixation movements between the pauses of the eyes to examine the print are extremely brief, lasting a little over one-hundredth of a second on the average (10 to 23 milliseconds each) in the case of the mature reader. Both the speed of these jerks and the rhythm improve with maturity until the rate finally becomes established as an automatic habit.

THE FIXATION PAUSES

The chief questions concerning the fixation pauses are: How frequent are these pauses? What is their average duration, and how much is seen during the pauses when the eyes glance or explore?

A. *Span of Perception.*   The span of perception is the amount of print seen during a single pause of the eyes. In the human eye the field of vision is the area the eyes can view distinctly while they are fixed upon some given point. The field of clearest vision is the fovea in the center of the eye. Surrounding the fovea is the macula, the area of less distinct vision. The field of distinct vision has no clear-cut boundary, but shades off gradually on both sides.

Even for the mature reader, there is a physiological limit to the visual perception span because of the way the eyes are set in the head. Human vision has a range of about 165 degrees horizontally and about 60 degrees vertically.

As the reader glances at the print he sees some elements clearly, others vaguely in marginal vision. Each successive fixation brings new material into clear vision which before was seen only vaguely.

The size of the perception span is obtained by dividing the length of the average line in the text read by the average number of pauses in a line. The perception span, the distance between two fixation pauses, averages 13 to 14 letter spaces for good readers, 6 spaces for poor readers, with an average around 9 to 10 letter spaces in clear foveal vision, plus one or two more letters in shadowy vision.

The common belief that the eyes take in several words or even a whole sentence at a glance is fallacious because this is visually impossible. Either the eyes have to move along or the head has to turn in order to bring the next batch of print into the visual field.

But what effect does the nature of the content have on the length of the perception span in reading? Practically none, because even though a story is easy to read and highly interesting, the eyes still cannot exceed their physiological perceptual limit.

An interesting question is whether the type of training in beginning reading makes any difference in the ultimate size of the recognition span. Although there is no objective research on this point, apparently mature readers reach the same level in recognition span regardless of the nature of initial instruction.

B. *Number of Fixation Pauses.* The number of fixation pauses in a line of print depends to some extent on the length of the line, and the amount of print in any line varies with the size of type. The typical response of the person who is asked to estimate how many times his eyes pause in a line of print is "three or four." Actually, it is closer to seven or eight, even for college professors.

In a 60-letter line the seven or eight eye pauses will be spaced about eight letter spaces apart.

Earl Taylor found the following eye fixation averages for senior high school students and adults(15):

Fixations in 100 Words	
Senior high school	83
Adults	75
Average Span of Recognition	
Senior high school	1.21 words
College students	1.33 words

In a study made with photographic apparatus in the educational psychology laboratory at the University of California, Gilbert reported that ninth-grade students avaraged 87.4 fixations in 100 words; college students reading prose, 79.5 fixations in 100 words(8).

These findings from recent studies are at variance with older studies which estimated the number of fixation pauses in a line as ranging between three to five. The discrepancy may be due not only to the more exact measurements possible with modern photographic equipment, but also to the artificiality of the test conditions in photographic studies. If eye movements of mature readers were photographed while the reader was curled up with a book in a comfortable chair, the number of fixation pauses might prove to be smaller.

However, in one photographic study, fourth-grade pupils showed no difference in characteristic eye movement patterns and habits when they were using their readers and when they were using special material prepared for the test. The fact must probably be accepted that the eyes actually pause from seven to eight times in a line of print at the stage of maximum reading maturity.

C. *Duration of the Fixation Pauses.* How long do the eyes pause at each fixation point? For the mature reader these pauses have a duration of 250 milliseconds on the average. A good reader pauses not longer than one fifth of a second during each fixation pause; the poor reader requires twice as long.

Taylor found the average duration of fixation to be as follows(15):

Senior high school students	.24	of a second (about one fourth of a second)
College students	.23	of a second

In Gilbert's study the average duration of fixation pauses for ninth-grade students was 7.34/30 of a second or about $\frac{1}{4}$ to $\frac{1}{5}$ of a second; for a college student reading prose, 7.79/30 of a second (8).[1]

Although at maturity the number of the fixation pauses is quite constant regardless of the nature of the reading content, the duration of the pauses may be shorter in easier, more familiar material.

From these figures it is obvious that the total time actually spent in looking at the print is far greater proportionately than the time spent in the interfixation eye movements. The mature reader spends about 94 percent of his time on pauses, and only about 6 percent of his time in interfixation jerks or movements. The extremely rapid reader spends slightly less time proportionately on the fixation pauses.

RETURN SWEEP

The return sweep is just what the term implies, the return movement of the eyes from the end of a line to the beginning of the next one below in a right-to-left direction. This motion, too, through practice becomes part of the total reflex eye-movement pattern—brief, automatic, and rhythmical. In the case of the mature reader the return sweep is incredibly fast, requiring on the average not more than 40 milliseconds, or about $\frac{1}{25}$ of a second.

REGRESSIVE MOVEMENTS

The eyes backtrack or regress when the reader must retrace his steps slightly because he has met some difficulty and has not comprehended the text. Refixations occur near the left-hand end of the line for a second start in case the first impression following the return sweep was not clear.

Regressions may also be due to lapses of attention. The reader is obliged to retrace his steps to get new clues for a fresh start much like a person momentarily lost in the woods. There is nothing standardized about the regressive movements because these movements are governed

---

[1] Different prose selections were used in testing the college students.

by the difficulties, such as lack of word recognition and a shortage of vocabulary, encountered in reading. The number of fixations and regressive movements appears to be little affected by fatigue until after reading of several hours' duration.

Taylor found that senior high school students made 15 regressive movements, on the average, in 100 words; college students, 11(15). Gilbert reported the number of regressive movements for ninth-grade students to average 18.5 in 100 words; college students reading prose, 13.6(8). This is about once in every three or four lines; the immature reader, on the other hand, may show three or more regressive movements in a single line.

Regressive movements are a normal accompaniment of rapid reading; they become unfavorable symptoms only when the number is excessive.

Eye-movement behavior is symptomatic of level of reading maturity. The mature person shows smoother, more rhythmical movements, fewer pauses and regressions, and shorter pauses than children and adults with immature reading habits. High reading test scores are associated with low fixation frequency, low regression frequency, and brief fixation.

The diagrams in Figure 1 illustrate schematically the eye movements described on pages 21–24.

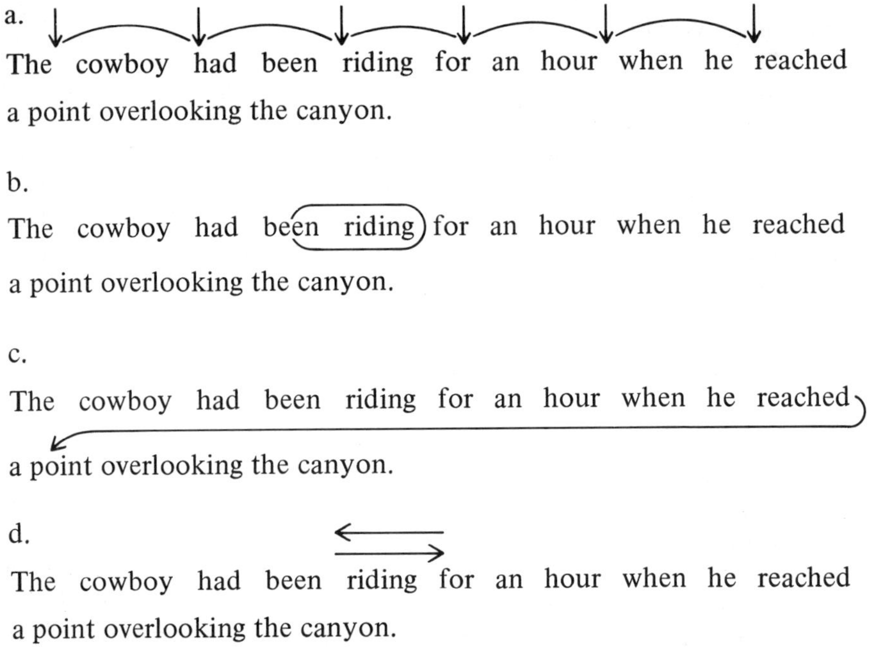

a.

The cowboy had been riding for an hour when he reached a point overlooking the canyon.

b.

The cowboy had been riding) for an hour when he reached a point overlooking the canyon.

c.

The cowboy had been riding for an hour when he reached a point overlooking the canyon.

d.

The cowboy had been riding for an hour when he reached a point overlooking the canyon.

Figure 1. Schematic diagram illustrating (a) fixation pauses and interfixation eye movements, (b) amount seen during one fixation pause, (c) return sweep, and (d) regressive eye movement. (Note that the line here is 54 letter spaces long.)

Eye Movements in Other Languages

What about the eye movements in the conventional printed page of other cultures, e.g., Hebrew in which the print goes from right to left, and Chinese which goes up and down the columns vertically? W. S. Gray made a survey of eye movements in reading foreign languages. Seventy-eight mature subjects read material in their mother tongue in 14 different languages. The material used was an old fable common to all of these languages except the Navaho (native American Indian) and a simple discussion of reasons why children and adults should learn to read and write. The results of two tests in both silent and oral reading showed striking similarity in the character of the eye movements in all languages. Dr. Gray concluded that reading patterns around the world were essentially the same regardless of the form and structure of the particular language or orientation of the lines of print(10).

That there is no essential difference in moving the eyes has been demonstrated in the cases of bright Oriental children who easily transfer their vertical eye movements to the horizontal direction required for English reading. A child who read Chinese fluently, but not English, entered the second grade of an American school and easily learned to read English within the year.

Physical Characteristics of Tactile Reading

Tactile and visual reading show the same fundamental characteristics. In reading Braille[2] the reader moves his fingers swiftly across horizontal rows of dots instead of moving his eyes across lines of print. As the right hand finishes a line, the left hand starts the next line, both hands moving steadily in a left-to-right direction across the lines of dots.

Good readers move their fingers horizontally with a minimum of up-and-down motion, while less skilled readers interrupt their horizontal movements by frequent up-and-down motions which may also form hooks. Good readers exert slight and uniform pressure while poor readers employ strong and variable pressure, much like the beginning sighted reader "staring each word to death"(12).

Interpretative Processes in Reading

As the words flash by, the experienced reader sees with his mind's eye a series of mental images—the result of thinking, inferring, and interpreting. Similarly, when viewing a movie he gains impressions of moving

[2] Braille is a system of embossed dots read with the fingers.

objects instead of seeing the succession of frames or still pictures that compose the film. The printed words are only so many black marks until the reader's mind interprets them, e.g.,

> The train ground to a stop.
> They caught the train.
> They climbed aboard.
> The Lone Ranger jumped on his horse and dashed away.

Similarly, singing is more than vocalizing *Do re mi,* and tennis is more than a succession of strokes.

Reading demands an alert mind. As Emerson said, "One must be an inventor to read well." Reading is a continuous puzzle because one can never anticipate precisely what word or combination of words will come next. Reading requires exploratory tries when new words or unusual meanings are encountered.

Reading requires inference, weighing the relative importance of ideas and meanings, and seeing the relationships among them; it is a process of forming tentative judgments, then verifying and checking guesses. To solve the problems in a passage the reader must be continuously in an alert, anticipatory frame of mind, suspending judgment, correcting and confirming his guesses as he goes along. What does the reader make of this puzzle? "Early morning _____ barracks _____ bugle _____ horses _____ watering trough _____." The term *train of thought* is nowhere more aptly used than when describing the thought process in interpretive reading.

The reader is somewhat in the situation of the automobile driver who is thoroughly accustomed to driving, knows all about the operation of the car, the road signs and regulations, but is never in exactly the same situation twice.

The thinking process in reading is similar to the reasoning and inferring that people must do in typical life situations. For example: It is supper time, and the family, consisting of mother, father, and teen-age boy are sitting around the dining table. A knock is heard at the door. Mother on answering finds a policeman standing there. Why has he come? Her first suspicion is that her boy may have gotten into some scrape or other. But no, the officer informs her that the boy has turned in a purse that he found, and he has come to give the boy the reward offered by the owner. Joy is registered all around at this turn of events.

The story of Sinbad's shipwreck on the Iron Mountain in the *Arabian Nights* provides a good illustration of the reasoning and inference required in every paragraph, in fact in every line. As the ship, lost in a storm, approaches the Iron Mountain the captain throws up his hands and weeps. He realizes that the force of the magnetic lodestone in the mountain is so violent that all the nails, bolts, and iron bands in the ship will fly out, causing the ship to break up and become submerged. The crew will perish and all the cargo will be lost. The mountain is covered with nails and bolts from vessels it has previously destroyed.

There is no question that this story holds the child's interest. He can hardly wait to see how it turns out, but whether or not he grasps the full meaning and reads it easily will depend on his background of experience, his ability to think and infer, as well as his skill in word recognition. A child who has heard about boats and shipwrecks will understand better why the captain gave up in despair as the ship was inexorably pulled toward the mountain. One who has played with magnets will grasp the significance of all this better than one who has not. The less mature child will interpret it all as something magical happening.

In interpreting print the reader makes use of his previous experience with words and language units, as well as his experience with the ideas and situations represented. On a higher level, reading requires seeing relationships between reading and other experiences and making applications of ideas gained from books.

Every experienced reader notes the greater ease of interpreting context with which he is familiar in contrast to material that is foreign to him. A teacher suddenly found himself required to read aloud the title of a journal article that was thrust into his hands, "Typology of Mithraic Tauroctones," but he was unable to read it, even though he could pronounce the words, because it was "all Greek to him." Here's a seven-year-old who can pronounce *prevention, duplicate,* and *elucidate,* even *gubernatorial,* but he cannot actually read these words because he does not grasp their meaning.

The thought processes in reading are subjective elements. Unlike the physical eye movements which can be measured directly, the nature of the thinking and interpretative processes during reading can only be inferred.

CLUES USED FOR GRASPING MEANING IN READING

The reader makes inferences from various clues: the foregoing sentences, the individual words and punctuation signs, and his knowledge of literary devices. Grasping meaning from the forepart of the sentence helps to predict what comes next. The more key words the reader comprehends in sentences the more efficiently he infers the meaning of the whole. A single word may be a clue to an entire sentence, and this word may be located anywhere in the sentence. The reader may even skip ahead to the end of the sentence for a clue to a word near the beginning of the sentence. The last word in the sentence may establish the correctness or incorrectness of the tentative inference.

Inferences are not limited to separate sentences but extend throughout a paragraph or an even longer unit. The meaning of adjacent sentences may help the reader interpret the meaning of the particular sentence before him. Sometimes, as one reads on in the paragraph, the vague meaning of what was encountered earlier becomes clearer, and a reinterpretation of the whole is necessary.

Punctuation marks, such as capital letters, the period at the end of a sentence, the apostrophe, and the question mark, also serve as clues to meaning.

USE OF REDUCED CLUES TO MEANING

A distinguishing trait of the experienced reader is his ability to use partial clues from the text for grasp of meaning. The mature reader works with greatest economy of time and effort, paying no more attention to the print than is absolutely essential to grasp the meaning. He has learned to respond to partial clues, the bare minimum needed for comprehension, instead of having to stare at each word in turn, as a beginner does. The most efficient reader gets the largest block of meaning with the fewest clues. Reading would be an irksome task without this use of partial clues, and the physical discomfort of reading word-by-word for three hours at a stretch would be unendurable.

The mature reader proceeds more or less subjectively; in fact, his reading is essentially paraphrasing as he anticipates through mental imagery the ideas to come even before the eyes have met the printed words, and fills in from his background of experience parts he does not actually see. The same process operates in listening to conversation: The experienced listener goes by clues; he can catch complicated meanings from hearing only parts of words or only the most significant words in sentences. This process of *cue reduction,* as it is called in psychology, is learned indirectly and incidentally like other aspects of reading behavior.

The Thought Span in Reading

As the eyes move across the lines of print the mind integrates the impressions of the words to form meaningful ideas. Contrary to the popular view, the mature reader does not interpret one eyeful of print at a time, but waits to perceive enough material to grasp a thought unit. The reader retains the impressions of a series of words until he is ready to make the interpretation.

The classical term for the forward sweep of the eyes ahead of the point of interpretation is *eye-voice span.* This phenomenon was first described by J. O. Quantz in a study published by Princeton University late in 1897 (14). Quantz noted that in oral reading, interpretation of print lagged behind the forward sweep of the eyes. The length of this span was not difficult to detect in oral reading because the distance could be measured between the point reached by the eyes in a line and the point in the line at which the voice was enunciating the words. Quantz found a high correlation between reading rate and width of the eye-voice span.

A few years later Dr. E. B. Huey described the *forward push* of association expectancy, in which the eyes pick up words ahead of their interpretation. He noted that the great advantage in this characteristic was that it permitted an uninterrupted stream of interpretation at a rapid rate with minimum error (11).

In the case of both oral and silent reading this span serves the same purpose, to insure maximum speed and accuracy in interpretation. As Dr. Buswell pointed out, an eye-voice span of considerable width is necessary for intelligent grasp of the material read, and for reading orally with good expression (2).

A wide anticipation span enables one to size up the situation before making a decision about the meaning of the series of words. A wide span also saves time, to the extent that it prevents regressing to correct errors. It depends on the operation of eye movements as described above, but skill in thinking meanings also influences the size of the span.

The A-span[3] is the mind's convenient way of dealing with uncertainties in the forthcoming combinations of words in sentences. This trait is especially serviceable in preventing errors in the meanings of words that are spelled the same but have different pronunciation and different meaning; also for interpreting word forms that have several different meanings. Dr. Buswell observed that when children failed to anticipate punctuation marks in oral reading they were totally unprepared for the voice expression required, e.g., a rising inflection in the case of the question mark. The good oral reader with a wide A-span grasps meanings in terms of thought units, hence he reads expressively to his audience much as though he were speaking.

The Braille reader depends on the A-span for rapid, errorless reading, just as the reader of print. Katherine Maxfield reported that better Braille readers read ahead on the next line with the left hand before the right hand had finished the preceding line. Immature readers in Braille, as those in sighted reading, have a short A-span. They keep the fingers of the right and left hands close together.

Actually the term eye-voice span is a misnomer for silent reading, either visual or Braille. In oral reading the A-span is the distance between the point to which the eyes have moved ahead in the line and the point which the voice has reached in pronouncing; in silent reading, the distance

---

[3] A-span, abbreviation for eye-voice span or anticipation span.

between the point to which the eyes have moved ahead and the point at which interpretation is taking place.

The A-span can be observed in oral reading by slipping a card over a line being read by the pupil and noting how far he can continue to read when perception is suddenly cut off. This span will indicate the amount of print the eyes fixated while the reading was going on.

The reader may have observed that he can look away from the page and even turn the page without disrupting the reading; when the lights suddenly go out while a person is occupied with his newspaper or a book, he can finish the sentence in the dark. To determine the presence of A-span in silent reading, place a card on the line being read and move it over to the right a word at a time. The card effectively cuts off vision of what lies ahead, preventing grasp of meaning in thought units, and often causing errors in interpretation of individual words.

Does the forward movement of the eyes have the same temporal relation to the lag of the inner voice in silent reading as in vocalized reading? There is no direct evidence on this point, but unquestionably the same relationship holds in both silent and oral reading.

During rapid silent reading the mind does not stop and wait as the eyes run on ahead; nor do the eyes suddenly stop at the end of a thought unit and wait for the mind to catch up. The whole process is so swift and fluent that a stream of thought moves steadily along, but it lags behind the progress of the eyes along the lines.

Although this phenomenon is reflected in the physical behavior of the eyes (or by the fingers in Braille reading), the length of the span is not controlled by the eye or finger movements, but by the reader's thought processes. For this reason the A-span cannot be photographed like the eye movements.

The steady, uniform tap-tap-tap of the eyes in pausing a number of times in each line of print was noted in an earlier section. Is this steady moving and regular pausing changed by the A-span? No, the A-span is quite independent of this mechanical motor process which is merely the vehicle for conveying the print to the mind for interpretation. However, there is a direct correlation between the minimum number of fixation pauses in a line and the width of A-span because both are indications of reading maturity.

The schematic diagram of Figure 2 illustrates the eye-voice span or A-span in reading as described above. Compare this diagram with Figure 1a.

ANTICIPATORY SPAN IN OTHER ACTIVITIES

The A-span is by no means limited to reading lines of print or Braille. It is found in all situations requiring interpretation of a succession of re-

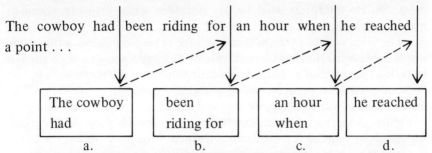

Figure 2. Schematic diagram illustrating the eye-voice span (A-span) in reading: a, b, c, and d represent points of interpretation as the eyes move ahead.

lated impressions rapidly without interruption or error. First of all, it is observed in listening to oral communication. The meaning is caught by listening ahead, not by listening for and interpreting each separate word as it comes along. The foreign-language interpreter makes use of the A-span right along in listening ahead for an earful before interpreting.

In speaking, also, the thought of the speaker runs some distance ahead of the point at which he is speaking in order to preserve coherence in what he is saying. Smooth sight reading in music is dependent upon this span. The expert performer holds in mind what the eyes perceive some distance ahead of the point where the music is being played to avoid mistakes and play expressively at the proper tempo. He can even keep on playing smoothly while turning the page because of eyefuls stored up on the previous page.

In telegraphy the operator receives the letters and fuses them together to form sentences for transmission at intervals. The A-span is also observed in stenography, and in typing from dictation and from copy. Another example is found in the experienced motorist who always drives "300 feet ahead." A trainer of jumping horses observed that the experienced horse anticipates the successive hurdles and prepares for them so as not to lose time in the combination of running and jumping.

CONTRAST BETWEEN THE EXPERIENCED AND THE IMMATURE READER IN A-SPAN

A wide A-span constitutes the most characteristic difference between the mature and the immature reader. Dr. Buswell's data proved that good readers had wider eye-voice span than poor readers at all levels of achievement. The mature reader keeps the eyes moving a distance ahead in the line so as to complete the thought before interpreting. Unlike the beginner, who tends to interpret each word one at a time, the experienced reader holds impressions of a series of words in mind before he makes an interpretation. He interprets what he has just seen while glancing ahead at what is to come.

The mind cannot perform this dual task in reading unless most of the words are familiar. Furthermore, a wide A-span presupposes a wide enough attention span to hold a series of words in mind until the meaning "clicks." So strong is the tendency to move ahead that, once it is habituated, the mature reader will find himself pushing ahead in new, difficult material, or in foreign-language reading, even though he fails to grasp the meaning. This is a form of habit response that is learned through continuous reading, much as the eye movements are learned without direct training.

The beginner and the retarded learner do not think word meanings relationally. The beginner's attention centers on decoding the individual words, e.g., the word *after* in the sentence "The boy ran *after* the ball." He scarcely dares to let his eyes glance over to the right of the point where he is dealing with a word. As a result he fails to phrase, hence to read fluently with expression, and to sense meanings easily. The adult reader of a new foreign language will note at once that his A-span drops back to near zero and he shows the characteristic behavior of a school beginner.

SIZE OF THE A-SPAN

How wide is the typical A-span in the case of the mature reader? The A-span is not of constant size but varies with the words and their meanings in the sentences. It varies in size depending upon the reader's familiarity with the vocabulary and the sense. This span is elastic, shortening or lengthening as the situation requires in order to get the correct meaning instantly. A-span is cut down automatically when any sort of difficulty is encountered. One of Dr. Buswell's subjects had a maximum span of 46 letters, but this was cut back to five when the word *hallucination* appeared.

The mature reader's span in silent reading ranges between 15 to 20 letter spaces, one third of a line at a maximum, two or three eyefuls of print. Quantz called attention to the varying length of the eye-voice span depending on the part of the sentence being read—fore, middle, or end part. The eye-voice span is longest at the beginning and shortest at the ends of the lines.

For 54 subjects Buswell reported an eye span of 15.9 letter spaces at the beginning of sentences, 13.4 in the middle, and 10.9 letter spaces at the ends of sentences. This difference was more marked in the case of good readers(2).

Fairbanks also found that the eye-voice span was shortest at the ends of sentences, but he found no difference in spans in the beginning and middle of sentences(7).

The span is shorter toward the end of the line because the train of thought is momentarily disrupted. Fortunately, the breaks at the ends of the lines do not constitute any marked disruption in the thought process because of the rapidity of the return sweep. The size of the span is also controlled by line length.

There is a human limit to the size of the A-span just as there is to the size of the perception span, but in the case of the first the limitation is mental—a matter of attention, experience, familiarity, and memory; in the latter case, the limit is physiological.

A period at the end of a sentence naturally marks the conclusion of a unit of thought, but the end of a span is by no means limited to periods. The point reached in the line when interpretation is made may or may not be at the end of a sentence or the end of a phrase.

What is the relative size of the A-span in oral and in silent reading? Buswell remarked that a comparison of the eye-voice span in oral and silent reading would be of interest, but even today this question cannot be answered for lack of objective evidence. The span is probably no larger in silent than in oral reading for the experienced reader, even though in silent reading he is interpreting faster.

One finding with a bearing on this phenomenon is the fact that a word not fixated with the eyes directly is recognized more easily if it is to the right of the fixation point rather than to the left. This is due to our habitual left-to-right reading direction.

Line length of no more than 27 to 30 letter spaces, such as those found in children's texts when two columns are printed on a page, do not provide for most efficient use of anticipatory span even for children in the middle grades.

Although the A-span in silent reading remains the most important feature of mature reading, it remains the least explored feature of the reading process, probably because the forward span in silent reading almost defies detection by objective means.

Speeding up in reading depends, in large part, on shortening the fixation pauses and lengthening the A-span, not on "speeding up the eye movements."

What is the relation between skimming and use of the anticipatory span in reading? There is none, because, strictly speaking, skimming is intentional paraphrasing through omission of material.

Relationship between Oral and Silent Reading

Oral and silent reading are assumed to be distinct processes, the reverse of each other, but the two processes have much in common. In both processes the reader is guided by clues to meaning from words and word parts. The mature reader has an A-span of similar length in both oral and silent reading. He tries to avoid regressing in oral reading but is not always successful. He uses the same return sweep in both processes. Except for pronunciation errors, the same sorts of mistakes are made in oral as in silent reading.

Earlier studies of O'Brien (13) and Cole (5) indicated that the average number of fixations in oral reading was greater than in silent reading, regressive movements were slightly more frequent, and the length of fixations was, on the average, greater in oral reading than in silent.

The difficult element in oral reading is the pronunciation of each word distinctly enough to be understood while the reader holds in mind the meaning of the passages. The task is easier to the extent that the reader is familiar with the vocabulary and the context.

Practice in oral reading contributes directly to fluency in silent reading because it familiarizes the reader with words and recurring phrases. There is no evidence that oral reading necessarily spoils eye movement habits for silent reading.

The mechanics of oral and silent reading are much the same so far as eye span and thought span are concerned, but the articulation required in oral reading necessarily slows down the process. For a person of average literacy, oral reading is only about 60 percent as rapid as mature silent reading: 150 words a minute (oral), 250 words a minute (silent).

Relation between Reading and Spelling

Although reading and spelling employ a common vocabulary, the two processes are essentially different. Reading requires recognition of the meanings of words; spelling is the opposite because it requires calling to mind the sequential order of letters in words and matching the letters to the sounds, e.g., *branch, bunch, brunch.* In spelling the pupil tries to recall the letters that compose the word; in reading, on the contrary, he studies the words, trying to figure them out from various clues.

In reading the more mature pupil gets along with partial impressions of words, tending to skip endings. In spelling he must give equal attention to all parts of the word he is writing.

The two processes come together at the point of word study when the pupil is trying to learn the association between the sounds and the letters that represent them, attempting to identify or recognize recurring sound elements in words for correct pronunciation of whole words or for partial sounding clues.

REFERENCES

1. Anderson, Irving H., and Walter F. Dearborn. *The Psychology of Teaching Reading.* New York: Ronald, 1952.
2. Buswell, Guy T. *An Experimental Study of the Eye-Voice Span in Reading.* Supplementary Educational Monographs, No. 17. Chicago: University of Chicago Press, 1920.
3. Buswell, Guy T. *Fundamental Reading Habits.* Chicago: University of Chicago Press, 1922.
4. Carmichael, Leonard, and Walter F. Dearborn. *Reading and Visual Fatigue.* Boston: Houghton Mifflin, 1947.
5. Cole, Luella. *The Improvement of Reading with Special Reference to Remedial Instruction.* New York: Holt, Rinehart and Winston, 1938.
6. Davis, Frederick B. "Fundamental Factors of Comprehension in Reading." *Psychometrika* (1944), 9:185–97.
7. Fairbanks, Grant. "The Relation between Eye-Movements and Voice in the Oral Reading of Good and Poor Silent Readers." Studies in the Psychology of Reading 1, University of Iowa Studies in Psychology, No. 21, *Psychological Monographs* (1937), Vol. 48, No. 3.
8. Gilbert, Luther C. *Functional Motor Efficiency of the Eyes and its Relation to Reading.* University of California Publications in Education (1953), Vol. 11, No. 3, 159–232.
9. Gray, C. T. *Types of Reading Ability as Exhibited through Tests and Laboratory Experiments.* Supplementary Educational Monographs, Vol. 1, No. 5. Chicago: University of Chicago Press, 1917.
10. Gray, W. S. "Reading Problems That Merit International Study." UNESCO Educational Studies and Documents, No. 20, 41–47. Paris: UNESCO, 1956.
11. Huey, E. B. *The Psychology and Pedagogy of Reading.* New York: Macmillan, 1908.
12. Lowenfeld, Berthold. "Psychological Problems of Children with Impaired Vision." *The Psychology of Exceptional Children and Youth* (William Cruickshank, Ed.) New York: Prentice-Hall, 1955. Chapter 5.
13. O'Brien, J. A. *Silent Reading.* New York: Macmillan, 1921.
14. Quantz, J. O. *Problems in the Psychology of Reading.* Psychological Review Monograph Supplement (1897), Vol. 2, No. 1. Princeton, N.J.: Psychological Review Co.
15. Taylor, Earl A. Bulletin of the Washington Square Reading Center. New York, 1954.
16. Thorndike, E. L. "Reading as Reasoning," *Journal of Educational Psychology* (1917), 8:323–32.
17. Vernon, M. D. *A Further Study of Visual Perception.* Cambridge, England: Cambridge University Press, 1952.
18. Walker, R. Y. "A Qualitative Study of the Eye Movements of Good Readers." *American Journal of Psychology* (1938), 51:472–81.

PART II

READING
READINESS
DEVELOPMENT
AT HOME
AND SCHOOL

Two major topics are treated in this part. The first concerns home environmental factors related to success in primary-grade reading. Some of the home environmental factors related to later reading success are: the oral language patterns used by the family members, the mother-child interaction, and the various prereading activities which are provided in the home. Prereading activities may include reading to the preschool child, providing him with books in the home, taking him on interesting family trips, and giving him manipulative materials with which to work.

The second topic deals with reading readiness development and early reading. One article discusses methods for reading readiness development which also can be used as an introduction to beginning reading. It shows how it is often difficult to differentiate between those activities which are used for reading readiness development and those used for beginning reading instruction. Miller (Selection 1) describes some characteristics of culturally disadvantaged children discovered as the result of two research studies on the relation of home environmental factors and primary-grade reading achievement. Certain aspects of the maternal and home environment which may cause children difficulty with beginning school experiences are described in an article by Hess and Shipman (Selection 2). Brzeinski, Harrison, and McKee (Selection 3) describe an interesting informal beginning reading program in kindergarten conducted in Denver which mainly used materials developed by McKee and Harrison. These special materials can be used for reading readiness development and combine the use of initial consonant sounds and oral context.

The following questions can be used to set purposes for the reading of the articles in Part II:

How is the home environment of disadvantaged children different from that of children in the middle class?

What aspects of the home environment are the most related to intellectual development and to success in primary-grade reading?

Should reading instruction be presented in kindergarten?

If reading instruction is begun in kindergarten, should it be of an informal or formal nature?

4 The Home Environment of Culturally Disadvantaged Children*

Wilma H. Miller

The difficulties that culturally disadvantaged children often experience with school learnings have been the subject of much research and writing during the past few years. Obviously, disadvantaged children have long been members of society, but the cognizance of their plight which is evidenced by current society certainly is one of the truly remarkable features of present educational research. The writer has had a unique opportunity to study the home environment of culturally disadvantaged children during two research studies which she has conducted in the midwest during the past several years (4). As a result of these studies and an extensive survey of the literature in this field, a number of generalizations about the home environment of disadvantaged children can be made.

Comments from the Literature

The majority of the researchers who have studied cultural deprivation have found comparable results. The homes of disadvantaged children

*This selection was written expressly for this volume.

were found to lack the physical stimuli that are needed for vocabulary and concept building. Their homes also were found to be noisy, congested, and inadequate in many respects(2). The parents of culturally disadvantaged children typically were found to employ a predominantly restricted language style, a manner of speaking in which a person uses simple sentence structure, few adjectives and adverbs, few complex verb forms, and an imprecise vocabulary(1). Furthermore, the parents of disadvantaged children rarely have been found to talk with their preschool children and to offer explanations for family rules. Rather, they expect compliance with family rules which may lead to their child's later passivity(1).

Culturally disadvantaged children also were found to employ a restricted language code which they have learned through the imitation of the language of their parents and older siblings. They therefore are unable to understand the more elaborated language style used by the middle-class oriented public school system(1). They also have impoverished vocabulary and concepts because of the lack of physical stimuli in their homes. As a result of this impoverished vocabulary and experiential background, culturally disadvantaged children usually have entered school with insufficient readiness for all school learning, and they have experienced more and more difficulty as they progressed through the elementary grades(2,3).

Maternal Behavior

As a result of talking with more than 40 mothers of culturally disadvantaged children during one-hour home interviews, some general impressions about maternal behavior can be stated.

The mothers employed a predominantly restricted language style with the use of simple sentence structure, simple verb forms, imprecise vocabulary, and incorrect grammar. A number of the mothers also employed a status-oriented control system, a type of family regulation in which the mother does not give her child a rationale for rules but merely expects compliance from him. A mother's use of a status-oriented control system may be a major reason for the passivity that disadvantaged children often display in school.

Some of the mothers of disadvantaged children used a passive teaching style in showing their children how to perform a simple task in the home. When a mother employed a passive teaching style, she did not outline the task in advance of her child's attempt to perform it nor did she give specific directions and positive reinforcement while the child was working on the task. The lack of instructive statements in the home may be another important cause of the disadvantaged child's lack of readiness for school instruction. A number of the mothers who were visited also did not take the time to talk with and listen to their children. Major reasons for this may be a mother's lack of time or her lack of awareness of the importance of communication.

Most of the mothers interviewed were very interested in their children and expressed great concern that their children do well in school. The main barrier for these mothers in preparing their children for school learning undoubtedly was a lack of competence rather than a lack of interest in the area. Many of the mothers asked the writer for specific directions to prepare their children for primary-grade instruction.

The Homes

The homes of the disadvantaged that were visited were located either in a midwestern rural area or a small midwestern city. All of the families had fathers living in the home who were predominantly elementary-school educated and who had semi-skilled or unskilled positions. The homes in the small midwestern city generally seemed to be more disadvantaged than did those in the rural area. All of the homes were lacking in the physical stimuli that are necessary for vocabulary and concept building. It is obvious that a preschool child cannot learn the word *picture* if there is no picture on the wall to serve as a referent for this term. Most of the homes were quite unkempt on both the outside and inside. However, the inside of the homes would be difficult to maintain in an orderly manner due to the lack of clothes closets, cupboards, and other areas in which to store the family possessions.

The furniture generally was meager and in poor repair. However, the writer saw a television set in every home that was visited. A number were color television sets, and the family life seemed to revolve around the television set which was on in each home when the writer arrived for the interview.

Some of the homes would be quite surprising to a person of the middle class. For example, one home in the midwestern city contained only one room with no partitions or drapes to divide the house. The living room furniture was found at the entrance of the house, while the bedroom furniture was placed near the middle of the house. The kitchen appliances and table were found in the back of the house.

The Culturally Disadvantaged
Children

Most of the families visited were large. The largest family had twelve children while the average number of children per family was approximately five. In general, the disadvantaged families in the rural area had more children than did the disadvantaged families in the small city.

At the time of the interviews all of the children were in kindergarten. The children generally employed a restricted language style with limited vocabulary, simple sentence structure, and some incorrect usage. Most of the children were quite shy and passive, but a few were both talkative and aggressive. In addition, many of them had difficulty in assembling a simple jigsaw puzzle that the writer brought to the home to assess maternal teaching style. The children generally seemed to be unsure of themselves and to have inadequate self-concepts.

Their daily home schedules were rather inadequate in comparison to the daily schedules of children in other social classes. The disadvantaged children engaged in less varied activities and had less parental supervision and interaction. For example, many of these children watched television for seven or eight hours per day. The children in the small midwestern city who went to afternoon kindergarten generally watched television for three hours in the morning, two hours in the late afternoon, and three or more hours in the evening. The disadvantaged children often went to bed much later than did children of other social groups. One disadvantaged child of kindergarten age usually went to bed at ten o'clock in the evening.

Typically, the culturally disadvantaged children were not ready for first-grade instruction. Their parents had not read to them very often, and they had few children's books to look at in their homes. Few of the children had ever been either to the public library or to a bookmobile. The children normally had poor visual and auditory perception skills and had engaged in few experiences that would help them to interpret effectively the stories in first-grade basal readers. A mother of nine children in the rural area indicated that her family had never gone anywhere. Undoubtedly the task of organizing a large family to take a trip even to a neighborhood park for a picnic is so difficult that it is seldom done. In addition, perhaps parents of disadvantaged children do not know of the learning that can be derived from a family excursion. Most of the children had used manipulative materials such as paper and crayons in their home, but few of them had used paints, scissors, or paste.

The rural disadvantaged children were given a readiness test in kindergarten and two reading achievement tests in first grade. Their readiness test scores indicated that they were less ready for first grade than were children in other social classes. They normally were in the "high-risk" category of readiness although a few of them did score well. In first-grade reading most of these children also did quite poorly. However, a few of them did achieve surprisingly well in first-grade reading, probably because of their first-grade teacher's positive influence.

Recently the writer tested the readiness of the small city disadvantaged children she studied. They also usually were found to be in the "high-risk" category of readiness although a few of them achieved a good readiness level.

Conclusions

The mothers of the disadvantaged employed a restricted language style, a status-oriented control system, and imperative statements. However, they were interested in learning how to help their children prepare for school.

The homes of the disadvantaged lacked physical stimuli for vocabulary and concept building, and the life of the home seemed to revolve around watching television.

The disadvantaged children usually were passive and had inadequate self-concepts. They also had poor visual and auditory discrimination skills and typically were not ready for first-grade instruction.

The attitude of the mothers of the disadvantaged seemed to indicate that an effort must be made to teach them how to prepare their preschool children for school instruction. Such training often must take place in the home because of young children whom they must care for. However, such training does not minimize the potential value of preschool projects such as the Head Start Program, which take the children out of their homes for compensatory education. Since the mother has contact with her child from the time of his birth, it does seem advantageous that she learn how to help him achieve readiness for school. She then would be able to help him several years before he normally would enter a program of compensatory education.

REFERENCES

1. Bernstein, Basil. "Social Class and Linguistic Development: A Theory of Social Learning," *Education, Economy, and Society.* New York: Free Press, 1961. Pp. 288–310.
2. Deutsch, Martin. "The Disadvantaged Child and the Learning Process," *Education in Depressed Areas.* New York: Columbia University Teachers College, Bureau of Publications, 1963. Pp. 1–5.
3. Deutsch, Martin. "The Role of Social Class in Language Development and Cognition," *American Journal of Orthopsychiatry,* XXXV (January 1965). Pp. 78–88.
4. Miller, Wilma H. "Relationship between Mother's Style of Communication and Her Control System to the Child's Reading Readiness and Subsequent Reading Achievement in First Grade." Unpublished doctoral dissertation, The University of Arizona, 1967.

5 | Early Blocks to Children's Learning*

Robert D. Hess
Virginia Shipman

The context of today's urgent need for preschool education, the central question is: Can we successfully intervene on a massive scale in the cycle of generation-to-generation transmission of poverty and semi-illiteracy? Any answer then at the present time would be based more on optimism that on experience and results. It would be naive, misleading, and irresponsible to make promises of easy success and instant results from large-scale programs intended to raise the educational level of children and families of low socioeconomic groups. There is some reason to be hopeful, but, at the present time, little basis for unrestrained enthusiasm.

Research now under way at the Urban Child Center of The University of Chicago is attempting to reach a great understanding of two related questions: (a) When we strip away personal concern and sympathy for human tragedy, and after we discard the political slogans, what *is* cultural deprivation and how does it get to shape and depress the resources of the human mind? (b) How does cultural disadvantage affect the mind of the young child?

*From *Children,* vol. 12, no. 5, September 1965, pp. 189–194. Based on a paper presented at the National Conference on Day Care Service. The research described is supported by the Children's Bureau, the Ford Foundation, and the University of Chicago.

Our hypotheses are these: first, that the behavior which leads to social, educational, and economic poverty is socialized in early childhood, that is, it is learned; and, second, that the central factor involved in the effects of cultural deprivation is a lack of cognitive meaning in the mother-child communication system.

We proceed on the assumptions (a) that the structure of the social system and the structure of the family shape communication and language; and (b) that language shapes thought and cognitive styles of problem-solving. In the deprived-family context, this means that the nature of the control system which relates parent to child restricts the number and kind of alternatives for action and thought that are opened to the child. Such constriction precludes a tendency for the child to reflect, to consider and choose among alternatives for speech and action, and develops modes for dealing with stimuli and with problems which are impulsive rather than reflective, which deal with the immediate rather than the future, and which are disconnected rather than sequential.

This position draws from the work of Basil Bernstein of the University of London. In his view, language conditions what the child learns, and how he learns, thus setting limits to his future learning.[1] He identifies two forms of communication codes or styles of verbal behavior: *restricted* and *elaborate.*

Restricted codes are stereotyped, limited, and condensed, lacking in specificity and in the exactness needed for precise conceptualization and differentiation. Sentences are short, simple, often unfinished; there is little use of subordinate clauses for elaborating the content of sentences: it is a language of implicit meaning, easily understood and commonly shared. It is the language often used in impersonal situations when the intent is to promote solidarity or reduce tension. Restricted codes are nonspecific clichés, statements, or observations about events, made in general terms that will be readily understood. By its nature, this mode limits the range and detail of concept and information involved.

Elaborate codes are those in which communication is individualized. The resultant message is specific to a particular situation, topic, and person: it is more particular, more differentiated, and more precise; and it permits expression of a wider and more complex range of thought, tending toward discrimination among cognitive and affective content.

Such early experiences affect not only the communication modes and cognitive structure; they also establish potential patterns of relationship with the external world. One of the dynamic features of Bernstein's work is his view of language as social behavior. As such, language is used by participants of a social network to elaborate and express inter-

---

[1] Basil Bernstein: Social class and linguistic development: a theory of social learning. In *Education, Economy, and Society* (A. H. Halsey, Jean Floud, and C. Arnold Anderson, eds.) Free Press of Glencoe, New York, 1961.

personal relationships and thus shape and determine these relationships. An understanding of the integral association between language and social structure is of critical importance for an understanding of the effects of poverty upon children. Within the individual family, this association emerges in terms of the principles which govern the decision-making activities, which, themselves, help regulate the nature and amount of social exchange.

Two Family Types

The interlacing of social interaction and language is illustrated by the distinction Bernstein makes between two types of families—those oriented toward control by *status* appeal, or ascribed role norms, and those oriented toward *persons*.[2]

In status-oriented families, behavior tends to be regulated in terms of role expectations. There is little opportunity in these families for the unique characteristics of the child to influence the decision-making process or the interaction between parent and child, the internal or personal needs of the children not being influential as a basis for decision. Norms of behavior are stressed with such imperatives as "You must do this because I say so," "Girls don't act like that," or other statements which rely, for justification, on the status of the participants or a behavior norm.

In the person-oriented family, the unique characteristics of the child modify status demands and are taken into account in interaction. The decisions of this type of family are individualized and less frequently related to status or role ascriptions. Behavior is justified in terms of feelings, preference, personal and unique reactions, and subjective states. This philosophy not only permits, but demands, an elaborated linguistic code and a wide range of linguistic and behavior alternatives in interpersonal interaction. Status-oriented families may be regulated by less individuated commands, messages, and responses than person-oriented families. (Indeed, by its nature, the status-oriented family relies more heavily on a restricted code; the verbal exchange is inherent in the structure, regulates it and is regulated by it.)

These distinctions may by clarified by two examples of mother-child communication, using these two types of codes.

Assume that the emotional climate of two homes is approximately the same, the significant difference between them being in the style of communication employed. A child is playing noisily in the kitchen with an assortment of pots and pans when the telephone rings. In one home, the mother says, "Be quiet," "Shut up," or gives some other short, peremp-

[2] Basil Bernstein: Family role systems, communications, and socialization. Unpublished paper prepared for the Cross-National Conference on Research on Children and Adolescents, University of Chicago, Chicago, Ill., February 20–28, 1964.

tory command, and answers the phone while the child sits still on the floor. In the other home, the mother asks: "Would you keep quiet while I answer the phone?"

The questions our study poses are these: What inner response is elicited in the child in each of these two situations, and what is the effect upon his developing cognitive network of concepts and meaning?

In one instance, the child is asked for a simple mental response. He is asked to attend to an uncomplicated message and to make a conditioned response (to comply); he is not called upon to reflect or make mental discriminations. In the other example, the child is required to follow two or three ideas; he is asked to relate his behavior to a time dimension; he must think of this behavior in relation to its effect upon another person; he must perform a complicated task in following the communication of his mother in that his relationship to her is mediated in part through concepts and shared ideas; and his mind is stimulated or exercised (in an elementary fashion) by more elaborate and complex verbal communication presented by the mother.

As objects of these two divergent styles of communication, repeated in various ways, in similar situations and circumstances, the two imaginary children would be expected to develop significantly different verbal facility and cognitive equipment by the time they entered the public school system.

In our project, we view the child as an organism which receives a great deal of information of many kinds, much more than he can accommodate. What he responds to, how he interprets stimuli, and how he reacts to it, the child learns in interaction with the environment. In other words, he is taught what to respond to, how to interpret messages, and how to respond. These patterns of cognitive activity, socialized in early experience in the home, become the basis on which the child's further cognitive development proceeds.

An analysis of language and social structure is necessarily concerned with the consequences of linguistic codes and their accompanying patterns of parental interaction upon the developing cognitive faculties of the child. It is our argument that person-oriented families tend to justify behavior and emphasize its consequences; and that status-oriented families ask for rote learning and acceptance of the status quo—that is, they use a more rigid learning and teaching model, in which compliance, rather than rationale, is stressed.

The Project

For our research, 160 Negro mothers and their four-year-old children were selected from four different socioeconomic levels: Group A came from college-educated professional, executive, and managerial occupational levels; Group B from skilled blue-collar occupational levels, with not more than high school education; Group C from unskilled or semi-skilled occupational levels, with predominantly elementary school education; and Group D from unskilled or semiskilled occupational levels, with fathers absent and family supported by public assistance.

These mothers were interviewed twice in their homes and brought to the university for testing in an interaction section between mother and child in which the mother was taught three simple tasks by a staff member, then asked to teach these tasks to the child.

One of these tasks was to sort or group a number of plastic toys by color and by function. The second was to sort eight blocks by two characteristics simultaneously. The third required mother and child to work together to copy five designs on a toy called "Etch-a-Sketch."

The objective of the project is to relate the behavior and performance of individual mothers to the cognitive and scholastic behavior of their own children. We expect to follow the children of the study through the first 4 years of school, to obtain data on a more complete range of behavior. At our present, relatively early, stage of analysis, data are being examined in terms of social class differences among the four socioeconomic groups of the study—professional (middle), skilled workers (upper lower), unskilled (lower lower), and public assistance (AFDC). At this point in the project, our data about the cognitive behavior and language skills of the children are limited.

The wide range of individual differences in linguistic and interactional styles of these mothers may be illustrated by excerpts from recordings of one of the structured teaching situations, the task of the mothers being to teach the child how to group, or sort, a small number of toys.

The first mother outlines the task for the child, giving sufficient help and explanation to permit the child to proceed on his own. She says:

> "All right, this board is the place where we put the little toys. First of all, you're supposed to learn how to place them according to color. Can you do that? The things that are all the same color you put in one section; in the second section you put another group of colors and in the third section you put the last group of colors. Can you do that? Or would you like to see me do it first?"
>
> *Child:* "I want to do it."

This mother has given explicit information about the task and what is expected of the child; she has offered support and help of various kinds; and she has made it clear that she impelled the child to perform.

The style of a second mother is not quite so easily grasped by the child. She says, in introducing the same task:

"Now I'll take them off the board; now you put them all back on the board. What are these?"

Child: "A truck."

"All right, just put them right here; put the other one right here; all right, put the other one there."

This mother relies more on physical signs and nonverbal communication in her commands; she does not define the task for the child; the child is not provided with ideas or information that he can grasp in attempting to solve the problem; neither is he told what to expect or, even in general terms, what the task is.

A third mother is even less explicit. She introduces the task as follows:

"I've got some chairs and cars. Do you want to play the game?"

The child does not respond.

The mother continues: "O.K. What's this?"

Child: "A wagon?"

Mother: "This is not a wagon. What's this?"

The conversation continues with this sort of exchange. Here again, the child is not provided with the essential information he needs to solve or to understand the problem. There is clearly some coercion, on the part of the mother, for the child to perform; but the child has not been told what he is to do.

Each teaching session was concluded with an assessment by a staff member of the extent to which the child had learned the concepts taught by the mother. His achievement was scored in two ways: first, the ability to place or sort the objects correctly: and second, the ability to verbalize the principle on which the sorting or grouping was made.

Social Class Differences

There were marked social class differences in the ability of the children to learn from their mothers in the teaching sessions. Children from middle-class homes ranked above children from the lower socioeconomic levels in performance on these sorting tasks, particularly in offering verbal explanations as to the basis for sorting. Over 60 percent of middle-class children placed the objects correctly on all tasks. The performance of children from the other groups ranged as low as 33 percent correct. Approximately 40 percent of the middle-class children who were successful were able to verbalize the sorting principle. Children from the lower socioeconomic groups were, on the whole, less able to explain the sorting principle. These differences clearly paralleled the relative abilities and teaching skills of the mothers from the different groups.

The differences among the four socioeconomic levels were apparent not only in sorting and verbal skills, but also in the mother's ability to regulate her own behavior and her child's in performing tasks which require planning or care rather than verbal or conceptual skill.

These differences were revealed by the mother-child performance on the "Etch-a-Sketch" task.

An "Etch-a-Sketch" toy is a small, flat box with a screen on which lines can be drawn by a device within the box. The marker is controlled by two knobs: one for horizontal movement, the other for vertical. The mother is assigned one knob, the child the other. The mother is then shown several designs which are to be reproduced. Together, they attempt to copy the models.

The products are scored by measuring deviations from the original designs. The mother decides when their product is a satisfactory copy of the original designs.

These sessions were recorded, and the nonverbal interaction was described by an observer. Some of the most relevant results were these: middle-class mothers and children performed better on the task (6 points) than mothers and children from the lower groups (9.2; 8.3; 9.5). Mothers of the three lower socioeconomic groups were relatively persistent, producing more complete figures than the middle-class mothers; mothers from the middle class praised the child's efforts much more than other mothers did, but gave him as much criticism; the child's cooperation, as rated by the observer, was as good or better in low socioeconomic groups as in the middle-class pairs; and there was little difference between the groups in affect as expressed to the child by the mother.

In these data, as in others, the mothers differed relatively little in the affective elements of their interaction with their children. The gross differences appeared in the verbal and cognitive environments which they presented. The significance of the maternal environment lies not only in the lack of verbal exchange but also in the kind of interaction that develops between learner and teacher. Mothers of blue-collar classes appear to be socializing passive learning styles on the part of the child, teaching him to be docile in such learning situations—in contrast to the more active, initiatory behavior of the child from the middle-class home.

One Question, Several Responses

The women in the study also varied in their perception of school. Applying Bernstein's concept of status-oriented and person-oriented families to our question, we analyzed maternal responses to the question: "I imagine your child is old enough to go to public school for the first time. How would you prepare him? What would you tell him?"

One mother, who was person-oriented and used elaborated verbal codes, replied as follows:

> "First of all, I would remind her that she was going to school to learn, that her teacher would take my place, and that she would be expected to follow instructions. Also that her time was to be spent mostly in the classroom with other children, and that she would consult with her teacher for assistance on any questions or problems that she might have."
>
> "Anything else?"
>
> "No. Anything else would probably be confusing for her at her age."

In terms of promoting educability, what did this mother do in her response? First, she was informative, presenting the school situation as comparable to one already familiar to the child; second, she offered reassurance and support to help the child deal with anxiety; third, she described the school situation as one which involves a personal relationship between the child and the teacher; and fourth, she presented the classroom situation as one in which the child was to learn.

A second mother responded as follows to the same question:

> "Well, John, it's time to go to school now. You must know how to behave. The first day at school you should be a good boy and should do just what the teacher tells you to do."

In contrast to the first mother, what did this mother do? First, she defined the role of the child as passive and compliant; second, the central issues she presented were those dealing with authority and the institution, rather than with learning; third, the relationship and roles she portrayed were sketched in terms of status and role expectations, rather than in personal terms; and fourth, her message was general, restricted, and vague, lacking information about how to deal with the problems of school, except by passive compliance.

These responses illustrated the tendency for status-oriented families and relationships to restrict the linguistic codes used in communication. The child who comes to school with a status orientation is prepared to engage in rote learning with passive acceptance of school authority in the learning situation. His initiative and participation in the learning possibilities of the school are meager. Not all such children accept the authority of the school in this unquestioning fashion, but they have few alternatives except to resist and rebel. The range of choice open to them is limited by the nature of the cognitive and interactional environment in which they have had experience.

A more detailed analysis of the mothers' responses to this question grouped their statements as *imperative* or *instructive*. An imperative statement was defined as an unqualified injunction or command, such as: "Mind the teacher and do what she tells you to do," or "The first thing you have to do is be on time," or "Be nice and do not fight." An instructive statement offers information or commands which carry a rationale or justification for the rule to be observed. Examples: "If you are tardy, or if you stay away from school, your marks will go down," or "I would tell him about the importance of minding the teacher. The teacher needs his full cooperation. She will have so many children that she won't be able to pamper any youngster."

Cultural Deprivation

Against this background let us return to the problem of the meaning, or perhaps more correctly, the lack of meaning in cultural deprivation. One of the features of the behavior of mothers and children of lower socioeconomic class is a tendency to act without taking sufficient time for reflection and planning. In a sense, one might call this impulsive behavior, not the acting out of unconscious or forbidden impulses, but a type of activity in which a particular act seems to be unrelated to the act that preceded it, or to its consequences. In this sense, it lacks meaning; it is not sufficiently related to the context in which it occurs, to the motivations of the participants, or to the goals of the task.

This behavior may be verbal or motor and it shows itself in several ways. On the "Etch-a-Sketch" task, for example, the mother may silently watch a child make an error, and then punish him. Another mother will anticipate the error and warn the child that he is about to reach a decision point; she will prepare him by verbal and nonverbal cues to be careful, to look ahead, and avoid the mistake. He is encouraged to reflect, to anticipate the consequences of his action and in this way avoid error.

Recall the example of the mothers and the telephone calls: one child was prompted to relate his actions to those of another person and to a time dimension, to delay, to observe, and to consider the consequences; the other was given a command that called for no reflection and did not require him to relate his behavior to the context in which it occurred. This is a model of a conditioned response, rather than a problem-solving strategy. A problem-solving approach requires reflection and the ability to weigh decisions, to choose among alternatives. The effect of restricted speech and of status orientation is to foreclose the need for reflective weighing of alternatives and consequences. The use of an elaborated code, with its orientation to persons and to consequences (including future), tends to produce cognitive styles more easily adapted to problem-solving and reflection.

The objective of our study is to discover how teaching styles of the mothers induce and shape learning styles and information-processing strategies in the children. The picture that is beginning to emerge is that the meaning of deprivation is a deprivation of meaning—a cognitive environment in which behavior is controlled by status rules, rather than by attention to the individual characteristics of a specific situation, and one in which behavior is not mediated by verbal cues or by teaching which relates events to one another and the present to the future. This environment produces a child who relates to authority rather than to rationale; who, although often compliant, is not reflective in his behavior; and for whom the consequences of an act are largely considered in terms of immediate punishment or reward, rather than future effects and long-range goals.

Program Implications

If this picture is substantially correct, there are several implications for preschool programs.

For example, it would argue that enrichment for the sake of enrichment may miss the point—that it is not additional, or even more varied, stimulation that is needed, but experiences which give stimuli a pattern of sequential meaning. It argues that such programs must not merely teach the child new words, but must show the child how ideas and events are related to one another. And it argues that the transition that a child must make from a cognitive style of immediate reactivity to one of problem-solving must be made by experiences with authority, not with machines.

When the data are more complete, a more detailed analysis of the findings will enable us to examine the effect of maternal cognitive environments in terms of individual mother-child transactions, rather than in the gross categories of social class. This analysis will not only help us to understand how social class environment is mediated through the interaction between mother and child, but will also give more precise information about the effects of individual maternal environments on the cognitive growth of the young child.

6 Should Johnny Read in Kindergarten?* — Yes

Joseph E. Brzeinski
M. Lucile Harrison
Paul McKee

A study of 4,000 Denver school children sought to learn whether beginning reading could be taught effectively in kindergarten. The children, whom we followed from kindergarten through the fifth grade, were randomly assigned by their schools to comparable control groups (1,500 pupils) and experimental groups (2,500 pupils) for kindergarten instruction. The teaching of the two groups was similar except for one major difference: The children in the experimental groups were given special reading instruction for 20 minutes a day.

This instruction consisted of seven types of learning activities:

1. *Spoken context.* From sentences or short paragraphs read or spoken by the teacher, the pupils practiced using context to figure out several words that would make sense where the teacher had omitted a word. (Johnny drank his _____. milk, juice, water)

2. *Initial consonant sounds.* The children gained awareness of beginning consonant sounds by sorting objects according to the initial sounds of their names, by naming words that began with the same sounds as words spoken by the teacher, and so on.

*From *NEA Journal,* vol. 56, March 1967, pp. 23–25. The research reported herein was supported by the Cooperative Research Program of the Office of Education, U.S. Department of Health, Education, and Welfare.

3. *Forms of letters.* They learned to recognize capital and small letters by matching and naming them in games.
4. *Context and initial consonant sounds.* The pupils practiced using the context of a sentence or paragraph read or spoken by the teacher and a beginning consonant sound supplied by her to think of the correct missing word. (Tom wants to cut a board in half. He needs a tool that begins with the same sound as *sit* and *sat*. He needs a _____. saw)
5. *Sounds and forms of letters.* The forms of letters were related to the sounds they make by grouping pictures of objects according to the beginning letters of their names, rearranging incorrectly placed picture cards in their proper groups, and so on.
6. *Context and displayed initial letter.* The children practiced using context and a viewed letter to figure out the missing word in a sentence or paragraph read or spoken by the teacher.
7. *Context and displayed word.* The teacher read or spoke a sentence or paragraph in which the word omitted was the only one that would make sense. At the same time she displayed the entire printed word on a card and asked the pupils to name the word.

The children in the control group followed the regular kindergarten program, typical of those in many parts of the country.

When the children entered first grade, both the experimental groups and the control groups were divided into two subgroups.

Group I — The Control Group (750 pupils)

Regular program in kindergarten
Regular program in the first and later grades

Group II — The Delayed-Experimental Group (750 pupils)

Regular program in kindergarten
Experimental program in early first grade
Adjusted program in the first and later grades

Group III — The Short-Term Experimental Group (1,250 pupils)

Experimental program in kindergarten
Regular program in the first and later grades

Group IV — The Experimental Group (1,250 pupils)

Experimental program in kindergarten
Adjusted program in the first and later grades.

We followed the four groups through the fifth grade. Group I provided a base against which to compare other groups. Group II enabled us to compare groups who received the same instruction introduced at different times. Group III showed the effect on the children's performance of shifting to regular instruction after one year of experimental instruction. Group IV was the full-scale experimental group, having a teaching program adjusted to the children's level of achievement throughout the study.

The regular reading program was similar to those programs suggested in teachers' manuals of most basal texts.

We evaluated and analyzed the experimental and control groups from the standpoint of every relevant variable: chronological and mental age when the child is first taught reading; his sex, IQ, and family characteristics. We gave particular attention to the relationship between age when first taught reading and the other variables as it affected reading achievement.

The findings were:

1. Beginning reading can be effectively taught to large numbers of typical kindergarten pupils. The Denver children readily learned letter-sound associations for commonly used consonants and acquired skill in identifying new printed words by using context and beginning-letter-sound associations.

2. The gains made by the experimental group could be maintained only by following up the kindergarten year with an adjusted teaching program in the subsequent grades. The children who received the experimental instruction in kindergarten and who had an adjusted program in later grades (Group IV) registered the highest reading achievement. We found the adjustment to be vital if the advantages of early reading instruction were to be preserved beyond the second grade.

3. The experimental kindergarten group (Group IV) showed the greatest initial and long-range gains in both reading comprehension and reading vocabulary. They also did better in other areas that depended on reading proficiency.

4. The children in Group IV read with greater speed than any of the other groups when tested at the end of the third grade.

5. Those children who were given the experimental instruction in the first grade, rather than in the kindergarten, and then were given an adjusted program in subsequent grades (Group II), did second best in reading achievement.

6. No evidence was found that early instruction in beginning reading affected visual acuity, created problems of school adjustment, or caused dislike for reading.

A little girl in one of the experimental classes who came from a broken home and was living with her grandmother was emotionally disturbed and could not enter into most of the activities of the class. During a demonstration, the teacher advised the demonstrator not to ask for responses from that child. But shortly after the demonstration teaching began, the child showed interest and literally demanded to be heard.

She could and did respond to the program with more success than many others. When she found how well she was doing, she grinned from ear to ear for the first time in the new school. After a few more successful responses, she actually cried for joy. From that time on, her emotional problems began to disappear. She had found herself in this program.

This investigation gives reassuring evidence that early reading instruction need not be harmful to children. Instead, the evidence shows that it can have a positive, measurable, continuing effect. Undoubtedly, potential dangers do exist, but the experimental methodology we used has shown that they can be avoided through employing a proper procedure. The possible hazards do not constitute an excuse for opposing change or for inaction.

A surprising and most important aspect of the study is the finding that most *average* youngsters in a large city public school system can profit from beginning reading instruction in kindergarten. Advanced reading achievement was not limited to precocious, gifted children from high socioeconomic backgrounds. The children in this study had the wide range of abilities and representative backgrounds usually found in large urban schools.

No elaborate screening or readiness testing was used. However, teachers were advised to delay starting any child they felt to be too immature to begin the program with the whole group.

One teacher told us about a small boy who, she had decided, was not mature enough to begin with the group. She found other areas of interest for him to work in while she taught reading to the experimental group. It soon became obvious, however, that the boy kept listening to the teacher and was so interested in what was going on that he ignored the substitute program planned for him. Each day he edged a little closer to the experimental group until one day he saw an empty chair and joined the group. He soon caught up with the others, and eventually passed them in achievement.

The implications of the study seem clear. School systems must re-evaluate the goals they have established for their kindergartens. Emerging psychological theory, recent research evidence, and the present study suggest that children profit from early educational stimulation. As a result of changes that have occurred in their environment, children today appear to have a greater aptitude for learning. Methods and materials of instruction are better.

Other school systems might well experiment with early introduction in language, writing, science, or number skills, to name but a few possibilities.

MODERN ELEMENTARY READING APPROACHES

The third part of this book contains articles on the modern approaches to elementary reading instruction. The language-experience approach which makes use of child-dictated and child-written experience stories is described. The language-experience approach is an excellent way to initiate reading instruction and to supplement later reading instruction. The basal reader approach also is described. This approach provides children, especially those in the primary grades, with an excellent way to learn all of the word recognition and comprehension skills. The individualized reading plan makes use of reading materials which are self-selected and self-paced by the children who are using them. This is an excellent way for children to reinforce the reading skills which they have learned by using another reading method. The best features of the language-experience, the basal reader, and the individualized reading approaches can be combined in what is called a combination or an eclectic reading approach.

Allen, a publicizer of the language-experience approach, gives a noncritical description of the approach and describes how it effectively can be used (Selection 7). The language-experience approach also is explained in an article by Miller (Selection 8), and she describes some of its uses and limitations.

In two articles, Brown (Selection 9) and Moir and Curtis (Selection 10) describe some of the aspects of the basal reader approach and indicate some of its limitations. The point is made that some of the limitations of the basal reader approach occur when it is not used in the way in which it was designed to be used. Staiger (Selection 11) describes how the basal reader approach can be used in elementary reading instruction.

Barbe (Selection 12), a proponent of individualized reading, describes how it effectively can be used. The conducting of an individualized reading program also is described in an article by Carlton and Moore (Selection 13) in which they answer questions about it. In two articles Groff (Selection 14) and Rollins (Selection 15) discuss some additional aspects of how to begin the individualized reading plan in an elementary classroom.

In one article, Blakely and McKay (Selection 16) illustrate one way in which individualized reading can be used in combination with another approach to develop an eclectic reading program. Stauffer (Selection 17) also discusses how several reading approaches can be used in combination to utilize most effectively the best features of each approach.

The application of linguistic principles to elementary reading instruction are described. Linguistic principles are related to the science and structure of the English language. The initial teaching alphabet and its implications for beginning reading instruction are described in several articles. The initial teaching alphabet (i/t/a) is an artificial orthography employing 44 symbols with a regular phoneme (sound)-grapheme (symbol) relationship. Words in color, a system which uses color as an aid to word recognition, also is discussed. Words in color often can be used effectively with another approach to beginning reading since it emphasizes the decoding aspects of reading. An approach emphasizing neurological dominance which sometimes is used with disabled readers is discussed in one article.

The contributions of linguistics to teaching elementary reading are described in an article by Cooper (Selection 18). Downing (Selection 19) has conducted the research in England on the use of the initial teaching alphabet for beginning reading instruction. He discusses the results of his research over a period of six years. Kirkland (Selection 20) also describes a research study which she conducted dealing with the use of both the initial teaching alphabet and traditional orthography in a beginning reading program.

Sister M. Raphael (Selection 21) describes the advantages of using words in color to teach the decoding aspects of reading. Hammill and Mattleman (Selection 22) describe the value of using programmed reading instruction in the primary grades. Olson, Olson, and Duncan (Selection 23) critically evaluate a possible relation between neurological dominance and reading disability in their article.

The following questions may serve to guide the reading of the various articles in Part III:

How can the language-experience approach most effectively be used in the primary grades?

Are the limitations of the basal reader approach inherent in the approach itself or in the way in which it is used by some elementary teachers?

Is an individualized reading program difficult to organize for an inexperienced teacher?

How can an eclectic reading approach be formed from several other reading approaches?

How can the science of linguistics make its maximum contribution to the teaching of elementary reading?

What is the chief advantage of the use of the initial teaching alphabet in beginning reading instruction?

How can programmed reading be used in the elementary grades?

7 | A New Approach to Reading*

Roach Van Allen

> The teacher who walks in the shadow of the temple, among his followers, gives not of his wisdom but rather of his faith and his lovingness.
>
> If he is indeed wise he does not bid you enter the house of his wisdom, but rather leads you to the threshold of your own mind.
>
> Kahlil Gibran
The Prophet

Professional educators today often echo Kahlil Gibran, the Lebanese prophet. We repeat glibly: learning must be based upon the experiences of the learner; the teacher must accept the child where he is; a child's perception of himself is a key factor in learning anything at any level; and flexibility in the educational program is essential to the development of the child's personality and interests. But much as we agree with these principles, most of us seem unable to teach accordingly. We continue to bid children enter the house of our own wisdom. We try to "give" them a reading program that is best for them. The gift, in too many cases, is a highly structured one that many young children do not understand.

We select materials to be used for direct instruction before we see the

*From Wilson Library Bulletin, vol. 39, October 1964, pp. 154–159. Reprinted by permission from the October 1964 issue of the Wilson Library Bulletin. Copyright © 1964 by The H. W. Wilson Company.

children we are to teach. Most of these materials were prepared in detail even before these children were born. They leave little room and little time for the personal language of children. Everything important has been prepared, predetermined and prepatterned: selection of content, order of presentation, and frequency of word repetition; which context clues to use; what consonant and vowel sounds to teach and when, etc. Questions are formulated and answers are determined prior to pupil contact with the reading materials, so most student response is limited to simple comprehension. Limited attention is given to the child's interaction with the ideas of the authors. The total language used is identical for all children, regardless of individual language experiences. Adjustment to individual differences is made through *pacing,* not through the use of varied materials.

Does teaching reading with this format place unnecessary limitations on children's achievement? Do *all* teachers have to struggle with these limitations? Can we remove some of the limitations and still have an organized, well-developed reading program?

The Language Experience Approach

Teachers and administrators in San Diego County, California, and many other places are convinced that there are ways of working with children to help them move into reading as a natural, normal extension of their own language experiences. Such methods are called the language experience approach in reading instruction. The description of this approach was formulated during the progress of the San Diego County Reading Study Project.[1] Most of the elements of the program had been in existence in classrooms as supplementary to the basal reading program, but few teachers had ever used the framework of the language experience approach as a major one.

The design of the San Diego County Reading Study Project included two other approaches to reading instruction: basal reader and individualized reading.[2] With each approach there was an attempt to observe, record, and analyze "what happens" to children's attitudes and achievements when the philosophy of any one of the three approaches is used as the major focus in an elementary classroom. The study also attempted to find out "what happens" to teacher attitudes and ability to change from one approach to another. The results of this extensive and penetrating

[1] San Diego County Department of Education. *Report of the Reading Study Project,* Improving Reading Instruction, Monograph No. 1. Superintendent of Schools, San Diego County, Calif., 1961.
[2] San Diego County Department of Education. *Description of Three Approaches to the Teaching of Reading,* Improving Reading Instruction, Monograph No. 2. Superintendent of Schools, San Diego County, Calif., 1961.

study are too voluminous to report here, but they are summarized in order to help the reader understand the high level of interest that has been generated for further description and implementation of the language experience approach.

Results of the San Diego Project

1. There are many effective ways of teaching reading in our schools. Teachers using all three approaches obtained "better than average" results as measured by standardized reading tests.
2. With an adequate in-service education program, teachers can and will change their point of view and practices in teaching reading.[3]
3. All three approaches were improved when teachers participated in a quality in-service educational program.
4. The way a child sees himself as a reader is a much greater factor in reading achievement than the use of any specific method of instruction. Therefore, any approach which seeks to involve the learner in a meaningful way will effect good achievement for the largest number of children.[4]
5. Within a school district, or within a school building, teachers should be permitted to select from various approaches the one (or combination of several) that is best suited to his teaching personality, the materials available, and the background and interests of his children.
6. The level and quality of social interaction between teacher and pupils has as much to do with achievement as the method used. Children who really understand what they are doing develop higher reading competencies, regardless of the method employed. Teachers should employ approaches which promote the highest level of teacher-pupil interaction.[5]
7. The use of predetermined controlled vocabulary in reading instruction is not as significant as was once thought. The unnatural sentences resulting from such control may present so many other difficulties for children that they may be harder to read than sentences using natural language.
8. There is a closer relationship between phonics and writing than between phonics and reading. Increased understanding of the phonetic elements of our language is best developed through activities which deal with the language letter-by-letter, syllable-by-syllable, and word-by-word. This suggests a planned program of spelling and writing to accompany reading from the beginning stages and continuing through the grades. Phonics instruction which is not reinforced with writing experiences is wasteful and inefficient.
9. Studies of reading instruction should be carried on as cooperative ventures if they are to make an impact on practice in any geographical area. No

[3] San Diego County Department of Education. *A Teacher Inventory of Approaches to Teaching Reading.* Monograph No. 3. Superintendent of Schools, San Diego County, Calif., 1961.
[4] San Diego County Department of Education. *An Inventory of Reading Attitude,* Improving Reading Instruction, Monograph No. 4. Superintendent of Schools, San Diego County, Calif., 1961.
[5] Anna L. Hoihjelle, *Social Climate and Personality Traits of Able Teachers in Relation to Reading Instruction.* Unpublished Dissertation, University of California, Berkeley, 1962.

district which was involved in the San Diego County Reading Study Project had, by itself, the personnel and other resources for such a comprehensive study.

The Fundamentals of the Approach

The basic ideas and fundamental concepts of the language experience approach in reading are rooted in antiquity. Great teachers have always expounded theories and implemented their ideas through practices which we describe as *creativity, discovery, interaction, self-concept, human dignity,* and *independence.* In the area of reading instruction in the United States, there have been attempts to keep the communication skills (listening, speaking, writing, and reading) together in the instructional program so that language learning could reinforce the thinking process described in the above terms. William H. McGuffy, in his *Eclectic Readers,* attempted to keep oral language and written language at the heart of reading development. During the same period, William T. Harris, superintendent of schools, St. Louis, Missouri, wrote the *Appleton's School Readers.* In his message to teachers, he said: "Children should be furnished with slates and pencils on their first entrance to school, and should be taught to write or 'print' as they are taught to read."[6]

It was when we became more and more specialized in curriculum planning and development of materials for instruction that reading instruction was separated from other language experiences to the point that the others tended to be neglected. In its simplest definition, the language experience approach in reading instruction is an attempt to keep listening, speaking, writing, and reading experiences together during instruction, especially at the beginning levels. The "togetherness" of skill development makes possible the child's continued use of his own experience background and personal language as he begins to understand both the English language in its printed form and the thinking processes involved when he comes in contact with the ideas and language of other authors.

More than other approaches, a language experience approach uses the thinking of individual children in the development of materials which promote skill development.

Language Experiences To Be Developed

The language experiences that must be developed to assure effective communication were defined during the San Diego County Reading Study

[6] William T. Harris, *Appleton's School Readers, The First Reader.* New York, American Book Company, 1877, p. 2.

Project and are used as guides for teachers who employ the language experience approach. These language experiences include:

Group One: Extending Experiences with Words

1. Sharing experiences—the ability to tell, write, or illustrate a personal experience.
2. Discussion experiences—the ability to interact with what other people say and write.
3. Listening to stories—the ability to listen to others and to relate what is said to one's own experiences.
4. Telling stories—the ability to organize one's thinking so that it can be shared orally or in writing in a clear and interesting manner.
5. Dictating words, sentences, and stories—the ability to choose, from all that might be said orally, the *most important* part for someone else to write and read.
6. Writing independently—the ability to record one's own ideas and present them for others to read.
7. Making and reading books—the ability to organize one's own ideas into a form that others can use. Also, the ability to use ideas which appear in books.

Group Two: Studying the English Language

1. Developing speaking, writing, and reading relationships—the ability to conceptualize that reading is speech that has been written and then reconstructed.
2. Expanding vocabulary—the ability to expand one's vocabulary through listening, speaking, reading, writing (including spelling).
3. Reading a variety of symbols—the ability to read in one's total environment: clock, calendar, dials, thermometer.
4. Developing awareness of common vocabulary—the ability to recognize that our language contains many common words and patterns of expression that must be mastered. One must be able to recognize them at sight and spell them correctly in writing.
5. Improving style and form—the ability to profit from listening to, reading, and studying the mechanics of well-written materials.
6. Studying words—the ability to find the correct pronunciation and meanings of words and to spell the words in written activities.

Group Three: Relating Ideas of Authors to Personal Experiences

1. Reading whole stories and books—the ability to read books for information, recreation, and improvement of reading skills.
2. Using a variety of resources—the ability to recognize and use many resources in expanding vocabulary, improving oral and written expression, and sharing ideas.
3. Comprehending what is read—the ability to gain, from oral and written exercises, skill in following directions, understanding words in the context of sentences and paragraphs, reproducing the thought of a passage, reading for detail, and reading for general significance.

4. Summarizing—the ability to get the main impression, the outstanding idea, or the details of what has been read or heard.
5. Organizing ideas and information—the ability to use various methods of briefly restating ideas in the order in which they were written or spoken.
6. Integrating and assimilating ideas—the ability to use reading and listening for personal use.
7. Reading critically—the ability to determine the validity and reliability of statements.

The goals of broad language experiences as stated above cannot be separated into *reading goals, writing goals, speaking goals,* and *listening goals.* To attempt to do so is to ask the child to perform, at an early age, the most difficult tasks of the scholar: integrating learning into meaningful behavior. To take reading out of its rightful place in the total language experience program is to ask children to do what is impossible for many of them. It requires that the teacher use valuable time to put back together what did not need to be separated in the first place.

The Child's Reading Concepts

The teacher's task is to create a learning environment in which certain concepts emerge in each child's thinking:

I CAN TALK ABOUT WHAT I CAN THINK ABOUT

The thoughts of each child are the basic ingredients in a program of improving all phases of communication. Hopefully, the thoughts and the language of other people will influence the learner, but they are not as basic to the beginnings of reading as are the thoughts and words which the child himself brings to the learning situation. Meanings are inside, not outside, the learner.

WHAT I CAN TALK ABOUT I CAN EXPRESS IN SOME OTHER FORM

Forms of expression vary a great deal, but in most school situations they include painting, drawing, modeling, construction, and *writing.* Infrequently, teachers use such forms as dramatic play, rhythms, and dramatization, but these generally relate more to an interpretation of someone else's ideas rather than an expression of one's own. Painting and writing remain the most used and the most personal forms of recording meanings from speech; but all other forms are important to use for variety in the classroom.

ANYTHING I RECORD, I CAN RECALL THROUGH SPEAKING OR READING

Experiences with both picture writing and writing with letters help the child to recognize that one is much more precise than the other. But the abilities required for effective written communication emerge not from lessons, but from the child's experiences with writing, painting, drawing, construction, rhythms, and other forms of communication. This whole development is based on oral communication which stems from the desire of a thinking individual to share his ideas with others.

I CAN READ WHAT I WRITE, AND WHAT OTHER PEOPLE WRITE FOR ME TO READ

The child who can, from the beginning, relate speaking, listening, and writing to the reading process, can carry on a conversation with an author. He can listen to what he has to say, agree and disagree, accept and reject ideas, and integrate his own ideas with those of the author. Thus, for him, *reading* is not a separate study in school, but a natural part of activities dealing with sending and receiving messages.

AS I TALK AND WRITE I USE SOME WORDS OVER AND OVER AND SOME WORDS NOT SO OFTEN

Most children enter school with a large speaking vocabulary. They use common words with ease and with a variety of meanings. The teacher's task is to help each child to recognize the visual forms of the words he is using, realize that all the children in his class use many of the same words he uses, and recognize the use of common words in what other people write for him to read.

AS I WRITE TO REPRESENT THE SOUNDS I MAKE THROUGH SPEECH, I USE THE SAME SYMBOLS (LETTERS) OVER AND OVER

Teaching the child to symbolize his speech sounds, rather than teaching him to assign a sound or sounds to symbols selected by the teacher, is the experience approach to learning the phonetic elements of his own language.

Phonetic understanding develops from a "say it" to "see it" sequence. This insures that the *real language experiences* of each individual, including skills in listening, speaking, word recognition, and spelling, is comprehended.

EACH LETTER OF THE ALPHABET STANDS FOR ONE OR MORE SOUNDS THAT I MAKE WHEN I TALK

At first the teacher records the oral language. As the child writes on his own, his understanding matures to include the many variations in the English language. The variable phonetic system of English requires that the child learn the elements of phonics with procedures that emphasize the *oral* prior to the *written* aspects of the language. When the child realizes that every word begins with a sound that he can write down, he can begin to read and write. His learning continues as he develops an awareness of such language characteristics as common word endings, syllables, consonant blends, diagraphs, dipthongs, and other aspects of word structure. Thus begins a long-range learning experience which continues throughout life.

MOST OF THE WORDS I SPEAK AND WRITE ARE THE ONES THAT OTHER PEOPLE USE WHEN THEY SPEAK AND WRITE THE THINGS THAT I READ

Children who conceptualize this idea are released from the fear that they cannot read a story. They realize that most of the words used are the same ones which they use in their own speech and writing. If the story deals with an idea that has some meaning to the reader, he should be able to extend and enlarge his own meaning through reading. Children who use writing to gain an understanding of the nature of their language are able to deal with the ideas of authors when reading. This contrasts with reading situations in which the author's ideas are lost in the confusion of trying to analyze words and relate speech sounds to printed symbols.

The Teacher's Conceptual Framework

It is not enough for the teacher to help each child conceptualize a few simple truths about language as stated above. The fundamental responsibility of every teacher who proposes to use a language experience approach is to establish a conceptual framework to guide him in the selection of activities, experiences, materials, and evaluation procedures. Such a framework will help the teacher determine goals for individuals without losing the unity desirable for an instructional program:

1. The basis of children's oral and written expression is their sensitivity to their environment both within the classroom and in the world at large. The teacher's continuing responsibility is to help children become aware of the world in which they live.

2. Freedom in self-expression, oral and written, leads to self-confidence in all language usage, including grammar, punctuation, capitalization, and spelling. When a child works with and reworks his own language, he makes significant gains in understanding the strengths and weaknesses of that language. The reworking of other people's language in the form of "exercises" makes little or no difference in the self-expression language of a child.

3. There is a natural flow of language development in children who are engaged in a program of instruction. The child's oral expression is stimulated and strengthened through art expression, careful observation, viewing of films and strips, and listening to stories and poems. Written expression flows easily from oral expression. Motivation for improving language form and usage comes as children's writing is used for others to read. As children continue to write, they are influenced by what they read. Good reading material leads to good language usage.

4. Making class books, listening to stories, storytelling, sharing, dictating to each other, and other language experiences help children build confidence in expanding ideas and refining language skills. The classroom is a day-long laboratory of language experiences. Good language experiences add depth of meaning to the social studies, raise thoughtful questions in science, individualize interpretations in art and music, promote accuracy in mathematics, and provide freedom of expression in creative writing.

5. Utilization of the child's own language as one of the bases for reading instruction results in a high degree of independence in writing and reading. At all levels, children should have frequent opportunities to read their own writing to the total class, to small groups within the class, and to other groups within the school. In preparation for oral reading, the child can devote his energies to clarity of expression, effectiveness of presentation, interpretation of punctuation, and other details necessary in good reading. During the process, he increases his sensitivity toward the well-written materials of others and develops a true appreciation of our best authors.

One might continue indefinitely to describe an approach to reading instruction built upon a base as broad as the language experiences of the children we teach. The future development of the approach will not depend on what is said here, but rather on the changing role of reading in enriching the lives of children, in facilitating learning in all curriculum areas, in promoting good citizenship, and in strengthening each child's concept of himself as a contributor of ideas to an emerging and growing society.

8 | A Critical Appraisal of the Language-Experience Approach to Reading*

Wilma H. Miller

The language-experience approach is considered by reading specialists to be one of the main approaches to teaching beginning reading in the United States today. This approach has proven itself very useful in many instances, but it also has some limitations which must be carefully considered when it is used as the major reading approach in a primary-grade classroom.

Background of the Language-Experience Approach

For a number of years, the experiences of first-grade children have formed the basis of some reading materials in beginning first-grade reading instructions. Every first-grade teacher is familiar with the experience chart, a group-composed manuscript. However, the language-experience approach has been refined and publicized in recent years by Dr. R. Van Allen, formerly Director of Curriculum Coordination of San Diego County, California, but now of The University of Arizona. Dr. Allen apparently

*From *Wisconsin State Reading Association News,* vol. 11, February 1968, pp. 4–8.

first noticed this approach being used with bilingual Mexican-American children in a border area of Texas. Since these children did not have the background of experiences to bring to the interpretation of the basal readers, their teachers were using dictated or child-written experience stories as the major basis of their reading materials. The teachers of these bilingual children also discovered that they were able to read their own language patterns much more effectively than they could read the language patterns found in the basal readers.

When Dr. Allen moved to San Diego County, he brought the idea of a refined language-experience approach with him. The approach was subjected to considerable experimentation in many first grades in San Diego County. One major research study conducted there indicated that the language-experience approach, the basal reader approach, and the individualized approach were all excellent methods for teaching beginning reading. However, the results further indicated that the language-experience approach and the individualized approach also developed a keen interest in learning to read on the part of the first-grade children (1).

Description of the
Language-Experience Approach

The language-experience approach can be crystallized by the following statement which Dr. Allen uses in his materials:

What I can think about, I can talk about.
What I can say, I can write.
What I can write, I can read.
I can read what I write, and what other people can write for me to read (2).

In kindergarten or in beginning first-grade, the children dictate many individual or group stories to their teacher who acts as a scribe. These stories capitalize on the in school or out of school experiences of the children and are recorded by the teacher using the language patterns of the children. The group-dictated experience charts are transcribed by the teacher on large chart paper. In using the group-composed experience charts, the teacher will read the chart to the class several times while emphasizing left-to-right progression. She will also have the children read various words or sentences from the chart. The individually dictated experience stories are often typed by the teacher using a primary typewriter and given back to the child who dictated them.

Various art media are used to illustrate the individually dictated experience stories which are the unique feature of the language-experience approach. The children occasionally use a drawing or painting to motivate the telling of an experience story, but more often the dictated story is illustrated by the child who dictated it. The illustrated experience stories are later bound into a booklet for which the child has designed a gaily decorated cover. Each child then "reads" his booklet of experience stories at school and at home.

By using both group-composed experience charts and individually dictated experience stories, the children in kindergarten or beginning first grade are able to conceptualize reading as "talk written down" and are able to learn a number of sight words in an informal manner.

As the children progress through first grade, they continue to use experience charts and stories as the major method of learning to read. They continue to dictate charts and stories to their teacher, but as they learn more and more words they can begin to write their own experience stories. Of course, in this beginning writing stage they still need considerable help from the teacher with the spelling of words, but the children are encouraged to spell the words in the experience stories as they think the words should be spelled. During the first grade, the children using the language-experience approach will read the experience stories that they themselves have composed as well as those of their classmates. The children will also read many stories from basal readers, but this reading is done on an individual basis for no ability grouping is found in the language-experience approach except for flexible short-term grouping. The children also will read many trade books in first grade.

There is no control of vocabulary in the language-experience approach for the child learns sight words found in his own experience stories or in the group-composed experience charts. Dr. Allen believes that the common service words will be learned by all children eventually since they are found in the dictated stories at some time during the early primary grades. Reading skills are taught in an incidental individual way in this approach, with phonics being taught on a "say it" to "see it" basis, the opposite of that found in the typical phonics program which emphasizes the "see it" to "say it" approach.

By the time the children have reached second grade, Dr. Allen assumes that they will be writing many experience stories with little help from the teacher. The children will be continuing to read their own experience booklets and the experience booklets of their classmates. They will continue to read stories from basal readers at their own reading level, whether it is the first grade, second grade, third grade, or perhaps the fourth grade levels. The second-grade children will also read trade books on their own reading level. The children will continue to learn the necessary reading skills on a basically individual basis.

The language-experience approach deemphasizes the use of experience booklets for reading material as the children approach the intermediate grades. It becomes mandatory at this level that the experience stories become supplementary instead of the basic reading materials.

Advantages of the
Language-Experience Approach

The language-experience approach has many unique features which make it very valuable. Perhaps one special advantage of this approach is that it enables children to conceptualize "reading is talk written down" during the early stages of reading instruction. This is a concept that many more mature readers do not seem to easily attain.

Another major advantage of this approach is that it insures that children have the background of experiences to bring to their reading since the experience charts and stories utilize their own experiences. This is a very important asset to the slow learning child or to the culturally deprived child.

The children can read their own language patterns very effectively, and the use of these more mature language patterns will not lead to the language regression that is sometimes the case when the basal readers are used in first grade. It has been found that older disabled readers, even those in junior high school, can easily read their own language patterns when given an opportunity to do so by a teacher who is using the language-experience approach as a remedial method with them. The approach also has a beneficial motivating effect to the disabled reader.

The language-experience approach can also be called an integrated language arts approach since it very effectively stresses the interrelationships among the four language arts of listening, speaking, reading, and writing. It particularly stresses the relationship between oral language and reading since the dictated experience charts and stories form the integral part of the approach at the early stages. It also stresses the relationship between reading and writing effectively since the child-written experience stories play an important part in the approach at its later stage.

The children's creativity is greatly enhanced when they are using this approach. The illustrations for the experience stories and the covers for the experience booklets give the children an opportunity to effectively explore various art media. The children who have used this approach usually are very adept at writing their own creative stories and often exceed children who were taught by other reading methods in creative writing ability.

Finally, the language-experience approach seems to develop a true interest in reading in the children who have used it.

Limitations of the
Language-Experience Approach

The major limitation of the language-experience approach is its lack of sequential skill development. Research has shown that word attack skills, perhaps especially phonetic skills, are much more effectively taught in a systematic sequential manner. Dr. Allen's belief that children will learn word attack skills when they feel a need to do so seems to be a rather naive concept.

Undoubtedly most elementary teachers are not sufficiently aware of the many facets of the complex reading process to be able to teach reading without some guidance. The language-experience approach seems to be much too unstructured to be used as the main approach for teaching reading by only but the most experienced and confident teachers of reading.

In this approach, the children do not have the control of vocabulary and systematic repetition of new words that is found in the basal readers. Using the language-experience approach the children learn vocabulary words from experience charts and stories, and the teacher can never be completely certain that they have learned the words that they will need to know how to recognize when reading basal readers and trade books.

In the language-experience approach there is no ability grouping, except for flexible short-term groups. While this may be an advantage in that it does not stigmatize the slow learning child, it certainly becomes a limitation when one considers how wasteful it is of teacher time and energy. Especially at the beginning stages when the teacher must act as a scribe for the individually dictated stories, it is almost a monumental teacher task to give each child the individual help that he needs. This is an especially important limitation when the class size is over twenty.

To function most effectively the language-experience approach assumes that primary-grade classrooms are very well equipped, and that the teachers are able to provide many enriching experiences for the children. The approach is based on the concept that the children will have much to say and to write about. Therefore, they must have an enriching and motivating classroom environment, must have the opportunity to go on many educationally valuable school trips, and must have available material with which to make their experience booklets. The classrooms must have available many basal readers and trade books also.

The language-experience approach cannot function effectively as the major method for teaching reading much beyond the primary grades since the children must begin to read in the content fields and cannot be limited to reading about their own experiences at this point.

Summary

It is to be hoped that every elementary teacher has a working knowledge of the language-experience approach since it can serve many valuable purposes in the classroom. It seems particularly valuable in introducing beginning reading in first grade and as a supplementary approach in all the primary grades. It is also very valuable to use with disabled readers as one means of introducing or carrying on a program of corrective reading.

REFERENCES

1. Allen, R. Van. "Three Approaches to Teaching Reading," *Challenge and Experiment in Reading.* International Reading Association Conference Proceedings, Volume 7, 1962, 153–156.
2. Department of Education, San Diego County. *An Inventory of Reading Attitude.* Monograph Number 4 of the Reading Study Project. San Diego: Superintendent of Schools, 1961.

9 | Whither Basal Reading?*

Charles M. Brown

Extensive consideration, of late, has been given to newer methods of teaching reading, especially individualized reading. Claims for the values of individualized reading programs have been made which indicate, in some cases, remarkable results. Does this mean the end of basal reading programs?

In order to determine a partial answer to such a question, the reading program in the elementary schools of a large city school district in Los Angeles County was recently analyzed to determine its nature and degree of success. This district includes twenty-one elementary schools, five junior high schools, three high schools, and one junior college.

The Reading Program

The program, as observed, was very similar to that recommended by most authors of basal reading series. Little or no formal reading or reading readiness work was carried on in the kindergarten, which concentrated on its more traditional role of preparing children to work in a group.

*From *Education,* vol. 82, September 1961, pp. 3–5. Reprinted from the September 1961 issue of *Education.* Copyright 1961 by the Bobbs-Merrill Company, Inc., Indianapolis, Ind.

In the first grade, instruction was carried on by means of a pre-primer approach, preceded by experience chart work. At the time the observations were made, all first-grade children had at least started the first pre-primer. Some of the youngsters were well into the primer.

The methods employed in the program included introduction of the story, presentation of the new vocabulary through discussion and use of the blackboard, guided silent reading, oral re-reading, and follow-up.

Instruction was carried on in group situations where the teacher worked with a small group of ten to twelve youngsters, while the remainder of the class was busily engaged in appropriate independent reading activities. The auditory and visual-auditory aspects of phonetic analysis were handled at the appropriate level in the first grade with children who had already developed the beginnings of a basic sight vocabulary. Workbooks were employed as part of the follow-up work, and were regularly corrected by the teacher and reviewed with the children.

Throughout the primary grades, a similar program on appropriate levels of difficulty was observed. Considerable attention was given to the various facets of reading, including vocabulary development, structural analysis, phonetic analysis, reading for comprehension, oral reading with expression as an indication of interpretation, an examination of the motives of story characters and insights into their feelings.

Considerable time was devoted in the primary grades to free reading or library-type reading from classroom libraries, supplied through a central curriculum library and through teacher loans at the public library. Most classrooms had from fifty to one hundred books available for the pupils.

In the intermediate grades continuation of the basal reading program was observed, with the addition of differentiated instruction in various levels through the use of carefully selected workbooks. Again, room libraries were available, and wide reading was apparent.

In the intermediate grades the advanced stages of structural analysis were employed, as well as reviews of phonetic analysis. Considerable attention was given to refinements of comprehension, including an examination of the motivation of story characters and critical reading in which the motives and qualifications of authors of the stories were examined.

Evaluation

The program of reading instruction as described above is the very type which individualized reading advocates would replace. The critical question, then, is how successful it has been.

The following tables indicate the success of the program in terms of achievement test results. Table 1 reveals that the mean achievement in reading comprehension and reading vocabulary, at the third grade level,

TABLE 1

Third Grade Reading Achievement

Grade Placement 3.9

Year	N	Reading Comprehension			Reading Vocabulary		
		Mean	Q_1	Q_3	Mean	Q_1	Q_3
1957–58	1427	4.6	4.2	5.0	4.8	4.0	5.5
1958–59	1459	4.6	4.3	5.1	4.9	4.2	5.6
1959–60	1570	5.1	3.9	5.8	5.0	5.0	5.7

as measured by the *California Achievement Test,* was well above the standardization norms. The figures in the Q_3 column indicate that more than seventy-five percent of all children in the third grade in this district scored above the national mean.

Table 2 gives the results on the STEP Reading Test for the fifth and eighth grade. The means were well above the standardization norms of the fiftieth percentile, as can be seen from the table below.

In most instances the Q_1 figure is significantly above the twenty-fifth percentile. The Q_3 figures indicate that perhaps the test did not measure the ceiling ability of approximately twenty-five percent of those tested.

What of the intellectual ability of these children? Table 3 gives the mean IQ for grades two, four, and seven, which comprise essentially the same individuals who were given the reading tests in grade three, five, and eight, the succeeding year. The mean IQ for all groups was slightly above 100. The Q_1 and Q_3 columns of this table indicate a somewhat narrower range of ability than one would expect, particularly at the lower end.

Conclusions

From the observations made and the data obtained, it would seem that the basal reading program enriched, as it was, in the manner advocated by

TABLE 2

Results for Fifth and Eighth Grades

Grade II	Date Given	N	Mean	Q_1	Q_3
1958–59	April	1442	93% ile	45% ile	99% ile
1959–60	March	1545	89% ile	28% ile	99% ile
Grade VIII					
1958–59	February	1527	73% ile	54% ile	91% ile
1959–60	February	1601	77% ile	57% ile	57% ile

TABLE 3

Intelligence Test Results

Grade	Year	Test	Mean	Q_1	Q_3
II	1958–59	Kuhlman-Anderson	105.1	99.6	108.7
IV	1958–59	Otis	103.1	94.8	111.7
VII	1958–59	CTMM	105.5	99.2	114.6

most basal reading authors, had produced excellent results in this stable, conservative community. It is problematical whether an individualized reading program would improve these results to any appreciable degree.

One of the reasons for this conclusion is the extent of wide outside reading done by the children, both under the direction of the school and on their own. Records indicate that library circulation in this community has more than kept pace with the growth in population for the past ten years.

It would seem unwise to recommend a change from a successful basal reading program to any other type of reading program.

10 | Basals and Bluebirds*

Hughes Moir
William J. Curtis

Another school year has passed, "O' Best Beloved," and we look forward to an inspiring new one in the fall. Millions of children will return from the world of reality to their classrooms to be inculcated with that mystery of organization called the reading textbook. How strange that children should be exposed to the trivia of the publishing world's efforts to be all things to all people. What is there for children to take from this confusing literary conglomeration? Dick and Jane in their sweet home with that nauseous dog and pony? A ride to the local post office to see its operation? What about an upper-grade poem like Frost's "Mending Wall"? These should excite the little urchins, all set about with fever blisters and great gray-black palms.

"The needs of children be hanged, we're here to teach them something, and grammar and reading skills are what they need," says Mrs. Dickson, a snappy educator who has learned it is fashionable to pooh-pooh learning theory. Mr. "Man-on-the-Street" must wonder at the crazy, mixed-up system that has developed in our schools.

I'm a Bluebird.

Oh, I look like any other ten-year-old boy—ordinary hands and face that are usually a little dirtier than my mother would like; a loose molar;

*From *Elementary English,* vol. 45, May 1968, pp. 623–626. Reprinted with permission of the National Council of Teachers of English and Hughes Moir, Assistant Professor, Children's Literature, College of Education, University of Toledo, Toledo, Ohio, and William J. Curtis.

brown hair that is a little longer than last year; and about average height and weight. I'm interested in baseball and football, riding my bike down to the hobby store to look at the latest electronic kit. All the things that I guess I'm supposed to be according to adults. There are other things that I'm interested in that I never talk about with other people. I guess just because I don't know anyone who'd be interested. Things like what I see on T.V. You know, the war in Viet Nam, Negro protests, people getting killed in our city, other people dying of starvation when I have so much to eat, God, and things like that.

But every day—except Saturday and Sunday and vacations—at 9:15 I'm a Bluebird.

Of course it's much better to be a Bluebird than to be a Robin or a Sparrow. Especially a Sparrow. Everybody knows they're the dumb ones— the kids that can't read. The Bluebirds are the kids in the best reading group. The funny thing is, year after year, there are always about the same number in each group and the same kids in each group. Oh, the names of the groups change each year—Miss Hearn called them Squirrels, Chipmunks, and Rabbits; Mrs. Knight called them Groups One, Two, and Three. Anyway, we're all taught from the same book. At the same time, we all have to do the same pages in the workbook. We all have to look at the same new words on the flannel board that Mrs. Dickson made in one of her college classes. The only difference is the smart group is a week and a half ahead, so if you listen closely you know all the answers.

I guess this is another thing I'm confused about, except that this doesn't seem as important as the other things I mentioned.

How someone can help kids learn more about their world is the big question. Books are usually considered important, but most kids are too busy in school for books. The reading methods that have been designed keep the teacher busy confusing the children about points of little interest or importance to anyone, especially active children.

Take the reading group as an example. Ten pupils of varying ability are brought together to read a passage in a book that no one in the group has selected. What about interest? But, even to consider interest is a digression—these students are presented new words that may or may not be new and told to commit them to memory. Why? Because the teacher said so, not because the students don't know them—the teacher doesn't know if the students know them or not. She thinks a publisher in Chicago or New York knows more about educating these children than she does. Too bad! Mrs. Dickson could really be a good teacher; that is, when she told the children about her vacation in Hawaii during the summer she was great. She was showing her slides about Hawaii during one class and she was an excellent narrator. She even skipped math that day, but *not reading!*

"These are the new words for today, boys and girls."

Up on the red flannel board are our new words. I guess this is another thing I'm confused about—the new words. Today we are supposed to learn "company," "thimble," "request," "America," and "explore." Who says these are new words? I've been able to read these for at least a year now —ever since I ran across them in books I read during library period. Of course, I heard them a long, long time ago from my folks, or on T.V. Anyway, Mrs. Dickson makes them look real pretty. She has put the words on the red flannel board in all different colors. The purple one is a little hard to see, but the yellow and green ones are. . . .

"Are you having trouble with any of them, Richard? I see that you look somewhat confused."

"Well, I can't quite make out the purple one very. . . ."

"Can anyone in the group help Richard with this word?"

"That's easy. It's 'rescue.'"

Beth smiles smugly.

"But I couldn't see the. . . ."

"Let's talk about today's story, boys and girls. Have any of you heard of Lewis and Clark?"

Today is a little different because we're reading out loud in our reading group. Yesterday we had silent reading. The whole class. Even Mike Mitchell who can't read anything except comics. Mike always gets called on to answer the questions that Mrs. Dickson asks. He never has the right answer. Mrs. Dickson always gets upset because she thinks Mike is goofing around drawing pictures and things like that. The trouble with Mike is that he can't read the story. Ask anyone in class. They'll tell you. Anyone, except Mrs. Dickson.

". . . in 1818 and Lewis from 1774–1809. They're famous Americans who were important in our history."

I guess this is another thing I'm confused about. Mrs. Dickson is always telling us dates. I don't see why this is so important to her. In fact, I don't see what this has to do with helping me to read any better. I remember reading *No Other White Man* last year. I couldn't begin to remember when they were born or when they died. Mike found an article in *National Geographic Magazine* that showed maps and pictures of where they went and what they saw. When I told him about the book, he showed me the article —it was great! Why, I remember the part about when they were . . .

"Pay attention, Richard. Susan is on page ninety-four."

After introducing new words to the group, teachers generally get down to the meat of the reading program. Oral reading. It comes after silent reading but is quite as silly. Ten kids sitting there waiting to make mistakes in front of their peers, and the teacher eagerly correcting all the mispronounced words. She makes lots of mistakes too, but then no two people talk exactly alike and that is what the teacher forgets. She uses "ya know," "goin'," "em," and "t" for "to" but what a ruckus would develop if the children told her. What a boring experience to sit and listen for twenty minutes to a poor story that you've already read! Of course, teachers figure that they are helping the children.

That's another thing. I don't understand why it is that I've got to listen to Susan to read. She reads O.K. I guess, but I've already read the story and so has everyone else—yesterday when the whole class read it to themselves. And I already know all the words, and I already know the story, too!! I already know. . .

"Richard? What's the matter with you lately? You look a little tired. Do you feel sick?"

"I'm O.K."

"Oh, you've finished already, Susan? Would you please go on, Frank."

I remember two weeks ago when me and another guy went to Sands Point. That's an amusement park down river a ways. We hitched a ride with his cousin and spent the day there riding the Whip, the Hammer, and the Roller Coaster, Boy did I get sick! I remember there was . . .

"Please go on Arnie. Richard! Are you sure you're all right?"

"Sure."

"Well, then please pay attention. Go ahead, Arnie."

I guess that's another thing I'm confused about. This is kind of like the rides down at Sands Point. You get on, ride round and round, and then . . .

"Please go on, Richard."

. . . after you've gone around a certain number of times . . . They do have a certain number, you know. Ten is the number on the giant Ferris Wheel . . . did you know that it was invented by a French engineer by the name of . . .

"Richard! Have you lost your place again? I do wish you'd pay attention to what's going on. You know how important this. . . ."

I guess that's another thing I'm confused about. . . .

"We're on page ninety-five, the last paragraph. It's your turn to read."

There's no reason to take you through my paragraph. It was about when Merriweather Lewis was a little boy and his mother told him to always make his parents proud of him. To do his best. You know . . . to be good. Sandy got to read the part about the expedition across the Northwest. That was the best paragraph.

Then comes those exciting workbooks! They are designed by publishers to increase profit and detract from teacher involvement with the learners. Naturally, educators call this reinforcement and pile it on because it's good for them. What fun to keep them busy and especially not to let them talk! For talking is the one great fault of children. They talk about stupid things like space travel, monsters, building things, and great ad-

ventures in living. Of course these are at the most trivial level and not
worth the effect of expansion. School is where we must discipline, not
discuss! Meanwhile, back to the workbooks. Most of what we find in the
workbook is erroneously assumed to improve reading skills. It neither
improves reading nor confronts the issue.

"Would you all take out your workbooks, please. Susan, may I see
yours first?"

Here we go round. . . .

"Richard, I don't know what's the matter with you. Will you please
pay attention."

This really confuses me. Pay attention. Mrs. Dickson is correcting
Susan's book. I know that she won't get to me until after she has corrected
Arnie's, Dawn's, Harold's, Cindy's, Marty's, and Ruthie's books. What is
there to pay attention to? But . . .

"May I see yours now, Richard."

Here comes the red pencil again. Why red? Why not . . .

"Very good, Richard. You only missed two. Perhaps tomorrow you'll
get them all correct. Now, please go to your seat and write the correct
answers ten times. Then begin your board work."

A smiling face! Miss Hearn use to write "Very Good" at the top of the
page. Mrs. Merrill wrote "A" or "B" or "C." Mrs. Knight, I guess, was
smartest. She used a rubber stamp that made a star on the top if we got
them all right or almost all right. In red ink, though.

Children become better readers by reading materials of vital interest
to them. This is much too simple an answer for most educators so they
fumble around with workbook exercises, oral reading, and vocabulary
presentation. In the final analysis very little is accomplished by the basal
approach but the exceeding hatred or disinterest in reading by most elementary children. There is an answer but teachers ignore it with gusto!
The individualized approach using literature. But it's too hard for the
teacher of forty students so we created the basal reader that results in
forty mental dropouts! Hurray for us! . . . and on to another fruitful year
of basal reading!

Ten o'clock. Finished just in time for recess. Just enough time to get
a drink and go to the bathroom. Maybe Harve will be there so we can talk
about our project we're working on at home. We're trying to figure out a
way to put together a. . . .

RRIIIIIINNNNNNNNNGGG!!!!!!!

There's Harve.

"Whadcha do this morning, Richie?"

"Aw, nothin'. We had reading."

11 | How Are Basal Readers Used?*

Ralph C. Staiger

Millions of copies of basal readers are being used in schools throughout the country. In order to collect information on the attitudes of school people toward some aspects of basal reader use, a questionnaire was sent to teachers, supervisors, consultants, and superintendents in many different types of schools in all 48 states and Hawaii in January of 1957. The findings are reported in this article.

Since the sample of schools was not a random one, it would be unsound to conclude that these proportions are truly representative of practices throughout the country. A sample of 474 responses from all 48 states and Hawaii, however, can be a useful indicator of practices.

The questionnaire was designed to offer as little resistance as possible to the respondent. It contained eleven questions, ten of which could be answered by check marks. A stamped self-addressed envelope was included. Six hundred fifteen questionnaires were mailed and 474 or 77.07% were returned. This was considered an adequate return.

The questionnaire read as follows:

1. Which plan do you use? (a) One series of readers basally (b) Two series

*From *Elementary English,* vol. 35, January 1958, pp. 44–46. Reprinted with the permission of the National Council of Teachers of English and Ralph C. Staiger. [This older article is included because no current article is available in this area. However, it is an important area of research. — W.H.M.]

of readers cobasally (c) Three series of readers cobasally (d) More than three series of readers for basal instruction (e) No basal readers (f) Other.

2. Which series do you use in your basal program?

3. When a reading group changes from one series to another, when is the change usually made? (a) At any opportune time (b) After the preprimers (c) After the primer (d) After the first reader (e) After the 2-1 or 2-2 readers (f) After the 3-1 or 3-2 readers (g) Other.

4. Who decides whether a pupil or group changes from one series to another, if a change is made? (a) Teacher alone (b) Teacher and supervisor or consultant (c) Consultant alone (d) Administrator alone (e) Other.

5. Do you use for supplementary reading the basal readers of any publishers other than the above?

6. At the primary grade level, are you satisfied with the two-level (2^1-2^2, 3^1-3^2) editions of the readers?

7. At the intermediate grade level, do you believe that two-level readers (4^1-4^2, 5^1-5^2, 6^1-6^2) are desirable?

8. Did or will the additional expenditure involved in two-level readers influence your adopting them in the primary grades?

9. Did or will the additional expenditure involved in two-level readers influence your adopting them in the intermediate grades?

10. Do you encourage use of the workbook which accompanies the basal reader?

11. How do you recommend use of the teacher's manual? (a) As the prescribed course of study (b) As a guide (c) Useful occasionally (d) Rarely useful (e) Other.

Results:

PLAN USED

Of the 474 schools in this sample, 69% reported using one series of readers basally. Comments made on the questionnaire indicated that 17.7% of these were varying their procedures so that it was doubtful whether a one-series plan was actually being used. Some of the variations mentioned included different series at the primary and intermediate levels, varying practices in the different schools of one community, or even in different classrooms of one school, and the experimental use of a cobasal series in some classes. Eight percent of the single basal users took the trouble to specify that supplementary readers were an important part of their reading program.

That two series of readers were used cobasally was reported by 20.0% of the schools; 5.7% used three series cobasally, 5.1% used more than three series. We must be careful to interpret the data collected in the light of the foregoing findings, for the sample appears heavily loaded with single basal series schools.

PUBLISHERS

The materials used by the schools queried were many and varied, and all of the major publishers were reported, sometimes as single basal adoptions and usually in combination with other materials. Being used as single basic readers were the series of Ginn and Company, Houghton Mifflin and Company, Lyons and Carnahan and Company, Macmillan and Company, Row, Peterson and Company, Scott Foresman and Company, and Silver Burdett and Company. Twenty-nine other combinations were represented, including two, three, four, five, and six series combinations. In these groups were represented the readers of the American Book Company, D.C. Heath and Company, Laidlaw and Company, and the Winston Company, in addition to the readers listed above.

CHANGING SERIES

Teachers sometimes find that a group of pupils needs additional instruction at a given level. When a shift is made from one series to another by a reading group within a classroom, the data showed that no particular level is favored for making the change. 40.1% of the respondents indicated that such changes were made at any opportune time, no matter at what level the pupils are reading. The schools which use only one series cannot make such a shift, and therefore 33.1% of the responses showed that no change is made. Other responses showed that 4.6% of the schools favored changing after the pre-primer level; 4.0% after the primer, 3.8% after the first reader; 2.5% after the 2-1 or 2-2 readers, and 5.5% after the 3-1 or 3-2 readers.

DECISION TO CHANGE

The decision to change a pupil or group from one series to another was apparently considered important enough to warrant the teacher's consulting with a supervisor, principal, or consultant in 51.5% of the schools responding. The teacher alone made the decision in 17.7% of the schools. In no case did the consultant or the administrator alone make the decision.

Perhaps it would be well to recall that most of the returns were from principals and supervisors, and so might be colored according to their beliefs. It is possible that in practice more such decisions are made by the teacher than these results indicate.

SUPPLEMENTARY READING

An overwhelming proportion of the responses indicated that the basal readers of publishers other than those adopted were used for supplementary reading. Only 5.4% of the respondents said that this was not common practice, while 92.5% approved of using basal readers for supplementary reading.

TWO-LEVEL READERS

Two-level editions of second and third readers have been on the market for several years. Apparently they have been accepted by a majority of school people, for 89.9% of the returns indicated satisfaction with the two-level plan at the primary level, while 5.3% did not approve. A small number suggested the need for additional in-between books, even though this question was not asked. When the subject of the increased cost of two-level readers was considered, 85.9% of the returns indicated that cost did not influence their adoption in the primary grades.

One relatively new development in basal readers has been two-level readers at the intermediate grade level (4-1, 4-2, 5-1, 5-2, 6-1, 6-2). Opinions on the desirability of these books were 63.7% in favor, 27.2% opposed, with the remainder not answering directly. Opinions on the influence of the cost factor were somewhat different from those toward the primary level materials; 23.5% believed that the additional expenditure would influence their adoption, while 69.8% did not believe that cost would be a factor.

WORKBOOKS

Workbooks which accompany basal reading programs constitute an important feature of the program, according to publishers. Single basal users are more likely to make use of this part of the program, for 91.4% of single basal reader schools reported using workbooks, while 76.3% of cobasal schools and 49.0% of tribasal and other schools use workbooks. Many of the affirmative answers specified that correct use of a workbook was important to its educational value.

MANUALS

Teachers manuals are used in different ways in different schools. In 15.0% of the returns, it was reported that the manuals are recommended as a prescribed course of study, while 68.1% of the returns recommended the manuals as guides. Their usefulness for inexperienced teachers was indicated in some of the responses. Other returns showed that they are recommended both as a guide and as a course of study. This accounted for 9.9% of the returns. Less than one percent of the responses suggested that the guides were useful only occasionally.

Conclusions:

Although it is recognized that the sampling of 474 schools cannot be considered truly representative of all schools, the following conclusions appear valid:

1. While many schools adhere to the single basal series plan, a considerable number is making use of books in other series. These are used as cobasal readers, to be used in conjunction with the basal series, or as supplementary readers, to give pupils additional practice in reading. The great majority of schools use basal readers for some supplementary reading.

2. When more than one series of readers is used for basal instruction, the change is made when it will benefit the needs of the child rather than at any predetermined reader level.

3. The change from one series to another is usually made after the teacher has conferred with a supervisor or principal although in many cases the teacher alone makes the decision.

4. Two-level readers in the primary grades have won widespread acceptance. At the intermediate grade level they are not so well accepted, although many school people think they are desirable. The additional cost of these materials while taken into consideration in many cases, has not prevented them from being adopted in most schools.

5. The workbooks which accompany basal readers are more likely to be used when a school adopts a single basal reading series. The likelihood of workbooks being used when two or three series of readers are used is considerably less. The greater the number of basal readers used for instruction, the less likely the students are to use the accompanying workbook.

6. Teachers manuals have been accepted by most school personnel as an aid to teachers. While some schools use the manuals as the prescribed course of study, most consider them a guide.

12 | A Personalized Reading Program*

Walter B. Barbe

The teaching of reading is far different today from what it was only a few years ago. Public awareness of the importance of education and government support have contributed to more and better materials, a wider variety of methods of teaching reading, and more careful attention to the outcomes of instruction(1). Disagreement over how reading should be taught no longer is directed primarily toward which method, rather than upon such factors as when to begin and to what degree the methods should be used.

Personalized reading(2) is a classroom organizational pattern which allows a creative teacher the flexibility to use those techniques and materials which are needed at any particular time. The personalized program differs from individualized reading in that the rigid rules applied by some in individualized reading need not be followed. For example, basal readers may be used in the personalized program for the specific purpose of teaching a particular skill, although it is not likely that children will methodically go through a basal reader page by page, and attention will be given to sequential development of skills both in small groups and in total class group instruction.

A personalized reading program incorporates the conference tech-

*From Education, vol. 86, September 1966, pp. 33–36. Reprinted from the September 1966 issue of Education. Copyright 1966 by The Bobbs-Merrill Company, Inc., Indianapolis, Ind.

nique, used successfully in many individualized programs, without abandoning the gains made by the use of grouping in order to teach particular skills. The basic premise of the developmental program, that children are provided with interesting material and are taught at their level, is not violated in the personalized program. As a classroom organizational pattern, the personalized program offers the teacher the opportunity to utilize the techniques which she feels are most helpful to each individual child. The language-experience approach operates in the personalized program most effectively.

Philosophy of Personalized Reading

The essential part of the personalized reading program is that it allows for flexibility. Rather than state that every child must cover certain materials, or learn certain skills, a personalized program establishes no such rigid goals of learning. The key to a successful program is the teacher, not the method.

The personalized program allows the teacher great enough flexibility so that she can use those skills which she knows in order to teach reading most effectively. But at the same time the program is flexible enough to allow her to change methods and materials, and even to shift goals, if during the school year any one child or group of children is not making progress.

The elements of self-selection and self-pacing are essential to a personalized program. Opportunity is offered in the personalized program for the child to select for himself those materials from which he will learn. There are times when for a specific reason a teacher will assign particular material, but such an assignment is never made for a prolonged period so that the children become classified by the book from which they are reading. Self-pacing allows for goals to be set individually, rather than by some preconceived notion that each child should "finish the book" by the end of the year.

The goal of reading instruction in any program, of course, is to develop permanent interest and skills in reading. Only if our program succeeds in developing within children the desire to continue reading, and provides them with the skills to become ever better readers, can it be called successful. A personalized program, as all other programs, has intermediary goals, but the final goal of developing permanent interests and skills is more easily remembered when rigid intermediary goals are not established.

As Witty has stated, "Our aim should be to help pupils become skillful, self-reliant, and independent readers who will continue to enrich their understandings and satisfactions throughout their lives by reading"(3).

Classroom Organization

A personalized reading program can best be initiated at the beginning of the first grade. There is mounting evidence that the program is equally applicable to the junior and senior high schools.

Beginning with a language-experience approach in the first grade (4) the program moves from the experience charts and stories developed by the children to printed material in children's magazines and books. Materials such as the *Little Owl Series*(5) are effective at this next level. The children select the material for themselves from a classroom library, which in no way replaces the need for a school library but, instead, enhances the children's interest in reading and in the use of the central library.

Beginning in the first grade with very short periods of time, and becoming longer and somewhat more formally organized in the higher elementary grades, conferences are scheduled and held with each child. At the time of the conference the teacher discusses with the child material which he has been selecting, gives direction if he has been choosing material of too difficult a level or material which is too easy, and checks his comprehension and skill development.

The conference period in the personalized program is not used for instruction in skills, other than in an incidental way. Formal, sequential skill development is planned in a personalized program. Skills are taught generally in small groups, in total class groups or to individuals, at times other than the conference time. This instruction may be from material in the basal reader or any other source.

The teacher keeps a record of the materials which the child has read. The personalized program, as the individualized program, can become overly burdened with teacher-kept records. Having the children keep a record of the books which they have read, and showing them to a teacher at the time of each conference, eliminates much of this problem. The use of some kind of skills check list(6) also makes it possible for the teacher to more easily keep track of skill development, as well as be reminded of the sequence of skill learning so that it is not overlooked.

Evaluation of Programs

Sartain(7) has summarized the research on individualized reading. He concluded that individualized reading:

1. "Can be somewhat successful under certain circumstances."
2. "Successful teaching in individualized reading requires especially competent teachers."

3. "Less capable pupils are less likely to achieve success in the individualized situation."
4. "Children read more books under the plan of self-selection with individualized instruction."
5. "The personal conference between the pupil and the teacher is of particular value."
6. "Individualized reading does not allow adequate time for the setting of thought-provoking purposes for reading, nor for the introduction of new vocabulary."
7. "The lack of a planned sequential skills program makes teachers uneasy about a wholly individualized organization."
8. "Teachers using a wholly individualized approach are constantly pressed for time to provide the conferences that pupils need."

A personalized reading program suffers from many of these same problems, as indeed so does the basal program, but by being more flexible in terms of materials which can be used (i.e. basal texts and children's magazines, as well as library material) and providing for a sequential skills program, some of the problems of the individualized program may be overcome. Clearly, children do read more books under the individualized and personalized program, like reading better, and the teacher is freer to do those things which she knows will be helpful to individual children.

As has been stated: "We should encourage every teacher to become the best teacher she can be. The methods which she uses should free her to do the best possible job, rather than limit her effectiveness"(1). A personalized reading program offers a classroom organization which allows the well-trained and dedicated teacher the flexibility necessary to provide effective reading instruction for each child.

REFERENCES

1. Editorial, "Is There a Best Method for Teaching Reading?" *Highlights for Teachers,* No. 1 (Sept., 1965), pp. 1–3.
2. Barbe, Walter B., *Educator's Guide to Personalized Reading Instruction* (Englewood Cliffs, N.J.: Prentice-Hall, 1961).
3. Witty, Paul A., "Individualized Reading: A Postscript," *Elementary English,* Vol. 41, No. 3 (March, 1964), p. 217.
4. Lee, Doris M., and Allen, R. V., *Learning To Read through Experience* (2nd ed.) (New York: Appleton, 1963).
5. Martin, Bill Jr. (editor), *Owl Series* (New York: Holt, Rinehart and Winston, 1964–65).
6. *Reading Skills Check Lists,* (3124 Harriett Road, Cuyahoga Falls, Ohio).
7. Sartain, Harry W., "Research on Individualized Reading," *Education,* Vol. 81, No. 9 (May, 1961), pp. 515–20, reprinted in Walter B. Barbe (editor), *Teaching Reading: Selected Materials* (London: Oxford, 1965), pp. 378–83.

13 | Individualized Reading*

Lessie Carlton
Robert H. Moore

What Is Individualized Reading?

Individualized reading consists of providing freedom for the pupil to select, from a variety of sources in the classroom, materials which are interesting and challenging but which he can read without too much difficulty. Reading is not regarded as a distinct subject but as a tool to be used in all learning situations. Children are encouraged to select materials which are related to what they are studying in science, social studies, and many other fields.

What Is the Teacher's Responsibility?

The teacher must see that children have access to materials they need and want to read; he must help them to develop the skills needed to read the materials they select; and he must determine the effectiveness of the program. He is a resource person, a coordinator, and an evaluator.

*From *NEA Journal,* vol. 53, November 1964, pp. 10–12.

When Is the Best Time To Begin an Individualized Reading Program?

There may not be any one "best time." Individualized reading has been introduced successfully as early as the first grade. One teacher, after she felt that her pupils were ready for preprimers or primers, spread the different books out on a table and invited each child to choose any one that he thought he might like to read.

Are Any Special Materials Needed for an Individualized Reading Program?

No. Almost any kind of reading material will do—library books, magazine articles, newspapers, textbooks. The essential criteria are that the pupil can understand it and that he learns something from his selection. For example, when a sixth grade class is studying about the weather, one pupil may read a book written for third graders, another may read a selection from an encyclopedia, and a third may read a college text.

How Does a Teacher Acquire Enough Materials for an Individualized Reading Program?

Some schools are using five copies each of six different supplementary reading books which cost little if any more than thirty copies of the same book. In many schools, children are encouraged to purchase inexpensive paper-bound books which they may want to exchange with one another. School libraries and bookmobiles are excellent sources for a wide variety of suitable materials. The teacher may also use books from the public library or carefully screened books brought from home.

How Does a Teacher Know Which Books To Give a Pupil?

The teacher does not give books to the pupil; he brings many books into the classroom and lets the pupil select his own reading. The teacher often makes suggestions, if suggestions are wanted or needed.

How Can a Teacher Be Sure That
a Pupil Is Reading at the
Level He Should Be?

The pupil need not be reading "at his level." Sometimes a child with a sixth grade reading ability can get a great deal of pleasure and significant information from a book supposedly written for third graders. Most material, of course, should provide challenge and lead to improved reading skill.

Can Children Be Expected To Select
Their Own Reading Material Wisely?

Children's selections are often guided by the specific subject they are studying, by what they enjoy reading, or by some felt need. In general, they select books that they can read with understanding. They will naturally want to read an occasional fairy tale or adventure story for enjoyment, a practice which should be encouraged.

How Do Pupils Develop a Basic
Vocabulary in an Individualized
Reading Program?

The answer depends on what is meant by a "basic" vocabulary. The oral vocabulary that a child brings to school is basic for him. Individualized reading programs provide many different experiences that help children to expand their oral and reading vocabularies.

Pupils dictate stories that the teacher writes down on a chart or a chalkboard. This activity helps them to recognize written words. In their reading, they come across unfamiliar words which the teacher may help them to understand or which they may look up in the dictionary. In these ways, they can learn hundreds of words in less time than it would take them to memorize a prescribed vocabulary of thirty or forty words such as *what, that, when, where.*

How Are Word Recognition Skills
Incorporated into Individualized
Reading Programs?

As the children read to themselves or to each other, the teacher goes about the room giving individual help. He may, for instance, have each pupil read to him for about five minutes at a time. He may notice that Johnny needs help in pronouncing the letter c. The teacher remembers that Bill and Mary also need help with the same problem. The three pupils can then be grouped together and given help with correct pronunciation, which is important to developing word recognition skills.

What Is the Advantage of Using Individualized Reading Instead of the Basal Reader Approach?

In individualized reading, the problem of developing interest in reading is reduced because each pupil reads what he can read and what he wants to read. On the other hand, the basal reader is too difficult for some and too easy for others; furthermore, its content may have no relation to the children's interests or personal experiences.

How Does the Teacher Evaluate Pupil Progress in an Individualized Reading Program?

Progress is evaluated both informally and formally. As the teacher moves from pupil to pupil listening to each one read, he can make an informal evaluation. He can also evaluate how well the children are assimilating content by having them discuss what they are reading. The progress of the pupils may be determined more formally by means of achievement tests given at regular intervals.

Why Do Some Studies Show Little Difference in Results between Individualized Reading Programs and the More Traditional Approach of Using Basal Readers with the Groups?

The reason for the small difference may be that what often passes for individualized reading in these studies is not truly individualized reading.

For example, one teacher who claimed to be using individualized reading required her pupils to select their reading materials exclusively from the school library. In fact, she went so far as to tell them which shelf to choose from.

Another teacher who said she used individualized reading permitted her pupils to read the books they had selected only after they had read their regular textbook assignment.

What Are Some of the Outstanding Advantages of the Individualized Reading Approach?

No child is labelled as being in a "slow" reading group. In classrooms using individualized reading, at least theoretically the needs of all the pupils are met, regardless of their reading level.

Pupils who can read at an advanced level of comprehension do not have to mark time by reading materials that are too easy for them. Pupils who make their own selection of reading matter develop not only a desire to read but also responsibility for their own learning.

14 Helping Teachers Begin Individualized Reading*

Patrick Groff

Individualized reading is a subject of growing discussion in the professional literature. This development parallels, in a sense, an increase in the number of teachers who are seeking to adopt an individualized reading program. As a result, it is becoming more and more likely that elementary school principals will be asked by their teachers to evaluate this approach to the teaching of reading and to give guidance on its use in the classroom.

On the surface, individualized reading appears simple. But all of the experts in individualized reading agree that it is not something to be taken lightly or gone into frivolously. The seemingly uncomplicated nature of the approach is deceptive. Any type of reading program can degenerate more quickly if misunderstood or misapplied. To rush headlong into individualized teaching of reading without careful study and preparation is to court certain failure and a consequent disillusionment about the value of the approach. It is far better to begin deliberately and gradually.

On the other hand, there is no doubt that individualized reading can be successful under the proper conditions and with the use of appropriate procedures. The objection that children taught through this kind of pro-

*From *National Elementary School Principal,* vol. 43, February 1964, pp. 47–50. Copyright 1964, National Association of Elementary School Principals, National Education Association.

gram will fail to learn to read is not substantiated by the research. Evidence continues to mount that with individualized reading, normal or above normal gains in reading vocabulary and comprehension can be expected, along with greater—although less measurable—advances in creative and critical reading, in positive attitudes toward and appreciation of books, and in the self-direction and self-control of the reading situation. All of these gains are improbable, nevertheless, if the prerequisites for the success of the approach are overlooked in planning for its use.

There are many questions about individualized reading that must be considered if the teacher would insure both his success and satisfaction in using this approach. Through individual or group conferences, the principal should make sure that his teachers are aware of the problems in successfully using individualized reading. He should take the initiative in seeing that teachers are prepared to explain the program to parents and should be sure that the school patrons understand the purpose of individualized reading.

The following twelve questions and comments indicate the kind of information and procedures which will help both teachers and principals in planning and initiating a program of individualized reading.

Teachers should be led to ask themselves:

1. Do I understand the purposes and techniques of individualized reading? For example, what are the five essential parts of the program? (Planning; individual silent reading and oral reading with partners; pupil-teacher conferences; sharing what has been read; and cooperative evaluation of these procedures. Details about each of these aspects of individualized reading may be found in the references below.)

2. Will it be possible for me to see individualized reading in action? Will at least two teachers in our school be using it so we can exchange visits and ideas?

The principal can be instrumental in encouraging teachers to work in teams on individualized programs. The support and encouragement teachers can give each other will help a great deal in making the program successful. If no other arrangements can be made, the principal might take over a teacher's class so he can observe in another classroom. If possible, provisions should be made for teachers to see individualized reading in action in other schools.

3. Do my principal and supervisors understand individualized reading?

The principal of any school in which an individualized reading program is contemplated should be familiar with the theories and practices of individualized reading as described in the references below. Knowledgeable supervision of a constructively critical nature is crucial to this approach.

4. Does my school have available the professional literature from which I can learn the details of individualized reading?

The following are some of the primary sources that both the teacher and the principal should consult. They should all be readily available in the professional library of the school that uses individualized reading.

Barbe, Walter B. *Educator's Guide to Personalized Reading Instruction.* Englewood Cliffs, N.J.: Prentice-Hall, 1961. 241 pp.

Brogan, Peggy, and Fox, Lorene K. *Helping Children Read.* New York: Holt, Rinehart and Winston, 1961. 330 pp.

Darrow, Helen F., and Howes, Virgil M. *Approaches to Individualized Reading.* New York: Appleton, 1960. 102 pp.

Draper, Marcella K.; Schwietert, Louise H.; and Lazar, May. *Practical Guide to Individualized Reading.* New York: Board of Education, 1960. 158 pp.

Duker, Sam. *Bibliography on Individualized Reading.* Brooklyn College, 1962.

Groff, Patrick. *Annotated List of Comparisons of Individualized Reading with Ability Grouping.* National Council of Teachers of English (508 South Sixth Street, Champaign, Ill.), 1962.

Jacobs, Leland B.; Miel, Alice; and others. *Individualizing Reading Practices.* New York: Teachers College, Columbia University. 1958. 91 pp.

Lee, Dorris, and Van Allen, Roach. *Learning To Read through Experience.* Second edition. New York: Appleton, 1963.

Robinson, Ruth, *Why They Love To Learn.* Charlotte, N.C.: Heritage, 1960. 172 pp.

Veatch, Jeanette. *Individualizing Your Reading Program.* New York: Putnam, 1959. 242 pp.

Articles on individualizing reading in *Elementary English* and *Reading Teacher* for the past few years.

5. Can my school provide enough books for me to make individualized reading work effectively?

Jeanette Veatch, in the book cited above, states that there must be a minimum of three books per pupil in the classroom library for an individualized reading program to work successfully. The number of books available will be greater if teachers teamed together in using the approach can pool their books in a commonly accessible place. Children can bring in personal books, library books, magazines and other reading materials. Many other suggestions about book collections are given in the references above.

6. Do I know enough about children's books to use individualized reading? Does my school have sources from which I can learn about children's literature?

The school's professional library should include at least the following books on children's literature. Of course, nothing can supplant a good college course in children's literature.

Arbuthnot, May Hill. *Children and Books.* Chicago: Scott, Foresman, 1957. 684 pp.

Huck, Charlotte S., and Young, Doris A. *Children's Literature in the Elementary School.* New York: Holt, Rinehart and Winston, 1961. 522 pp.

Larrick, Nancy. *A Teacher's Guide to Children's Books.* Columbus, Ohio: Merrill, 1963. 316 pp.

Tooze, Ruth A., and Krone, B. P. *Literature and Books as Resources for Social Studies.* Englewood Cliffs, N.J.: Prentice-Hall, 1955. 456 pp.

7. Do I know where to find the right book for the right child at the right time? Does my school have references which will assist in this search?

The teacher using individualized reading must be especially concerned with seeing that the books brought into the classroom meet both the children's interests and their reading ability. Analyses of the pupils' interests and abilities should be made frequently to guide the use of the following book selection aids.

Basic Book Collection for Elementary Grades. Ninth edition. Compiled by Miriam S. Mathes. Chicago: American Library Association, 1961.

Best Books for Children. Fifth edition. Compiled by Patricia H. Allen. New York: Bowker, 1960.

Bibliography of Books for Children. Washington, D.C. Association for Childhood Education, 1960.

Children's Catalog. Tenth edition. New York: H.W. Wilson, 1961, with supplements.

Dawson, Mildred A., and Pfeiffer, Louise. *Treasury of Books for the Primary Grades.* San Francisco: Chandler Publishing Company, 1959.

Austin, Mary K. *Good Books for Children.* Revised edition. University of Chicago, 1962.

Groff, Patrick. *Recent Easy Books for First Grade Children.* San Diego State College, 1962: the author.

Recommended Children's Books. New York: Wilson Libraries Journal, 1961.

8. Do I know enough about the techniques of teaching reading to use individualized reading? Can I teach reading without guidance from a teacher's manual?

With individualized reading, the teacher does not depend on the teacher's manual for direct guidance as he does when using a textbook for reading instruction. Consequently, he must know and understand at least the following aspects of reading methodology: word analysis and recognition; comprehension and study skills; flexibility of speed; oral reading; and appropriate independent review. Teachers need to self-evaluate frankly whether or not they will be able to develop these skills in an individualized reading program.

9. Can I find the time necessary to make an individualized reading program a success in a class of normal size?

There are many time-consuming aspects to individualized reading: for example, holding conferences, record keeping, directing sharing sessions, and teaching needed skills in groups. A well-organized time schedule should be developed. Further, in almost all cases it is better to begin by individualizing the reading of a small subgroup composed of dependable, industrious children. The amount of time needed for conducting individualized reading can be determined at this point.

10. Am I psychologically suited for this type of teaching? Is my personality such that I would feel a great loss of security if I could not depend on the teacher's manual for day-by-day directions?

Each individual teacher must judge for himself in the light of his experience, education, and personal characteristics whether or not he is suited to use individualized reading. The principal should, of course, be able to provide certain professional insights into this intricate and subtle problem.

11. Will I be able to explain the individualized reading program to parents?

Teachers, as well as principals, should be able to explain the advantages of an individualized reading program over ability grouping in terms of: pupil achievement; provisions for individual differences; pupils' attitudes toward reading; pupils' self-direction and control; and long-range effects. Teachers and principals should also be prepared to explain how the program differs from simple "free" reading.

If the teacher reads carefully in the above references, he should be able to explain these points to the satisfaction of most parents. The bibliography from the National Council of Teachers of English by this writer can be especially valuable in providing evidence that individualized reading does, in fact, develop reading skills.

12. Can I answer the objections that have been made to individualized reading?

The faculty of any school using individualized reading should be prepared to answer the various charges that have been made against this approach. Among the objections which are made are these:

Individualized reading procedures are too disorganized, irregular, and time consuming for the average teacher.

Individualized reading is too unsystematic to allow for sequential learning.

Individualized reading does not develop children's reading tastes and interests.

Parents do not want their children to use individualized reading.

Reading achievement is low. Reading skills are neglected and faulty word recognition habits and weak study skills result.

There is no possibility for group learning with individualized reading.

Most teachers do not have the personality or the knowledge of books, children, and reading procedures to use individualized reading.

Most authorities are opposed to individualized reading; therefore, it must be wrong.

"Flexible grouping" will adequately take care of individual differences.

There is not enough control or repetition of vocabulary. The reading level of tradebooks (non-textbooks) is unknown. There is no provision for reading readiness.

Discipline problems develop with individualized reading. Most children do not have the self-direction or control to work under this approach. They are inattentive and develop slovenly work habits.

Most classes are too large for individualized reading to be used effectively. There are not enough books in most schools to make individualized reading work.

Individualized reading will not work with slow learners.

Individualized reading will not work in the primary grades, especially the first grade.

The scope of this discussion precludes an adequate answer to these objections. Again, the teacher and principal should refer to the above references for help. Most of the questions are pertinent and reasonable; a few are misguided or obstructionist. In any case, the teacher using such an unconventional approach as individualized reading must be prepared to defend his heterodox procedures against such charges.

15 How Do I Begin an Individualized Reading Program?*

Kaye Rollins

"Just how do I begin an individualized reading program? I've heard it's a new approach to reading, but where do I start?"

Many teachers have pondered over these same questions just as I did. This is the way I began the most successful and satisfying experience in my teaching career. Perhaps it will help you.

First of all I felt a need to change my reading program. The children just didn't seem to enjoy reading. It was a chore to them instead of a very rewarding experience. I didn't feel that I was doing a good job of teaching the three-group method either. I was as bored as the children.

I heard about a class that was being offered in individualized reading at a near-by college. It was through this class that I spent many hours studying individualized reading. The more I read, the more enthusiastic I became over the program. I could hardly wait to introduce it to my sixth grade class. When I felt I had enough background material and an attitude of self-direction and independent work habits had been firmly established, then I presented the program to my students.

*From *Education,* vol. 82, September 1961, pp. 36–38. Reprinted from the September 1961 issue of *Education.* Copyright 1961 by the Bobbs-Merrill Company, Inc., Indianapolis, Ind.

Presenting the Plan

At the beginning of our reading period, I asked the pupils to close their books and I began asking questions. "What kind of books do you like to read?" "Why do some children enjoy reading more than others?" "If you had your choice what kind of books would you like to read?" The discussion went on for thirty minutes or so. The children aired their opinions about reading.

At the end of the discussion I asked the pupils whether they would like to read library books of their own choosing rather than series of readers. They were more enthusiastic over the idea than I had hoped. We spent the remaining part of the reading time planning the time of reading, establishing a procedure for checking books in and out, caring for the library corner, and deciding on methods of evaluating material read. It was also necessary at this time to make clear that each child's progress depended on his own efforts and willingness to accept his share of responsibility. I was there to help them improve in reading.

Ample books were obtained from the district library for every child's interest and ability. The children also brought books, magazines and the daily newspaper from home.

Self-Selection

The students chose the books that they wanted to read. They were given ample time to browse. When some children had difficulty choosing books, I would offer suggestions. However, they would make their own decisions. No pressure was exerted to hurry and decide. But once a book was decided on a plan was made whereby each child agreed to finish the book chosen unless he had good reason to change. He had to discuss this reason with me.

Records of Reading

Each child kept a record of the books he read. In his notebook he wrote a short review of each book after it was completed. He kept a list of "difficult" words along with each review. Each child also had a book wheel which helped him to see the different areas in which he read. If a child read nothing but books of adventure he was encouraged to broaden his reading scope, but it was not forced.

I feel that children, like adults, enjoy certain types of stories. If they are forced to read books they don't enjoy, then the whole idea of individualized reading is destroyed. But sometimes it is necessary to encourage some children to "taste" other books to see if they might enjoy something different. In most cases children were willing to branch out and then return to their favorite area.

When the program was first initiated a weekly reading survey was used. On this sheet the children had to account for the number of pages read each day and the amount of time they spent browsing, reading their book, or the newspaper. The purpose of this was to make the "time wasters" utilize their reading time. After a few months this survey was not necessary because the dawdlers had become avid readers.

My role as a teacher changed. Instead of teaching children how to read, they were taught to read. My time was spent in guiding, helping, and working with children individually in conferences rather than in groups.

Personal Conferences

The individual conferences were a pure joy! It was through these conferences that I really got to know my children. While I was working with the children one by one at my desk, the rest of the class would read silently in their own books. In the conferences I checked the child's reading list, vocabulary list, and the progress he had made since the last conference. He would discuss stories or books that had been read. The child would read orally. Comprehension was checked by asking the child to tell part of the story or book. Skills were also taught at this time based on individual needs. After the child left I would jot down in a notebook the book, page, material read by the student, and notes on the conference.

Our weekly schedule was set up for conferences on Monday, Tuesday, and Wednesday. On Thursday I worked with small skill groups. Friday was used for oral book reports. Children were allowed to report to the class about their book through the use of dioramas, dramatic play and pictures.

Results

It wasn't long before everyone in the class thoroughly enjoyed reading. Even the poorer readers would sneak out their books if they had a spare moment.

The success of this program showed up in several ways. (1) The children had a greater incentive to read more. Parents called saying how wonderful it was to see their child wanting to read instead of wanting to watch television. (2) The quality of reading improved. There was greater growth in reading skills and vocabulary. (3) There was a definite carry over of reading skills to other parts of the curriculum. (4) The children enjoyed this type of program.

What greater joy is there in teaching than to see children want to learn. In an individualized reading program every child progresses at his own rate. He is getting help and skills when he needs them and not when the teacher thinks he should have them. He is learning to appreciate the pleasure found in books.

Individualized reading is a new approach to reading. It isn't the only plan of teaching reading, but it is fresh and most rewarding. Wouldn't you like to try it?

16 Individualized Reading as Part of an Eclectic Reading Program*

W. Paul Blakely
Beverly McKay

Although some of the more partisan advocates of Individualized Reading have presented it as an all-or-nothing program, there have been expressed authoritative opinions that it may contribute rewardingly, along with elements of other recognized types of reading instruction, to an eclectic reading program. Witty wrote,

> It seems that a defensible program in reading will combine the best features of both individual and group instruction in reading. . . . A defensible reading program . . . recognizes the value of systematic instruction, utilization of interests, fulfillment of developmental needs, and the articulation of reading experience with other types of worthwhile activities.[1]

Likewise, Strang raised the question whether it is necessary to choose between individualized and basal reader approaches, and identified the effective teacher as one who, whatever the major approach used, introduces all the necessary features of a successful reading program.[2] Artley,

*From *Elementary English,* vol. 43, March 1966, pp. 214–219. Reprinted with permission of the National Council of Teachers of English, W. Paul Blakely, and Beverly McKay.
[1] Paul Witty, "Individualized Reading—A Summary and Evaluation," *Elementary English,* 36 (October, 1959) 450.
[2] Ruth Strang, "Controversial Programs and Procedures in Reading," *The School Review,* 69 (Winter, 1961) 420–21.

Robinson, and Barbe are among the other specialists who could be cited to the same effect.[3, 4, 5]

To give further substantiation to these opinions, and to provide a source of guidelines for schools and teachers wishing to use individualized reading in an eclectic reading program, the authors undertook the following investigation during the school year 1962–63. It was the purpose of the investigation to discover what means are being used to supplement a basal reader program with individualized instruction in grades four, five, and six.

The investigation was carried out by means of a questionnaire which was constructed for the purpose and sent in the quantity of five copies each to the elementary supervisors or comparable officials in fifty Iowa school systems. The school systems were selected arbitrarily and subjectively, with geographic distribution within the state and elimination of very small systems being given consideration. Each of the fifty officials was requested to distribute the five questionnaires to teachers in grades four, five and/or six whom he believed to be using individualized reading procedures along with a basal reader program.

A return of 124 questionnaires of the 250 thus distributed, was received. The return percentage of 49.6 should be interpreted bearing in mind that some officials may have had no teachers in their systems eligible to receive the questionnaires under the terms specified, and others may have had fewer than the five for whom questionnaires were supplied.

Of the 124 questionnaires returned, eleven answered negatively the first question, "Do you use individualized reading as part of your reading program, *along with a basal reading series?*" (This happened in spite of the stipulation in the accompanying letter to the elementary supervisor or other official which was intended to prevent it.) This comparison of eleven with 113 (total, 124) in no way represents the prevalence or scarcity of the practice being investigated, of course.

Individualized reading was identified in the first question as follows:

> Individualized reading is not new! It refers to the procedures involved when reading time is spent by children reading materials which they themselves select, with teacher guidance when necessary, and the activities associated with such reading: pupil record-keeping, individual teacher-pupil conferences, and individual or group instruction in reading skills when need arises.

---

[3] A. Sterl Artley, "An Eclectic Approach to Reading," *Elementary English,* 38 (May, 1961) 326.
[4] Helen M. Robinson, "News and Comments on Individualized Reading," *The Elementary School Journal,* 60 (May, 1960) 411–420.
[5] Walter B. Barbe, *Educator's Guide to Personalized Reading Instruction.* Englewood Cliffs, N.J.: Prentice-Hall, 1961, pp. 223–224.

Two respondents of the 124 described a program which was more or less strictly individualized reading rather than a use of it in combination with the basal reader program. This left a population of 111 respondents who indicated that they did use individualized reading along with a basal reading series, and on whose answers the following analysis is based.

The Role of Individualized
Reading in the Eclectic Program

In the questionnaire, the respondent was offered four possible procedures among which to indicate the one she was using; or, in case none of the four was appropriate, a fifth choice, "Other." An examination of Table 1 shows that the use indicated most frequently was that of a supplement to the basal reader, used regularly regardless of whether or not the basal reader has been completed. Other uses indicated with considerably less frequency were (in descending order) a special approach for retarded readers, to fill out a year or semester for any group which finishes basal readers, miscellaneous "other" uses, and to fill out a year or semester for only the superior group. (The percentages in the tables do not necessarily total 100. A respondent might indicate more than one response to most questions.) Among the "other" practices reported were use of individualized reading in a program of interclass grouping ("Joplin Plan"), use of the Science Research Associates Reading Laboratories, use of individualized reading for twelve weeks followed by the basal reader program, and use of individualized reading as a special approach for both the retarded and the superior readers. One teacher reported an individualized reading group which children might join when they demonstrated that they had acquired certain skills.

TABLE 1

**Method of Incorporating Individualized Reading into the Reading Program
Selected Iowa Schools, 1963**

Method	Teachers Indicating	Percent of Total
To fill out a year or semester for only the superior group	11	10
To fill out a year or semester for any group which finishes basal readers	24	22
As a special approach for retarded readers	30	27
As a supplement to the basal reader, used regularly even though the basal reader has not been completed	88	79
Other	19	17

Basis of Students' Book Selections

Respondents were asked, "How do students select books?" An analysis of the responses, which were not structured on the questionnaire, is shown in Table 2. The basis mentioned most frequently was interest, while teacher guidance, selection from a group which the teacher has selected as being at his level and suitable, and selection on the basis of relation to reading and other subject units being studied were mentioned less frequently. Miscellaneous other bases, mentioned from one to eight times each, were availability, appearance and physical characteristics, recommendations of friends, guidance of librarians, individual ability, and selection from books and stories suggested in the basal reader.

Sources of Books Available to Children

Ranking high as sources of books used by children in individualized reading, as mentioned by the 111 respondents, were the school central library, the public library, and the classroom library. Less frequently mentioned were the county library (in Iowa, usually associated with the Office of the County Superintendent of Schools) and the children's homes. Other sources, mentioned by a few respondents, were book clubs, the teacher, the S.R.A. Laboratory (a misinterpretation of the question), and

TABLE 2

**Basis of Students' Book Selections in Reading Programs
Selected Iowa Schools, 1963**

Basis	Teachers Indicating	Percent of Total
Interest	77	69
With teacher guidance	25	23
From group teacher has selected as being at his level and suitable	25	23
Relation to reading and other subject units being studied	20	18
From books and stories suggested in basal reader	8	7
Individual ability	8	7
Guidance of librarian	6	5
Recommendations of friends	4	4
Appearance, physical characteristics	2	2
Availability	1	1

TABLE 3

**Sources of Books Available to Children
Selected Iowa Schools, 1963**

Source	Teachers Indicating	Percent of Total
School central library	82	73
Public library	73	65
Classroom library	67	60
County library	24	22
Home	22	19
Book clubs	7	6
Teachers	6	5
S.R.A. Reading Laboratory	4	4
I.S.E.A. Library Service	1	1

the library service of the Iowa State Education Association (a sales, not a lending agency). The information concerning sources of books is presented in detail in Table 3.

Types of Materials Used

Table 4 shows that the most frequently mentioned types of materials used in the individualized reading part of the eclectic reading program

TABLE 4

**Types of Materials Used
in Reading Programs
Selected Iowa Schools, 1963**

Type	Teachers Indicating	Percent of Total
Fiction trade books	102	92
Non-fiction trade books	99	88
Various basal readers	83	75
Periodicals	73	66
Content texts	67	60
S.R.A. Laboratory	5	5
Newspapers	1	1
School newspapers	1	1
Comic-type	1	1

were fiction trade books, non-fiction trade books, various basal readers, periodicals, and content texts. The S.R.A. Reading Laboratory was mentioned by five percent of the respondents, while newspaper and comic materials were mentioned in three responses. It should be noted that fiction and non-fiction trade books were both mentioned by a large majority of the respondents.

Methods of Keeping Records of Children's Reading

The variety of methods of keeping records of children's reading associated with individualized reading is shown in Table 5. Mentioned most frequently were file cards, student notebooks, charts, and written reports. Thirteen percent of the respondents said that no records were kept. Mentioned once or no more than four times were the S.R.A. record-keeping procedure, graphs, check sheets, cumulative folders, and questionnaires.

Of the teachers reporting no record keeping procedure, one said, "I do not keep a chart or file. I believe if a child will read for enjoyment and not because of a star or a check, he is on the way to a life of reading, and not just a year or twelve years."

Types of Teacher-Pupil Conferences

One of the elements that usually distinguishes individualized reading from simple "free reading" is the provision for definite individual discus-

TABLE 5

**Methods of Keeping Records
of Children's Reading
Selected Iowa Schools, 1963**

Method	Teachers Indicating	Percent of Total
Filing cards	33	30
Student notebooks	29	26
Charts	28	25
Written reports	22	20
No records	14	13
S.R.A. procedure	4	4
Graphs	3	3
Check sheets	3	3
Cumulative folders	2	2
Questionnaires	1	1

TABLE 6

**Types of Teacher-Pupil Conferences
in Reading Programs
Selected Iowa Schools, 1963**

Type	Teachers Indicating	Percent of Total
Individual	28	25
Small group	27	24
Combination of above	35	31
No conferences	21	20

sion and instruction involving the teacher and the pupil. Table 6 shows that only twenty-five percent of the respondents indicated the use of individual conferences, while twenty-four percent indicated the use of small group conferences, and thirty-five percent, a combination. Twenty percent indicated that they held no conferences.

Activities That Take Place during Teacher-Pupil Conferences

Table 7 indicates that the activity taking place most frequently in the individualized reading conferences in the respondents' classrooms was the child's telling the story in his own words. Oral reading and question-answer sessions were mentioned by fifty-one and forty-one percent of the respondents respectively; while fewer mentioned checking for comprehension and vocabulary and helping in correcting difficulties, and discussion of story, characters, incidents, *etc.* Activities mentioned by one to six percent of the respondents were discussion of book to be read next, discussion of written report, pupil evaluation of his own achievement, taping of oral reading or reporting, and dramatization. Three respondents said they varied the activities to meet the needs of the children. The fact that a large number of the respondents mentioned several activities indicates that many teachers follow this practice, which is, of course, necessary for true individualization of reading instruction.

Occasions for Group Instruction

The inclusion in Table 8 of thirteen categories derived from answers to the question, "What occasions, if any, are used for *group* instruction specifically related to the individualized reading part of the program?" indicates the wide variety of such occasions. Those mentioned most fre-

TABLE 7

**Activities That Take Place during Teacher-Pupil
Conferences in Reading Programs
Selected Iowa Schools, 1963**

Activity	Teachers Indicating	Percent of Total
Child telling story in own words	68	63
Oral reading	56	51
Question-answer session	45	41
Check for comprehension, vocabulary, *etc.* and help in correcting difficulties	13	12
Discussion of story, characters, incidents, *etc.*	12	11
Dramatization	6	6
Taping of oral reading or reporting	3	3
Activities varied to meet needs of children	3	3
Pupil evaluation of own achievement	2	2
Discussion of written report	1	1
Discussion of book to be read next	1	1

quently were need of the group for help with a particular skill, opportunity for individual ideas or discoveries with the class, opportunity for oral book reviews, need to prepare the class to select and evaluate books, a number of students' having chosen the same or related material, need for the whole class to plan for a particular activity, need to introduce new concepts, and need to stress reading skills in teaching the content areas.

Group instruction or sharing provides an opportunity for interaction among students and the bringing together of ideas, opinions and concepts gained from their independent reading experiences. Instruction provided in groups, where common need or readiness warrants it, is also more economical of teacher time than individual instruction and thus more efficient.

Goals of the Individualized
Reading Part of the Program

As shown in Table 9 and as might be expected because of the nature of individualized reading, the most frequently mentioned goals of the individualized reading part of the eclectic reading program were love of reading and broadening interests. It is significant, however, that four of the next five items in rank have to do with skills of reading: increased comprehension, enriched vocabulary, greater independence in work, and mastery of skills. Skills areas mentioned less frequently are improved fluency and speed, improved self-expression, improved research skills, independent

TABLE 8

**Occasions for Group Instruction Specifically Related to the Individualized Reading Part of Programs
Selected Iowa Schools, 1963**

Occasion	Teachers Indicating	Percent of Total
Group needs help with a particular skill	19	17
Sharing individual ideas or discoveries with class	18	16
Oral book reviews	9	8
Preparation of class to select and evaluate books	9	8
Number of students choose same or related materials	8	7
Planning by whole class for a particular activity	6	5
Introduction of new concepts	5	5
Stressing reading skills in teaching the content areas	5	5
Follow-up activities	3	3
Wide interest shown in some phase of work	2	2
Oral reading to class	2	2
Panel discussions	1	1
Word building and analysis	1	1
None	27	24

application of word attack skills in context, and development of ability to select materials wisely. Mention by several respondents of increased knowledge and broadened background indicates another potential contribution of individualized reading.

Teacher Opinion of the Value of Individualized Reading as Part of the Reading Program

It is probably not surprising, in view of the selection process used in getting respondents in this investigation, that 108 of the 111 were favorable toward the use of individualized reading in conjunction with the basal reader program. Individual comments included the following: "Interest has been established within the slower group to stimulate their seeking the help needed." "In my opinion, the basic text does not provide very much challenge to the better readers and by individualizing the program you can make these people stretch their minds." "I feel that each child is progressing at his own rate and developing interests." "Individualized reading is essential! It is a self-motivator for application of skills taught. It removes the temptations of poor work-study habits, dawdling, and mischief. It provides for repetition of skill teaching. Its content leads children into joyful experiences with reading."

TABLE 9

**Goals of the Individualized Reading
Part of the Program
Selected Iowa Schools, 1963**

Goal	Teachers Indicating	Percent of Total
Love of reading	37	33
Broadened interests	36	32
Increased comprehension	22	20
Increased knowledge	20	18
Enriched vocabulary	19	16
Greater independence in work	14	13
Mastery of skills	13	12
Adoption of reading as a leisure activity	11	10
Development of literary appreciation and taste	10	9
Improved fluency	10	9
Increased speed	10	9
Increased amount of reading	8	7
Reading of wider variety of materials	8	7
Improved self-expression	8	7
Improved research skills	7	6
Independent application of word attack skills in context	7	6
Broadened background	5	5
Development of ability to select materials wisely	4	4

Conclusion

The results of the investigation reported here, based on questionnaire responses of 111 middle-grade teachers, give credibility and meaning to the assertion that individualized reading procedures may enrich and stengthen an eclectic reading program, offering contributions that complement the basal reader series.

17 | Breaking the Basal-Reader Lock Step*

Russell G. Stauffer

Preprimers are stilted in style. The sentences are short, the stories are short, and the pictures are large.

The stilted style is the result of controls. In these books the vocabulary, the length of the sentences, the length of the lines, the number of pictures in each story, and the interest area are all controlled. The main purpose of the controls is to teach children to recognize and remember printed words.

In most textbook series the first words presented are to be learned as sight words. That is, they are to be recognized and remembered by their configuration; they are not learned by phonetic analysis. Sight words are important because they serve as the visual foundation for learning how to attack other words by phonetic and structural analysis.

Teachers and others who are uninformed about the purposes of preprimers often reject them with distaste and caustic criticism. Yet during the past thirty years at least 90 per cent of the pupils who learned to read did so through a basal-reader program.

Today we know that it is possible to circumvent the use of preprimers, and sometimes primers, by using experience stories or charts. The experience chart presents a story dictated by individual pupils or by a group of pupils while the teacher records the account in manuscript writing.

*From *Elementary School Journal,* vol. 61, February 1961, pp. 269–276.

Some charts are written on the chalkboard, but many are written on newsprint so they may be used again. The charts vary in length and interest area and are often illustrated by the child who dictated the story.

This excellent approach creates desirable attitudes toward reading. It gives pupils an active part in the preparation of materials and capitalizes on the children's skill and interest in speaking. Through this approach children learn to read in much the same way that they learn to talk—by using immediate, personal experiences.

Role for Preprimers

The teacher who uses experience stories does not have to stop using preprimers. She may merely use them in a different way. Instead of using them to develop the children's reading vocabulary, story by story under her direction, she may give them to the pupils to read independently.

The procedure has at least two advantages. It gives the children an opportunity to try their fledgling-reading skills on carefully structured material, and it makes their first contact with readers a pleasant experience in which they discover that they can read an entire book—a preprimer—on their own. The reassurance and the enthusiasm that result from such an experience are priceless. Even a preprimer can become a magic carpet that transports children into the world of books.

It is easy to understand how pupils taught by the experience-story approach can use preprimers and primers for independent reading. It is also easy to see how independent reading of carefully structured material fosters self-selection and independent reading of simple story books.

Experience charts give each child an opportunity to learn words without limiting the experience, the interest area, or the vocabulary. Each child's interests, experiences, and language facility form the boundary of his possible progress.

Once the children's interests and curiosities are given freedom as they reread their own experience stories and those of their classmates, they will naturally seek out other material. The desire for additional material is beyond doubt one of the most important outcomes of a first-year or beginning reading program. Experience has shown that where this approach is used pupils complete the reading of preprimers and primers earlier than they do by other approaches. The reason is obvious: the books are used in a more meaningful way(1).

Self-Selection in Reading

Once the children are reading at a first-reader level, the emphasis should be shifted. The basic reader should be used for instructional purposes, not for independent reading. The use of experience stories should be sharply curbed and replaced by the wide reading program fostered by the self-selection method, or the individualized method.

The basic-reader approach now becomes the group approach and provides one method for directing reading as a thinking process. The self-selection method, using many books, is the individual approach and provides another method for directing the reading-thinking process. The effective use of both methods is the best way to teach all the skills needed for versatile, efficient, independent reading.

Self-selection is a more appropriate expression than *individualized reading.* The latter implies that the teacher who uses basic readers cannot help individual pupils, which is not true. First-grade teachers bristle, and rightly so, if they are accused of not knowing their pupils and not providing individual help. Yet many teachers do admit that they would do more individualizing of instruction if they knew how.

In self-selection it is the individual who seeks and selects. Actually in the end what each pupil learns, remembers, and uses is largely a matter of self-selection(2). But teaching should not deteriorate to a mere catering to whims and fancies so that learning becomes undirected and unmethodic. Quite the contrary, teaching should be firm and resolute. It should reflect research findings on child growth and development. It should indicate an ability to teach reading as a thinking process. It should show knowledge of children's literature. In schools where teachers have plunged into a program of self-selection, or so-called individualizing of reading instruction, without the necessary knowledge and skills the teaching of reading has become meaningless.

What are the essentials of self-selection? How does the method fit into, and modify, a basal-reader program?

The Teacher's Attitude

Most important in self-selection is the teacher's attitude toward the program. She must be convinced that children can and will select material in which they are interested and that is within their abilities.

She must believe that the children will read to understand what they select. As in group–directed reading, the pupils will have purposes, although their purposes are not declared to or through a group. Pupils will want to share what they have read. Whether the material is discursive or non-discursive, children are not interested in just reading. In situations where children are encouraged to do their own thinking, reading, and reflecting, they are eager to share with their peers.

The teacher must also recognize that interest in self-selection and in reading materials selected varies from individual to individual and from day to day. Performance is no more uniform than it is when other methods are used. For all pupils—the bright as well as the slow—the teacher has to give thought to providing materials, fostering interests, developing word-attack skills and comprehension skills. In providing materials and experiences the teacher must keep in mind each child's maturity. In short, the teacher does teach.

Teachers must know as thoroughly as possible the growth patterns, social and personal, of each child. Because the pacing of each pupil's progress is to be governed by his maturity, the teacher needs some yardstick of maturity. Given encouragement, children explore their environment and seek experiences appropriate to their maturity. For the teacher to provide materials and experiences in keeping with a pupil's maturity at a pace that assures success, she must make decisions about what to offer, when, how much, and how soon. To carry out this responsibility, she must be informed about the development of typical six-year-olds, their interests and their needs.

Provide Books—and More Books

If children are to seek and select, they must have books and materials from which to seek and select. The approach calls for books, magazines, newspapers, and other printed materials on various topics and at many levels of difficulty. Textbooks as well as story books are required.

Love for reading is not taught; it is created. Love for reading is not required, but inspired; not demanded, but exemplified; not exacted, but quickened; not solicited, but activated.

To succeed, the teacher must know materials. She must read much of the material, enjoy it, be enthusiastic about what she has read, and know to whom to recommend what.

Each child's interests vary and fluctuate: today a child may be entranced by a book about trains; tomorrow he may be held capitive by *Peter and the Wolf;* the day after, his enthusiasm may go to a book like *Big Top,* about the circus; and the day after that, his favorite may be a book about Mickey Mouse.

Although teachers are not amateur psychiatrists, they do come to know a great deal about children's needs and may at times want to recommend books like *The Lonely Doll* or *The Big Lonely Dog.* Children are insightful enough to appreciate how others meet problems similar to their own. They realize that they do not have to jump off a bridge to learn the consequences of such an act. Learning through the experience of others is not new to them, nor is learning through books and stories. For hardly a child comes to school who has not heard or read stories.

To Launch a Program

One of the first questions teachers ask about self-selection is "How do you organize the program?" To the disbelief of some and the amazement of others, a program of self-selection requires even more planning and more reflection than programs that are already structured. This is easy to understand.

Consider Farmer A. He is engaged by a landlord to run a farm and told to obtain the best yield possible. The responsibility and the challenge are great. He must study the soil, cultivate it, and enrich it as needed. He must sow the right seed and control the weeds. In time, he will have to harvest the crop and plan for the future. In short, he must be able and resourceful.

Now consider Farmer B. Also engaged by a landlord to run a farm, he is given a plan. He is told what fertilizer to use, what crops to plant where, how to harvest and market his crops, and how to prepare for next year. He, too, has a formidable task, but his responsibility is considerably different. For him, plans have been set up and decisions made.

In a program of self-selection, the basic tenet is to adapt instruction to each child's needs and interests. It would be well-nigh impossible to prepare a plan or a time schedule to fit every pupil in every classroom, but certain specifics that might be adapted to various situations can be defined.

Time

When a basal-reader program is modified by the self-selection approach, some decision is needed on how much time is to be allotted to the two approaches. It is recommended that the time be divided about equally: One week all the reading time may be devoted to group instruction using the basic reader. The following week all the time may be devoted to self-selection, or individualized instruction. A day or two a week for self-selection seldom accomplishes the aims desired.

Motivation

The pupil's motives for reading determine the kind of material to be read, the difficulty of the material, the amount of material, and what to do with what has been read. The pupil's motives take precedence over time or materials. The pupil decides what he wants to read about and why. He may consult with the teacher or a classmate to clarify his purposes. Or, in the course of participation in a group or class project he may discover individual purposes for reading.

To get started on an effective plan, a teacher needs to learn each pupil's motives. She can get the information in several ways. She can take an inventory of each pupil's interests by asking questions about what he does and what he likes. The questions may be asked orally of individuals or small groups over a period of two or three days. Another good technique is the three-wishes question: "If you had three wishes, what would they be?" Or pupils may be given a sentence-completion test. The Rhode Sentence Completions Test, for instance, has these items:

> My schoolwork . . .
> I want to know . . .
> Much of the time . . .

The teacher can give sales talks about books. Through her talks she can not only find out what books pupils respond to most enthusiastically but foster new interests as well. One of the best methods is to keep eyes and ears open throughout the day and note pupils' likes and preferences.

To say that there should be no schedule for self-selection periods is ridiculous. Havoc would result. The schedule is determined largely by the personal interests and needs of each child. If a child is working with another child or in a group, the interests and needs of the pair or the group set the pace.

This type of scheduling is based on the assumption that individuals are capable of responding in various ways and can select some ways in preference to others. In the self-selection schedule the pupils need to do more than make undirected, unmethodic preferences. The selections need to be consciously determined, deliberate, and in many ways reality-bound and goal-seeking.

As Stock and Thelen point out in their discussion of Bion's concepts, a work aspect and an emotionality aspect are involved in situations where personal needs are met. These aspects vary from individual to individual, from task to task, and within an individual or in the process of accomplishing a task (3).

In other words, at times a pupil may read and be very busy; at other times he does not seem to be able to get started or, once started, to keep going. Sometimes during a self-selection period a pupil may show short attention spans and irritability, while at other times he may work like a beaver.

Such variance in performance influences schedules. As long as the children are eager to work, they will read and learn. If the children are restless and emotionality appears dominant, behavior may be aimless, and the mood of the group may verge on disorder.

But the same pattern may be found when basic readers are used. On some days the pupils are ready and eager, on other days they are not. Self-selection is not a panacea. Self-selection does not mean that every pupil is busy reading every moment. During a self-selection period conditions and changes in performance are as much a part of the climate as they are in group situations when basic readers are used.

Scheduling in self-selection requires that the teacher keep track of an extraordinary number of individual schedules. One teacher reported the schedule of eight of her twenty-seven pupils:

"This morning John selected a book on stars. He'll probably need help with words throughout the reading period. He'll probably keep the book for two or three days."

"Mary just finished a book. She is slow in selecting something new and may not choose a book until tomorrow."

"Harold is reading the book *Surprise for Timmy:* he'll be busy all day."

"Helen and Arlene both had the same word-recognition difficulty; they'll be working as a team today."

"Howard and Carl and Jean are reading a play together; Howard read the play first and interested the other two."

This teacher kept a running record for each pupil. She made notes during the reading period and at the end of the day. Some teachers keep all the schedules in mind and make records only of special items that need extra planning. For example: "Have the librarian locate books on jets for Warren."

Discipline

If a child is to behave as an individual and yet respect the rights and comforts of the other members of the class, he must view his behavior as having a place among the behavior patterns of the other children. There must be some controls over each pupil's behaviors and over the behavior of the entire class, controls that result in a social system sound enough to maintain orderliness and stability of expectation.

Rules must be developed that encourage some behavior patterns and inhibit others. Controls must be developed in such a way that each pupil feels responsible for making the rules and learns to exercise some authority over himself. Certain pupils may be chosen to help manage the room.

The spirit motivating the class must be such that the success of one pupil is gratifying to all and the failure of one pupil results in a let-down feeling in the others. The feeling of unity must be strong. Each pupil must show respect for the purposes, values, and actions of every other pupil.

At first some pupils may find it difficult to assume responsibility and take part in group action. They may display anger or frustration, or they may be aimless, passive, and acquiescing. For these pupils both the teacher and the class must feel a responsibility. Controls must be exercised in so humane a way that a pupil's willingness to express himself and to participate in group actions will not be inhibited.

Skills

During self-selection periods skills are, of course, taught and maintained. Pupils need to learn where such materials as textbooks, tradebooks, magazines, encyclopedias, dictionaries, and newspapers are located and how to use them.

The old-time Friday afternoon library period did not require much self-analysis and understanding. But when a pupil is free to select day after day for eight or ten successive days, he is almost forced to examine his interests and decide more carefully what he wants to do.

Through self-selection pupils learn to be resourceful, to search persistently for answers, to distinguish between reading just for fun and reading to learn. They learn to read extensively and intensively. They learn to assemble and organize information. They learn how and when to share ideas. They learn to listen attentively so as to ask intelligent questions.

The children learn to keep records. Each pupil maintains his own record of the books he reads along with notes about the books. The children's records usually show the name of the book, the number of pages read, the date of reading, and the child's opinion of the book. The children prepare no formal reports. This procedure usually results in a more discriminating evaluation. One boy noted in his record, "This book's got it."

Evaluation

It is unfortunately true that one of the best measures of the success of a program of self-selection is the children's enthusiasm for the privilege of just reading. This is a shocking indictment of what apparently has been happening in classrooms where the basal-reader lock step has been used. Eagerness to read, enthusiasm for what is being read, and a desire to share what has been read are important measures of success in a self-selection program.

Other measures are a longer attention span; more reading and less frittering away of time; bigger vocabulary; more sensitivity to words both in and out of school; and a desire to share ideas.

When this approach is used, results on standardized reading tests usually show greater achievement over shorter periods of time than when only a basal-reader approach is used.

In summary, the modified basal-reader approach recommended here uses both basal readers and self-selection. All children need instruction in both group-type directed reading activities and individual-type activities.

Second, self-selection activity is supervised and organized. The self-selection period is not a time for aimless drifting. On the contrary, more pupil-teacher planning is required than when other methods are used.

Third, a pupil may select material to accomplish his own purposes. If he is a member of a group of pupils who have related interests, his purposes may reflect these interests. At times the entire class may want to accomplish an objective, and each class member may select materials to this end. Whether the purposes are a pupil's very own or reflect membership in a group or in the entire class, the teacher must honor the purposes selected.

Fourth, the teacher can motivate reading. She can set the stage for pupils to encounter a variety of experiences to fulfill various purposes for reading. She can promote certain ideas by her enthusiasm. Not only the materials she provides but the way she organizes new ideas will influence the children's self-selection. Ideas placed first usually get more attention. Not all planning is left to the whim and fancy of individual pupils.

Fifth, skills are taught. The self-selection program gives children experience in identifying individual purposes, in seeking and selecting material, in adjusting rate of reading to purposes and materials, in reflecting on and evaluating answers found, and in organizing and presenting materials to others.

REFERENCES

1. Stauffer, Russell, and others. *Away We Go* (Teachers Edition). New York: Holt, Rinehart and Winston, 1960.
2. Olson, Willard C. "Seeking, Self-Selection, and Pacing in the Use of Books by Children," *The Packet* (Spring, 1952), 3–10. (Published by Heath, Boston, Massachusetts.)
3. Stock, Dorothy, and Thelen, Herbert A. *Emotional Dynamics and Group Culture*. National Training Laboratories. New York: Published for the National Education Association by New York University Press, 1958.

18 Contributions of Linguistics in Teaching Reading*

Bernice Cooper

Linguistics is a broad but specialized field as are anthropology, sociology, psychology, and education. All of these are concerned with language: the linguist from the viewpoint of the structure of language, the anthropologist because man's culture has been transmitted through language, the sociologist because of society's dependence upon language, the psychologist because language is one way man expresses self, and the educator because language is one medium of recording knowledge. Consequently, all are related to reading.

Although the science of linguistics is not new, recently the application of linguistic principles to the teaching of all the language arts is being studied and recommended. It is found in writing about grammar, speech, foreign languages, written composition, and literature as well as the teaching of reading. Certainly, linguistics, the scientific study of language, is important to communication in its broadest sense, to language arts as an area of the curriculum and to reading as one facet of the language arts.

What principles from the science of linguistics may be incorporated in the teaching of reading? The problem is to understand linguistics as well as

*From *Education,* vol. 85, May 1965, pp. 529–532. Reprinted from the May 1965 issue of *Education.* Copyright 1965 by The Bobbs-Merrill Company, Inc., Indianapolis, Ind.

the related curriculum area and to examine both critically in an effort to determine those principles which offer direct and practical value for reading instruction. At the present time, these principles have not been determined satisfactorily. They require greater study in the future.

Basically, the suggestions made by linguists for beginning reading instruction seem to be an oversimplification of the reading process. The reading act is more complex than the recognition of the structure of words. This writer will attempt to focus attention on some of the specific suggestions for teaching beginning reading which may be questioned and to suggest how linguistics may be useful to the teacher of reading. Fries's *Linguistics and Reading* (1) will be used as the primary source of practices considered in this paper, for it offers a rather detailed description of materials and methods for teaching reading through the linguistic approach.

Letter Forms

1. Fries recommended habit-forming practices to develop high-speed recognition responses to the principle of our alphabetic writing during the "transfer" stage. The purpose of these practices basically is to develop the ability to see the significant contrastive features of the separate letters. He emphasizes that:

> There must be no attempt to connect the letters themselves with sounds. Nor should the groups of letters used in the practices of 'alike' or 'different', which happen to form 'words' for us who can read, such as IT, IF, FIT, HIT, AT, HAT, be treated at this preliminary stage *as words to be pronounced and connected with meaning* (1, p. 194).

For a number of years, many exercises in readiness materials have been planned to develop visual perception which includes an awareness of likenesses and differences. It must be recognized however, that these activities have usually been based on pictures of objects rather than letter forms.

An examination of the readiness books of eight publishers of basal readers revealed that seven of these included very few exercises with letters or words for visual discrimination purposes. In these seven, the number of exercises using letters or words ranged from none to nine. Most of those which were included were for the purpose of recognition of the names of the characters and perhaps three or four other words the child would meet in the preprimer.

Of course, teachers use other materials during the prereading period, but it must be concluded that a minimum of exercises is used with letters or words to develop likenesses and differences. Perhaps more exercises using letters and combinations of letters during the prereading stage would help to develop a keener and quicker recognition of letter forms.

Letter Groups

2. Fries stated that "this ability to identify the difference between three-letter groups is so important a skill at this stage that the variety of practices necessary for its full development should become the chief activity of the prereading child"(1,p.193). This skill does offer possibilities for the classroom teacher. However, whether it should become the chief activity of the prereading child may be questioned. All the goals of a reading program should be considered and attention should be given to all the skills with varied activities included from the beginning stages.

Capital Letters

3. Linguists suggest, too, the use of all capital letters in the beginning stages of learning to read; that is, during the time the reader is learning contrastive features and clusters of letter groupings(1,pp.190–191).

Why? Books are not printed in this form. Why should exercises to develop his awareness of contrasts and recognition of clusters (if used) not begin with the same forms, including lower case and capital letters as needed, which he will continue to use? Why begin with these forms and then have to shift to the use of lower case letters? This suggestion seems to create new problems for the teacher rather than alleviate old ones.

Spelling Patterns

4. The use of the spelling pattern, for example, (consonant)-vowel-consonant, has also been over-simplified. The recommended presentation of the spelling pattern of *at, bat, cat, fat, gat, hat,* . . . , . . . omits any suggestions as to how an awareness of the sounds represented by the different beginning symbols will be achieved(1,p.171). The same difficulty is apparent in *bat, bad, bag, ban,* . . . , . . . , when the ending is different (1,p.172). To one who reads, this seems simple; however, there is an intermediate step which must be provided for the beginner.

Or, consider the spelling pattern of *man, mane, mean*(1,p.201). Teachers generally use the single vowel, final *e,* and vowel diagraph principles to develop an understanding of the difference in words of this type. The linguist objects to these principles on the basis that they are structurally incorrect. However, the child needs some clue other than "great practice to respond automatically to the contrastive features that separate these three patterns"(1,p.201).

Getting Meaning

5. The act of reading implies getting meaning from the printed symbols. The teaching of reading without meaning is mechanical and dull. Lindemann said:

> *Nonsense letter groups are the test of a child's success in reading.* If he unflinchingly attacks those, he will, later on in his career, have learned how to attack 'big words' and words that others, not trained in this manner, might find strange or queer. Moreover, letters in short form without sense become words in longer combinations: *e.g., han* will become *handle, mag* will become *magneto* and *magnanimous* and *Jan* will become *January*(2).

But, one may ask, what happens to *han* in *elephant, change, shanty?* to *mag* in *imagine, image?* to *jan* in *Jane, jangle?* The carry-over of these letter groups to "big words" is an over-simplification. When this technique is relied upon, pronouncing words becomes an attempt to blend letter groupings which will not work in many cases as blending of individual letters will not work.

Although Fries stated that "even from the beginning there must be complete meaning responses"(1,p.204), some of his suggested combinations leave doubt as to whether they are meaningful; for example, BAT A FAT RAT—A CAT AT BAT—CATS BAT AT RATS(1,p.203).

Practical Uses of Linguistics

One has only to scan the vast amount of research in reading, to examine the changes which have been made in methodology and materials, and to observe the interest indicated by conferences and in-service programs to know that those responsible for the teaching of reading are eager and anxious to learn new ideas and techniques which offer possibilities for greater success in the classroom.

However, new ideas and techniques must be considered carefully in an effort to assure that they do indeed offer possibilities for improvement and are not merely an innovation with doubtful value. The questions raised in the above discussion are not intended to imply that linguistics has nothing to offer. Rather it questions the specific suggestions made particularly for beginning reading.

Two first-grade teachers in Clarke County, Georgia,[1] had a brief intensive course in linguistics during the summer of 1964. After approximately three months in the classroom following this instruction, they were interviewed by this writer concerning the application of linguistic principles to beginning reading instruction. Both felt that they needed to know more to be able to use this information as they thought they might.

However, one commented that she was now more conscious of the structure of the language and she listened to the conversation of the children with more awareness. She added that she used the linguistic principles more in oral language perhaps than in reading. Actually, she concluded that she could not say that she had consciously changed activities and methods in beginning reading instruction, but that the linguistic principles had become a part of her thinking and made a difference in her observations and suggestions concerning the overall use of language, including reading, in her classroom.

The second teacher emphasized her use of intonation, pitch, and stress in oral reading. And, although she said that she had always encouraged children "to read as they talk" she was now more conscious of the value of this approach. She also commented that she was using oral language such as book reports and dramatizations to a greater extent than before the course. She concluded, also, that she was more conscious of the structure of language in her teaching.

The reactions of these two teachers, although recognized as only two cases, reinforce the writer's conclusion that, at this time, perhaps the best way to take advantage of the knowledge of linguistics is for teachers to become better acquainted with the field. They would then be in a position to use this understanding in all phases of the curriculum dealing with language. This approach probably offers more to the future of reading instruction than the present attempts to translate linguistic principles into the specific methodology of teaching beginning reading *per se*.

In the meantime, more research is needed in this area.

REFERENCES

1. Charles C. Fries, *Linguistics and Reading* (New York: Holt, Rinehart and Winston, 1962).
2. J. W. Richard Lindemann, "Linguistics and the Teaching of Reading," a paper presented to the University of Georgia 24th Annual Reading Conference, June 27, 1968.

[1] Mrs. Evelyn Booth and Miss Lois Settle, Alps Road School, Clarke County, Ga.

19 Initial Teaching Alphabet: Results after Six Years*

John Downing

In June, 1960, the University of London Institute of Education and the National Foundation for Educational Research in England and Wales announced that they were "initiating an investigation into the early stages of learning to read, when the matter to be read is printed in a special form alleged to be easy to learn and leading to a full reading skill" (1). This announcement marked the beginning of six years of study of the initial teaching alphabet. Five of those years were devoted to controlled scientific research with the initial teaching alphabet in British schools. All this work is reported in *Evaluating the Initial Teaching Alphabet* (2), published in London in December, 1967.

The completion of this research represents the culmination of four hundred years of proposals, trials, and controversies over systems similar to the initial teaching alphabet, and the report relates the results of the more modern scientific research to these earlier attempts as well as to relevant research and theory on the psychology of the reading process.

There are many problems in applying the methods of experimental psychology to the real-life issues of the schools. Difficulties of this kind

*From *Elementary School Journal,* vol. 69, February 1969, pp. 242–249. Dr. Downing is Professor of Education, University of Victoria, British Columbia, Canada.

that arose in the experiments on the initial teaching alphabet in Britain are discussed in two recent articles on research methodology (3, 4). This brief summary permits only a list of the matching variables used in the first experiment, which began in 1961:

1. Environmental variables: These included location (urban or rural), age range of school (two types: infants' schools for pupils aged five to seven years and schools for infants and juniors combined, that is, pupils aged five to eleven years), number of pupils in school, pupil-teacher ratio, amenities of the school building, minimum age of admission, and the social class of the neighborhood.
2. Individual student variables: These were intelligence (non-verbal and verbal), social class, age, and sex.
3. Treatment variables: These included the materials and methods of teaching. The eclectic "Janet and John" series was used. The text was presented in the initial teaching alphabet in the experimental classes and in the traditional orthography of English in the control classes. The Hawthorne effect was taken into account. For example, workshops were held for teachers in the control group as well as for teachers in the experimental group.

In 1963, a second experiment in the initial teaching alphabet began in Britain. This experiment controlled teacher competency in addition to the variables listed. Each teacher worked half her day in the class that used the initial teaching alphabet and half in the class that used the traditional orthography. Both classes were in the same school.

In the first experiment, 158 classes were recruited originally, but the careful matching procedure reduced this number to 82 classes (41 used the initial teaching alphabet, and 41 traditional orthography).

The second experiment used sixteen pairs of classes. One class in each pair was taught the initial teaching alphabet; the other, traditional orthography. Because three schools followed inadequate procedures in sharing teachers, their data had to be excluded from the analysis, and this reduced the number of pairs of classes to thirteen.

In both experiments, for the first one and a half years, pupils' learning when the initial teaching alphabet was used was compared with pupils' learning when traditional orthography was used. Pupils who were taught the initial teaching alphabet were tested in the initial teaching alphabet. Pupils who were taught the traditional orthography were tested in the traditional orthography. The reading tests were parallel: the words and sentences in the initial teaching alphabet were the same as those in the traditional orthography.

The results of the first phase of the research were conclusive in both experiments. On every test the reading attainments of pupils who used the initial teaching alphabet were very much superior to those who used traditional orthography. Indeed, the difference was quite dramatic. For example, in the initial teaching alphabet classes, pupils were able to read by the end of the first year on average more than twice as many words of English as children who used traditional orthography.

In the second phase, the tests for the transfer of learning from initial teaching alphabet to traditional orthography also were the same in both experiments.

From the middle of the second year, all the pupils taught the initial teaching alphabet were tested in the traditional orthography, and their attainments were compared with the attainments in traditional orthography of the pupils who had learned only the traditional orthography from the beginning.

In both experiments, in the middle of the second year the pupils who had learned the initial teaching alphabet were not able to read in traditional orthography as well as they could read in the initial teaching alphabet which they had been learning. This was hardly surprising, but it is noteworthy that their reading attainments in traditional orthography were equal to those of the pupils who had been learning traditional orthography from the beginning of the experiment. Even more surprising were the later results of the first experiment: by the end of the third year, the pupils who had learned the initial teaching alphabet had traditional orthography reading attainments that were significantly superior to those of the control group pupils who had used only traditional orthography. The average pupil in the initial teaching alphabet classes was five months ahead of his counterpart in the traditional orthography classes after three years of school.

However, the results for this second phase—the transition from the initial teaching alphabet to traditional orthography—are not as clear as those for the first phase when attainments were measured in the same alphabet as the pupils were learning. One result of the first experiment has not been confirmed as yet by the second experiment. In the later experiment, the pupils who had begun with the initial teaching alphabet had attainments in reading traditional orthography that were equal to those of the pupils who had learned only the traditional orthography from the start. But the pupils who had begun with the initial teaching alphabet did not show at the end of the third year the superiority that was found in the first experiment. There is some evidence that the teaching pace of the second experiment was slower, and, therefore, the recovery from transition may come later. This second experiment has been extended for two more years to investigate this question.

The effects of the initial teaching alphabet on free written composition were studied in small subsamples of children from initial teaching alphabet and traditional orthography classes in Staffordshire, England. The written work of one week near the beginning of the third school year was analyzed. The schools were matched on the number of pupils and urban-rural location, and the pupils were matched on intelligence, sex, and social class.

It should be noted here that, in Britain, correct spelling and hand-writing are not demanded in the first three years of school when traditional orthography is used. Thus, in this respect, the treatment of the group taught the initial teaching alphabet was the same as the treatment of the group taught the traditional orthography.

The results for this part of the experiment were clear. The compositions from the initial teaching alphabet classes were superior on all measures used. The compositions of these classes were, on the average, 50 per cent longer and used 45 per cent more different words. This expansion of vocabulary was to an important degree due to the use of more advanced words. These results have been confirmed in a small study in Scotland (5), which also tested the quality of creative writing in the two alphabets. Independent judges consistently gave higher grades to the initial teaching alphabet compositions, although these had been re-written in traditional orthography to prevent the judges from knowing in which classes the compositions had been written.

Finally, the conventional English spelling attainments of all pupils in both experiments have been tested. Only correct traditional orthography spellings were accepted. Correct initial teaching alphabet spellings were treated as errors in all tests. It seems certain from these tests that the initial teaching alphabet does not cause poor spelling in traditional orthography. In both experiments, by the middle of the third year of school, the pupils in the initial teaching alphabet classes had attainments in conventional English spelling that were equal to those of the pupils in the traditional orthography classes. In the first experiment, by mid-fourth year the pupils in the initial teaching alphabet classes had significantly superior scores on standardized tests of conventional English spelling. But the second experiment did not show this finding, although the follow-up study may at a later stage.

The two experiments confirm each other in one most important conclusion. The initial teaching alphabet is definitely superior to the traditional orthography of English. The difference between the reading achievement of pupils taught the initial teaching alphabet and the reading achievement of pupils taught the traditional orthography is truly dramatic. For example, on both the Schonell Graded Word Reading Test (6) and the accuracy measure of the Neale Analysis of Reading Ability (7) the mean score for pupils taught the initial teaching alphabet is more than double the mean score for pupils taught the traditional orthography. In written composition, too, pupils taught the initial teaching alphabet demonstrate a very important superiority in breadth of vocabulary.

The unequivocal conclusion is that the traditional orthography of English is a seriously defective instrument for the early stages of reading and writing. As long as this traditional orthography is used in the early years of schooling in English-speaking countries, children's learning of reading and writing is bound to be much less efficient than it can be with a simplified and regularized writing-system such as the initial teaching alphabet. Of this, there can no longer be any doubt.

What action can be taken to remove this serious handicap on those who are learning to read and write in English? The results from the British research on the initial teaching alphabet summarized here show quite clearly that three main courses of action are open to us:

1. *More extensive adoption of the initial teaching alphabet*

The superiority of the initial teaching alphabet in comparison with the traditional orthography is so great that the continued use of the latter seems indefensible. However, educators need to be cautious in planning to replace traditional orthography with the initial teaching alphabet in their classrooms. The initial teaching alphabet is only an alphabet—not a complete teaching method. It can be taught well or badly. Materials printed in the initial teaching alphabet can use or abuse its advantages. Before adopting materials labeled "initial teaching alphabet," educators should study the materials carefully—even more carefully than usual, because the initial teaching alphabet itself is still quite new and experimental, and materials printed in it must be even more so. The author of this article has described in other articles(8,9,10,11) the important differences between various basal series in the initial teaching alphabet on the market. These differences are particularly important for American schools.

While the initial teaching alphabet is clearly superior to traditional orthography in the initial stages of learning, the research results are less clear with regard to the effectiveness of the initial teaching alphabet in transfer to traditional orthography.

At the transition stage, pupils taught the initial teaching alphabet read textbooks printed in the traditional orthography less well than they read the same textbooks in the initial teaching alphabet, though usually their reading in the traditional orthography is not worse than the reading of pupils who have used only traditional orthography from the beginning. In the first experiment, the transition usually occurred in the second half of the second year of school. In the second experiment, the teachers seem to have delayed transition somewhat, so that it is not clear whether the result of the first experiment at the end of the third year of school will be confirmed. In that first experiment, the pupils who were taught the initial teaching alphabet appeared to recover from a plateau effect in transition. By the end of the third year they had a lead of about five months in reading age in word recognition in traditional orthography over pupils taught the traditional orthography. Although this advantage seems to be important, the gain is not so dramatic as the gain found during the first two years, when the initial teaching alphabet was the medium of instruction and testing. This may lead some educators to ask whether it is worthwhile to use the initial teaching alphabet for the beginning stage. But to question the worth of the initial teaching alphabet on this basis is to ignore several educational benefits to be derived from the dramatically improved achievements of pupils taught the initial teaching alphabet while still working with that writing-system. Because the initial teaching alphabet clarifies the structure of English, the discovery approach to learning is facilitated, and children can express themselves more readily, more fluently, and more creatively in free written composition. Moreover, young boys and girls may develop a healthier self-image through the greater certainty of success derived from the simplicity and the regularity of the initial teaching alphabet. Again, it must be added, these gains may result if the methods and the materials used in teaching the initial teaching alphabet are planned to take advantage of the potential of the new writing-system in these respects.

In Britain, where the initial teaching alphabet was introduced in 1961, it is spreading steadily as each school principal considers the results of the research and makes his own decision, as is usual in the British education system. This growth in the use of the initial teaching alphabet will create new needs. New tests in the initial teaching alphabet will have to be standardized, and the norms for existing tests in the traditional orthography will have to be re-established as more and more children have prior experience in programs that use the initial teaching alphabet.

2. *Research and development to improve the initial teaching alphabet*

The results of British research also indicate that the writing-system of the initial teaching alphabet must be improved. While research supports the general principle of simplifying and regularizing English orthography, this principle has yet to be applied in full. Many years of further research may be necessary. Some of the needed improvements in the initial teaching alphabet have been indicated in a recent article (12). Birnie's (13) linguistic analysis of the initial teaching alphabet supports these proposals.

The need for further research to improve the initial teaching alphabet is no excuse for postponing the adoption of this initial teaching alphabet in its present form. The evidence on this point is conclusive. The traditional orthography of English is seriously inadequate in comparison with the initial teaching alphabet. Therefore, the present initial teaching alphabet should replace traditional orthography in printed materials for beginning reading until research has refined the form of the initial teaching alphabet.

3. *General and permanent correction of English orthography*

It is clear from the results of the British research on the initial teaching alphabet that the only completely satisfactory solution to the problem of the writing-system of the defective traditional orthography is permanent correction. If pupils did not have to transfer to traditional orthography, their dramatic superiority would probably continue into the later years of schooling. This is not a simple problem, and others besides teachers and young children would be affected by such a change. However, the British research report recognizes that, although there may be some practical problems in changing English spelling, research should begin immediately to determine what these problems are and how they might be overcome if these defects in English orthography are to be corrected. A study could be made of the difficulties found and how they were met in other countries when they introduced a more phonetic spelling.

Benjamin Franklin's prediction at long last has been fully vindicated by the British research. He wrote:

> Whatever the difficulties of reforming our spelling now are, they will be more easily surmounted now than hereafter; and some time or other it must be done; or else our writing will become the same with the Chinese as to the difficulty of learning and using it(14).

Indeed, in comparison with Chinese, English may soon be in a far worse position, for China has begun to reform its writing-system. Prime Minister Chou En-Lai's(15) pragmatic approach to opposition to the reform is an object lesson in determined progress toward the goal of a maximally effective writing-system for learning to read and write where universal functional literacy is recognized as the essential basis for a fully efficient technology. He states:

> An alphabet is a means of transcribing pronunciation. We make it serve us just as we make trains, steamships, automobiles and airplanes serve us. (And, from the point of origin, all these are imported.) It is also like using Arabic numerals for counting and calculating the Gregorian calendar of the Christian era for recording the year, kilometres for measuring distance, and kilogrammes for measuring weight. The adoption of the Latin alphabet will, therefore, not harm the patriotism of our people.

REFERENCES

1. University of London Institute of Education and National Foundation for Educational Research in England and Wales. *Some Reasons Why We Are Initiating an Investigation into the Early Stages of Learning To Read.* London: University of London Institute of Education, 1960.
2. John A. Downing. *Evaluating the Initial Teaching Alphabet.* London: Cassell, 1967.
3. John A. Downing. "Commentary: Methodological Problems in Research on

Simplified Alphabets and Regularized Writing-Systems," *Journal of Typographic Research, 1* (April, 1967), 191–97.

4. John A. Downing, Daphne Cartwright, Barbara Jones, and William Latham. "Methodological Problems in the British i.t.a. Research," *Reading Research Quarterly, 3* (Fall, 1967), 85–100.

5. John A. Downing, Thomas Fyfe, and Michael Lyon. "The Effects of the Initial Teaching Alphabet (i.t.a.) on Young Children's Written Composition," *Educational Research, 9* (February, 1967), 137–44.

6. F. J. Schonell and F. E. Schonell. "Graded Word Reading Test," *Diagnostic and Attainment Testing.* Edited by F. J. Schonell. Edinburgh: Oliver and Boyd, 1956.

7. M. D. Neale. *Neale Analysis of Reading Ability.* London: Macmillan, 1958.

8. John A. Downing. "Alternative Teaching Methods in i.t.a." *Elementary English,* 45 (November, 1968), 942–51.

9. John A. Downing. "Self-Discovery, Self-Expression, and the Self-Image in the i.t.a. Classroom." *Claremont Reading Conference Thirty-second Yearbook.* Edited by Malcolm Douglass. Claremont, California: Claremont University Center, 1968.

10. John A. Downing. "The Nature and Function of i.t.a. in Beginning Reading," *A Decade of Innovations: Approaches to Beginning of Reading,* pp. 149–61. Edited by Elaine C. Vilscek. Newark, Delaware: International Reading Association, 1968.

11. John A. Downing. "Recent Developments in i.t.a.," *California English Journal, 3* (Fall, 1967), 66–74.

12. John A. Downing. "Can i.t.a. Be Improved?" *Elementary English, 44* (December, 1967), 849–55.

13. J. R. Birnie. "Inconsistencies in i.t.a. and T.O.—an Examination of Four Popular Children's Readers," *Reading, 1* (December, 1967), 19–25.

14. Jared Sparks (editor). *Complete Works of Benjamin Franklin,* vol. 6, p. 295. Boston: Hilliard Gray and Company, 1840.

15. Chou En-Lai, Wu Yu-Chang, and Li Chin-Hsi. *Reform of the Chinese Written Language,* p. 21. Peking: Foreign Language Press, 1958.

20 | The Effect of Two Different Orthographies on Beginning Reading*

Eleanor R. Kirkland

During the past decade our methods of teaching reading have been criticized by such people as Flesch in *Why Johnny Can't Read,* and Walcutt in *Tomorrow's Illiterates.* These individuals attribute the "poor reading achievement" of our children to the "word recognition" method. Without citing any statistical source, Walcutt estimated that three of four Americans were not reading as well as they should or could.

Arthur Trace (6), author of *What Ivan Knows that Johnny Doesn't,* presented views similar to those of Walcutt. He, also, offered no objective evidence. The assertion made in both books, that children in today's schools do not learn how to figure out unfamiliar words or words not taught in the basal reader, deserves attention. Both authors assume that the only words children can read are those found in their basal readers. Trace recommended the development of basal readers "that have three to five times the vocabulary and at least twice as much text as the typical reading series now has. . . ." Both authors suggested that the increase in

*From *Reading and Realism,* IRA Conference Proceedings, 1969, pp. 667–671. Reprinted with permission of Eleanor R. Kirkland and the International Reading Association.

vocabulary be accomplished by using the extreme type of phonic drill which they favor.

Studies have indicated that the greatest number of poor readers is found in the first grade, but that only a smaller number is found in the second grades. Ninety-nine percent of the first grade failures, ninety percent of the second grade failures, and seventy percent of third-grade failures are due to poor reading ability(3).

The National Council of Teachers of English estimates that four million elementary school pupils have reading disabilities.

The variety of material available for reading instruction indicates the numerous attempts to solve the difficulties children ordinarily have in achieving reading skill in the first grade. Each of these programs can be evaluated as an attempt to meet the motivation with which a child enters school—to learn to read and write.

While no single factor can be isolated and pointed to as the one which limits learning, current studies have shown the spelling of our language to be a significant factor.

Linguistic solutions recently developed have attempted to simplify beginning reading materials by using regularly spelled words to avoid the orthographic complexity of English. In the eyes of the linguist, a child can read when he can recognize sound-symbol correspondences to the point that he can respond to the marks with appropriate speech(5).

Others besides the linguists, however, have turned their attention to the beginner. The augmented Roman alphabet, produced by Sir James Pitman to be used as an Initial Teaching Medium, represents an effort to shape an alphabet that has a symbol for each of the forty-four simple and complex consonant and vowel sounds of English.

The Purpose of the Study

The purpose of all basic writing systems is to provide a graphic code. When one has learned the code of the language signals and the code of the writing, one can then interpret written materials in terms of the language they represent. To read any writing efficiently, one must develop high speed recognition responses to the graphic signs as representations of significant language parts.

The purpose of this study was to determine if the Initial Teaching Alphabet, a more consistent medium for the teaching of reading, would result in superior success in word attack skills and comprehension when contrasted with the teaching of reading using the traditional orthography.

Design

PUPIL SELECTIONS

The design of the study provided for the inclusion of approximately 180 first grade children in the San Juan Unified School District, Sacramento County, California.

The first grade pupils were assigned to classes on the basis of an articulation card filled out by the kindergarten teacher at the end of the school year. The child's progress and his readiness for first grade were evaluated in the following way: (a) below average, (b) average, and (c) above average. The teacher also indicated whether the child could recognize and write his name, recognize colors, count objects to ten, handle scissors, cut and paste, and follow directions.

After the student cards were arranged according to the three classifications, the assignment was random, with the exception that a proportion of the groups falling in each of the three levels was assigned to each classroom. This method was used in all schools involved in the study. The purpose was to insure that each classroom was heterogeneous with respect to readiness for formal reading instruction.

One of the first grade classes in each of the schools selected to take part in the study was then designated as the i.t.a. class. The i.t.a. groups were generally considered as representative of the total first grade enrollment in the district.

The sample consisted of an experimental group from two schools and two control groups matched according to sex, age (within four months), and intelligence (within four points). Control 1 was made up of children from the same two schools as the experimental group; control 2 consisted of children from two different schools in the same district. The latter group was included to study further the Hawthorne Effect on the achievement of the children, and knew nothing of the study comparing the progress of the children in i.t.a. and those using t.o. Eller(2) states that "less tangible bias may result from the differences in teacher and pupil enthusiasm if the experimenters know that they are participating in a new and different program while the controls go about their work as usual." Kerlinger(4) says that "if a learning study is being done, one or more control groups are essential. Almost any change, any extra attention and experimental manipulation or even the absence of manipulation . . . but the knowledge that a study is being done is enough to cause the subjects to change." Borg(1), in speaking of the Hawthorne Effect, said, "any situation in which the experimental conditions are such that the mere fact that the subject is participating in an experiment or is receiving special attention will tend to improve his performance. . . . The Hawthorne Effect decreases as the novelty of a new method wears off. Studies extending over two or three years can be relied upon somewhat more in evaluating the effect of a new technique."

Preparation of Teachers

The teachers who volunteered to use the Initial Teaching Alphabet as the medium for reading instruction in first grade classrooms attended a summer workshop and received two days of orientation. This consisted of an introduction to the rules for spelling with i.t.a., and training in writing the symbols. The workshops also included the viewing of a film, *The 40 Sounds of English,* and a review of the materials to be used— readers, workbooks, and teachers manuals.

During the school year a meeting, conducted by the investigator, was held once a month to discuss the progress of the experiment, problems arising in the classrooms; and to evoke a general sharing of ideas. The meetings were attended by all of the i.t.a. teachers, the second grade teachers who had been selected to take the class on during the following year, the principals of the schools involved, the reading consultant, and on several occasions, the teachers of the Control 1 classes.

It was recognized that the meetings of the i.t.a. teachers might increase the Hawthorne Effect in this group. Meetings were therefore also planned for the teachers of Control 1. Resource people were called in, e.g., representatives from Allyn Bacon; films and filmstrips were previewed, and the reading consultant made a presentation.

The teachers of Control 2 were given no special treatment. There were no special meetings set up for them. They did attend the grade level meetings held by the district, however, as did all first grade teachers.

There were many visitors during the first year of the experiment. The study, being conducted in the San Juan Unified School District, was one of the first in the area. Consequently, teachers, administrators and educators came to observe. In order to make the teachers of Control 1 aware of the fact that they were also an important part of the experiment, an equal number of visitations were arranged if possible.

Preparation of Parents

In late August of each year, a special meeting was held for all of the parents of first grade children in the two schools which had i.t.a. and Control 1 classes. At that time, the parents were made aware of the study being conducted. The film *The 40 Sounds of English* was shown. Material was distributed explaining the i.t.a. program as well as a copy of the symbols used. The teachers who had attended the i.t.a. workshop explained the program. A time was set aside for a question-and-answer period.

At the time of the meeting the class lists had not been posted. The parents were therefore unaware of their child's placement. They were told, however,that if their child was in an i.t.a. group and they would rather not have him in that class, they should notify the principal. Parents who desired having their child in the i.t.a. class were put on a waiting list. In the three years of the study, only one parent asked to have his child removed from the i.t.a. class, and many parents requested that their children be placed in the experimental group.

Pupil Preparation

On the first day of school, the children in the i.t.a. classrooms were told that they were going to learn to read by using a special alphabet. This special alphabet had been designed to help them learn to read easier. When they could read very well using this special alphabet, then they would also be able to read in "grown-up" alphabet.

All labels and signs were written in i.t.a. It was recognized that the children would see the traditional alphabet elsewhere every day. At the beginning of the first year of the study, the number of library books written in i.t.a. were limited. Consequently, there were books on the library table or in the reading corner in the traditional alphabet. These were mainly for browsing. As more books became available in the special alphabet, they were put on display. Many old preprimers were prepared by the teachers for use in the reading corner by transliterating the material and pasting this over the original.

The study, being a longitudinal one, made provisions for collecting data for first grade children over a three year period, second grade children for two years, and third grade for one year.

Materials Used

The following testing measurements were used: the SRA Primary Mental Abilities Test at the beginning of first grade, Gates Primary Reading Test at the end of the fifth and ninth months of first grade, Gates Advanced Reading Test at the end of the ninth month of second and third grades, Botel Phonics Mastery Test during the seventh month of first grade, Stanford Achievement Test-Primary Reading during the last two years of the study, 76 Word Dictated Spelling Test of regularly written words devised by the investigator during the eighth month of first, second and third grades, and the Stanford Spelling Achievement Test at the end of the third grade. The Botel Word Recognition Test was administered to a subsample of the population on an individual basis by the investigator.

The reading tests, with the exception of the Stanford Primary Reading Tests, were given in the media in which the children were learning to read. After the transition to the traditional orthography was made, all tests were administered in t.o.

The experimental groups used the *Early-to-Read Series* by Mazur-kiewicz and Tanyzer. Supplementary material consisted of the *Downing Readers,* a large selection of library books in i.t.a., and during the third year of the study, *The Books for Me to Read* Series by Ainsworth and Ridout and *The Nicky Books* by Doris Dickens.

The control groups used the *Ginn Basal Reader Series* (both readers and workbooks) supplemented by the *Allyn and Bacon Basal Reader Series.* They also had available to them a large number of library books in t.o. Both groups had access to a central school library, the County Schools Library, and the Curriculum Center of the District for additional materials in the traditional alphabet only.

Conclusions

Since the study was conducted over a period of three years, in reporting the findings the first year will be called Phase 1 (1964–65), the second year Phase 2 (1965–1966), and the third year Phase 3 (1966–67).

An attempt was made to answer the following questions.

Question 1.   Is there a measurable difference in the reading ability of children being taught using i.t.a.?

The subtests used to measure reading achievement were Gates Reading Test—Word Recognition, Sentence Recognition, and Paragraph Recognition, and Stanford Reading Test—Word Reading and Paragraph Meaning.

The results were as follows: the three-year evaluation shows that girls in i.t.a. did advance more rapidly in reading and achieved significantly superior reading skills at an earlier time.

In contrasting the boys in i.t.a. with those learning to read using the traditional alphabet, it was not until the testing at the end of the year that there was a significant difference in the reading achievement.

There was a significant difference in favor of the girls in the experimental group for all three years in Word Recognition. In the Paragraph Meaning subtests of the Gates and Stanford Reading Tests (used to measure comprehension), the results were significant on the Stanford Reading

Tests. It should be remembered that this test was administered in the traditional orthography to all first grade children, whether they had made the transition or not.

During the first year of the study, the boys in the control group read equally as well as the boys in the experimental group at the end of five months instruction. The differences were significant in favor of the boys learning to read using i.t.a. in Word Recognition for the three years of the study, with the exception of February 1965 and May 1967 on the Gates Reading Test. On the Stanford Reading Tests, which was administered in t.o., the differences were significant in favor of the boys in i.t.a. in both testing periods (May 1966 and May 1967).

Results of the Botel Word Recognition Test, administered to a small subgroup, suggest that the experimental group was reading about one grade level ahead of the control group.

Question 2. Will the use of i.t.a. develop in the children a spelling "attitude" or skill superior to that of the children learning to read using the traditional alphabet?

The children in the experimental group developed superior skills (better described as encoding) in contrast to those of the control group. The significant superiority was first evident at the end of first grade when a test of regularly spelled words was given and maintained during the second and third grades. This significant superiority in spelling was also indicated by the results of the standardized test given at the end of third grade, which consisted of words both regularly and irregularly written.

Question 3. Does i.t.a. develop superior phonic word-attack skills? These skills, as measured by the Botel Phonics Mastery Test, levels A and B, consisted of Consonant Sounds, Consonant Blends, Consonant Digraphs, Rhyming Words, Long and Short Vowels, and Other Vowel Sounds.

During all three phases of the study, the girls were significantly superior on all subtests of the Botel Phonics Mastery Test, with the exception of Rhyming Words in Phase 3. In this particular instance, the girls in the control group did equally as well as the experimental group.

During Phase 2, the boys in i.t.a. showed a significant difference in all areas of the test. For the other two years there was little consistency. The boys in the experimental group were significantly superior to the boys who had learned to read using t.o. in only the Vowel Sounds and Other Vowel Sounds subtest of the Phonics Mastery Test.

On the basis of the findings, it is evident that the children in i.t.a. do learn the sounds of the vowels at an earlier stage than those learning to read in t.o.

Question 4.   It is assumed that first grade children lose some of their reading ability over the summer months. Does this assumption hold true for children learning to read using i.t.a., as well as those using t.o.?

The results of the retest of the Gates Primary Reading Test during the second week of second grade indicate that there was a loss in reading achievement over the summer months for all children in some subtests, and a gain in others for all three years of the study. In many instances the change, either up or down, was insignificant. The children in the experimental group dropped more often over the summer months than did the children in the control group.

The girls in the control group consistently gained in achievement over the summer months. None of the differences were significant, however.

Question 5.   Will the i.t.a. children at the end of the second and third grades retain their superiority in reading achievement?

The differences were only significant for the second grade girls in word-recognition, third grade boys in word recognition, and third grade girls in comprehension.

Question 6.   Which ability group will derive the most benefit from the use of i.t.a. as a media for learning to read?

The encoding and decoding achievement of the following groups was compared: (a) upper third according to intelligence, (b) middle third, and (c) lower third. The range of intelligence in the upper third was from 109–127 IQ; the middle third from 103–112 IQ, and the lower third from 67–104 IQ, as measured by the SRA Primary Mental Abilities Test.

When looking at the data collected, it was found that in the first grade, the i.t.a. girls in both the upper-third and middle-third showed significantly superior progress in all subtests of the Gates Primary Reading Test. The i.t.a. girls in the lower-third made significantly more progress in word-recognition. The i.t.a. boys in the upper-third also made significantly superior progress in all subtests of the Gates Reading Test. There were no significant differences for the boys in the middle-third or lower-third in any of the subtests.

At the end of the second grade, the i.t.a. girls in the upper-third showed a significant difference in both word recognition and comprehension subtests of the Gates Advanced Reading Test. There were no significant differences in either the middle-third or lower-third for the girls. The girls learning to read using the traditional alphabet who fell in the lower-third of the group did make a higher score in comprehension, but the difference was not significant.

The boys in the middle-third showed significantly superior progress in word recognition. No other significant differences occurred in any of the groups for the boys in second grade.

By the end of the third grade there were no significant differences for either the boys or girls, regardless of intelligence. Although the boys in the control group falling in the upper-third of the group did score higher in both subtests, the differences were not significant.

Question 7.   Quite often in a first grade classroom, when pupils are grouped according to reading ability, one finds an over abundance of girls in the top group, and more boys in the slow groups. Is it possible that the use of i.t.a. will develop just as many good readers among the boys as among the girls?

In most instances, the girls were found to be superior in reading ability to boys in both treatment groups. The results indicate that when using i.t.a. the girls were the best readers. On the other hand, while the girls in the control group did appear to be better readers in Phase 1 and 2, the boys in the control group achieved more success in first grade reading in Phase 3. The results were not always consistent with the teacher's comments. Teachers indicated that they seemed to have a fewer number of boys reading in the slow group when using i.t.a. than they had previously experienced. In the third year of the study, of the first four children who made the transition to the traditional orthography, three were boys. It is difficult to make generalizations from the data collected because there are many factors involved, such as age, readiness, language experience, and family background. According to the test results, however, it would be assumed that the girls in both treatment groups were better readers at the end of first grade.

Question 8.   Does the so-called "Hawthorne Effect" produce superior results due to teacher-pupil enthusiasm for method used, and what relation exists between this effect and the length of the study?

Several controls were built in to the study to take care of the Hawthorne Effect: (a) the duration of the study and (b) use of a second control group in school not involved in the study.

It was noted that in all of the tests administered to the first grade children in the first year of the study in which a second control was used, the scores of Control 1 were consistently superior to those of Control 2. Not only were the differences superior, they were significantly superior in favor of the control group within the same schools as the experimental group. The results show that the matched group from the schools in which i.t.a. was being used achieved more success during the first year of the study than did the group of children which came from two schools who knew nothing of the experiment and had gone about learning to read just as they had done in the past.

Borg states that the Hawthorne Effect decreases as novelty of a new method wears off. The results of the testing program during the remainder of the study confirmed this statement. In looking at the data, it was evident that the mean differences were much less in the second year. There were very few significantly different scores. There were several scores which indicated a superiority for the second control, but they were not significant.

Implications of the Study

The Initial Teaching Alphabet is not a panacea. While the findings of the study show that i.t.a. has brought some children an important advantage in their learning to read, it does not show it to be a cure-all for all of their reading problems. Needless to say, there were still children who made a poor response when i.t.a. materials were used.

Since many of the traditional second grade words included in the spelling program were regularly written, many of the children who had learned to read using i.t.a. had the ability to encode them. The focus, therefore, was on the study of spelling patterns and development of phonic and structural analysis skills as part of the spelling program.

This study has shown that the i.t.a. children do score significantly better in many of the decoding and encoding tests and their subtests in grades 1 through 3. It also has shown that the i.t.a. children do not score significantly less superior on these same measures.

In conclusion, this study has shown that first grade children make more progress in beginning reading (decoding) when using a more consistent and phonemically regular alphabet, such as i.t.a. The results of the Botel Word Recognition Tests suggest that they were reading one grade level higher than first grade children who had learned to read using the traditional orthography. As the children progressed through the second and third grades, the differences in the achievement between the experimental and control group narrowed and became less significant. By the time the children were tested at the end of third grade, the boys and girls who had learned to read using i.t.a. did not differ significantly in reading achievement from those in the control group, although several mean differences favored the former group.

Regardless of which media was used for teaching beginning reading, the girls made more progress in first grade. Surprisingly enough, the children who gained the most benefit from i.t.a. (those from the upper-third of the group according to intelligence) would probably have learned to read using any media or method. This is not to say, however, that they have not gained or benefitted from the use of i.t.a. The Initial Teaching Alphabet gave them a headstart; they read much earlier; they moved ahead faster; reading skills were introduced much earlier; and they were able to read much more widely.

Results of the Botel Phonics Mastery Test indicate that children learning to read using i.t.a. learned the sounds of the vowels much sooner. In spelling (encoding), the children in i.t.a. were significantly superior in first grade when writing regularly spelled words and continued to be significantly superior in the third-grade on a standardized test.

REFERENCES

1. Borg, Walter R. *Educational Research:* . . . . New York: McKay, 1963.
2. Eller, William. "A Research Pitfall: Jumping to Conclusions," in J. Allen Figurel (Ed.), *Challenge and Experiment in Reading,* IRA Conference Proceedings, 7, 112.
3. Gates, Arthur I. "The Teaching of Reading: Objective Evidence versus Opinion," *New Perspectives in Reading Instruction,* in Albert J. Mazurkiewicz (Ed.), New York: Pitman, 1964.
4. Kerlinger, Frederick N. *Foundations of Behavioral Research:* . . . New York: Holt, Rinehart and Winston, 1964.
5. Strickland, Ruth G. "The Contributions of Structural Linguists to the Teaching of Reading, Writing and Grammar in the Elementary School," *Bulletin of the School of Education,* Indiana University, Vol. 40, No. 1, 1964.
6. Trace, Arthur S., Jr. *What Ivan Knows That Johnny Doesn't.* New York: Random House, 1961.

21 Color: A New Dimension in Teaching Reading*

Sister M. Raphael, F.D.C.

Color has added a new dimension to the teaching of reading. Throughout the country, primary children, children with reading difficulties, and illiterate adults are learning to read through this new approach to reading and writing called "color reading" or "visual dictation."

Dr. Caleb Gattegno, a British educator, developed the color reading system called "Words in Color" (WIC). He first saw children in Switzerland learning music through the use of color and was greatly impressed with the results. Under this inspiration, he introduced a system of learning arithmetic in which color was of special importance. In 1957, while working in Ethiopia on a UNESCO project, he discovered the value of mathematics and color in the teaching of Amharic, the official language of Ethiopia. He was able to reduce the learning time for reading and writing its 251 signs from a minimum of 4 or 5 months to 10 hours. After experimentation with the phonetic languages of Spanish and Hindi, he tackled the nonphonetic English language. After five years of work, he first demonstrated the teaching process in Washington, D.C., in 1964.

*From *Catholic School Journal,* vol. 66, October 1966, pp. 56–57. Reprinted from the October 1966 issue of *Catholic School Journal* with permission of the publisher. This article is copyrighted. © 1966 by CCM Professional Magazines, Inc. All rights reserved.

The irregularity of the English spelling has long been recognized as the biggest stumbling block for beginning readers. This is a major argument of those who oppose the phonics method of teaching reading. Many children never overcome the confusion they encounter when letters are pronounced one way in one word and another way in other words. English, which is not phonetic, is full of such pitfalls.

For example, the same "oo" sound is represented by the ten different letter combinations in the following words: *to, too, two, crew, through, flu, true, fruit, shoe,* and *you.* Quite naturally, a child meeting these words for the first time and trying to decipher them with an ordinary phonics background will at least be confused, if not hopelessly lost. In "Words in Color" all the letters or combinations of letters which are pronounced "oo" are colored green. The color provides the key for reading the words.

Although Dr. Gattegno has identified more than 270 different sounds in the English language which uses only a 26-letter alphabet, he simplifies these to 47 main sounds. The colors represent sounds, one each for the 20 different vowel and diphthong sounds in English and one each for the 27 consonant sounds. Teachers who use this system must have 47 colors of chalk at hand to represent the main sounds. The color for a sound is the same no matter how the word is spelled. For example, the *n* in *no,* the *ne* in *phone,* the *kn* in *knew,* the *pn* in *pneumonia,* the *gn* in *gnat* are all lavendar, the *n* sound in color.

An advantage of WIC is that the learner is allowed initially to view our nonphonetic language as a phonetic language without changing the traditional spelling. Reading books accompanying the program are in black and white, and all writing done at the chalkboard is done with white chalk. The colored chalk is exclusively for the teacher's use.

Materials Needed

Three kinds of materials are required for color reading method: those for the teacher, those for the entire class, and those for the individual learner. The teacher has a teacher's guide which gives detailed suggestions for the content and sequence of the lessons. The entire class uses 21 charts in color with more than 600 words, eight phonic code charts in color, and word cards for more than 1200 words, printed in black on colored cardboard. Each student receives a word-building book, three reading books containing an 1100 word vocabulary, a story book, and worksheets.

The 21 charts progressively introduce the sounds of English, beginning with the most regular spelling and progressing through virtually all the regular and irregular signs of English. The set of eight phonic code charts is a systematic organization of the signs (spellings) occurring in English; four charts present the vowel signs with their various spellings;

and four charts present the consonants with their varied spellings. The word cards introduce words representing different parts of speech. Each part of speech is printed on a card of a special color. By putting the words together in sentences, learners discover the structural elements of complete sentences. If a word can be used as more than one part of speech, it is printed on more than one color card. Thus, the student learns inductively that every complete sentence *always* has some structural element and only sometimes includes others.

All of the materials for the individual learner are printed in black on white. As soon as the teacher has introduced the first sounds, the learner can recognize these words in his word-building book, can learn words made up of these sounds in the first of his three reading books, and can use words on his first worksheet. Since the learner works almost simultaneously with words printed in color and words printed in black, at no point in the program does progress depend on remembering colors.

The use of all the materials is flexible. Their use depends upon the needs and level of readiness of the students. This flexibility easily allows for taking care of individual differences.

Teachers working with WIC have not found that the number of colors is confusing to the learners. One color with its sound is introduced at a time. A new color with its associated sound is not introduced until complete mastery of previous colors and the associated sounds have been mastered. At times, the closeness of colors has been deliberate. For example, the colors for *b* and *d* are purposely close so that beginners learn immediately that they must recognize the letters by shape differences.

Color-Blindness Is No Problem

Since the system is based upon distinguishing between so many colors, the questions of what effect color-blindness might have naturally arises. Authorities agree that this is not a serious problem since present research reveals that less than eight percent of the boys and about 0.5 percent of the girls in the average first-grade classroom will have some degree of color-blindness. Furthermore, many color-blind children see most colors naturally, and those colors which are distorted will still be distinguishable from the others.

Proponents of the color reading program say that continuing experiments may enable an average kindergarten child to read up to 2000 words after six months. WIC is being tested throughout the country. In the spring of 1965 the program was being used in some 600 classrooms by approximately 15,000 students. The program has been met with approval where it has been used. In the Santa Fe public schools, the program is considered a success and has been added to the approved textbook list of the state department of education.

For Adult Illiterates

The WIC reading program has been used successfully to teach adult illiterates and nonreaders of all ages. The program is now being tested under the antipoverty program in work camps for adults and teen-agers. Various cities have also initiated the WIC system. Program for Action by Citizens in Education (PACE) in Cleveland, Ohio, has joined the Cleveland public schools, the Cleveland Public Library, and other community organizations in a "Right-to-Read Project." Their object of teaching adult illiterates and poorly schooled adults is being realized partly through the use of WIC.

22

An Evaluation of a Programmed Reading Approach in the Primary Grades*

Donald Hammill
Marciene S. Mattleman

Over ten years have elapsed since B. F. Skinner (1954) gave impetus to the increased use of programmed instruction. While other agencies such as the army and the church have tried this approach rather widely, schools have been slower to adopt auto-instructional techniques. However, the literature which pertains to the effectiveness of programmed instruction in teaching school subjects indicates that this approach is *as* effective as other approaches to teaching, that is children can and do learn as well with programmed instruction as with other modes(8). With regard to reading, the reports of McNeil(7) and Jones(4) point to positive gains of experimental groups over control groups where programmed materials were used. Results of large studies using the Sullivan Associates Programmed Reading (SAPR) materials undertaken in Colorado Springs(6) and Denver(1) as well as the findings of numerous pilot studies(5, 10, 3) suggest unexpected gains in reading after one school year's study in favor of the Sullivan programmed approach.

The studies using Sullivan materials which are reported mostly in *The Journal of Programmed Reading,* a publication of McGraw-Hill Publishing Company, cannot be taken as conclusive evidence of SAPR's su-

*From *Elementary English,* vol. 46, March 1969, pp. 310–312. Reprinted with the permission of the National Council of Teachers of English, Donald Hammill, and Marciene S. Mattleman.

periority in reading instruction over traditional methods. While providing interest to the teacher, these investigations, in general, did not make use of control groups nor did they take into account possible Hawthorne Effects.

The present research investigated the effectiveness of the SAPR approach as implemented in the School District of Philadelphia during the 1966–67 academic year. The efficacy of the method when used as the sole approach to reading instruction and when used in conjunction with basal readers for the period of one school year was probed.

Procedures

Two hundred and eighty children from 35 second and third grade classes in 16 different inner-city Philadelphia schools served as subjects. With few exceptions, the students could be considered low achievers in reading on the basis of performance on the pretest measures. Three groups, matched on achievement, were formed. Hereafter Experimental Group I (E_1) refers to subjects who received SAPR instruction exclusively ($n = 96$). Experimental Group II (E_2) refers to those who received SAPR instruction in conjunction with basal readers ($n = 85$). Control Group (C) refers to those instructed with basal readers only ($n = 99$). Analysis of variance was the statistical technique selected and the .05 level of confidence was chosen.

The *Stanford Achievement Test* served as the pre- and posttest at grade level two, and the *Iowa Test of Basic Skills* at the third grade. These measures were selected in order to coincide with existing school testing procedures. The reading comprehension subtest was utilized as the criterion measure and grade placement units were used in the calculations.

Findings

Posttest differences among treatment groups (Columns) did not approach the .05 level of confidence while, as expected, differences between grades (Rows) were highly significant. That is, although third grade readers were superior to second grade readers, no treatment showed appreciable difference from the others. Group means on the posttest measures at both grade levels for treatment groups are found in Table 1; the analysis of variance information is presented in Table 2.

Discussion and Implications

While these results indicate that SAPR was no more effective in reading instruction than the basal reading approach, findings should not be

TABLE 1

**Group Means on Posttest
Scores and Grades Two
and Three**

	E_1	E_2	C	Total
Two	2.2	2.3	2.2	2.2
Three	3.3	3.6	3.3	3.4
Total	2.7	3.0	2.7	2.8

interpreted as conclusive evidence that the SAPR materials could not be effective under other circumstances. One cannot investigate a current program without consideration of previous background and experience of teachers. Before new approaches can demonstrate their efficacy, teachers who implement the programs must be re-educated in the nature and purposes of innovated techniques. Without special training, teachers may lack necessary skills and insights to initiate experimental methods. The current study is a case in which limited initial orientation was provided and considerable ongoing training was not included for teachers of experimental classes. Teachers using the basal readers, by contrast, had at their disposal a manual which provided lesson plans in addition to a college course in elementary education which generally focused on basal reading.

The problem, however, is not merely one of comparison between two similar reading approaches. Programmed materials presume a new organization for dealing with content. In cases where basal materials are used, the teacher serves as an instructor. However, in the case of programming, the material is auto-instructional and the teacher serves a different role.

TABLE 2

**Summary of Analysis of Variance on
Posttest Data**

Source	df	MS	
Grade Level (R)	1	10286.2	92.6**
Treatment Group (C)	2	243.2	2.1
Cells	(1)		
CR	2	66.0	.6
Within Cells	274	110.6	
Total	279		

**Sig. at less than 1% level.

While it was not the intent of this study to focus on the teacher's role in student achievement, this variable is worthy of consideration in studies in which materials are compared.

In addition to differences in instructional techniques, SAPR applies some linguistic principles to reading. The vocabulary of the widely used basal readers and that of the linguistic approach varies. While testing materials in this study employed vocabulary from both basal and linguistic approaches, no achievement tests have yet been developed for dealing with these differences. Therefore, the possibility exists that the commonly used reading tests have limited usefulness in measuring improvement where varied approaches have been used.

A final comment should be raised with reference to comparisons between approaches to reading. The assumption usually is made that groups are "equal" when matched on CA, IQ, and reading ability. Yet, children, especially low achievers in academic areas, are likely to possess varied learning skills and deficits. Speaking to this point, Frostig(2) has commented:

> In each classroom there will be children with reading difficulties. A single method cannot be best for all these children. To use a somewhat coarse analogy, a comparable practice in medicine would be to compare two diets, one with low protein content and the other with low carbohydrate content, each of which has been given to an unselected population of patients containing both cases of kidney disease and cases of diabetes. (p. 24)

With this in mind, it would seem that future research should be directed not only toward determining the effectiveness of a given approach but also toward determining the characteristics of children for whom SAPR or any other approach is most effective.

REFERENCES

1. Department of Research of the Denver Public Schools. Progress report: Programmed reading in the primary grades. *Research Notes,* 1966, 1:1.
2. Frostig, Marianne. Testing as a basis for educational therapy. The *Journal of Special Education,* 1967, 2:1, 15–34.
3. Jackson, A. M. Programmed reading inspires culturally deprived students. *Journal of Programmed Reading,* No. 4, undated.
4. Jones, S. H. Programmed reading report, so far, so good. *Nation's Schools,* 1966, 28:1, 39–40.
5. Kates, H. Teachers use PR with basal program. *Journal of Programmed Reading,* No. 5, undated.
6. Liddle, W. Colorado Springs tests programmed reading. *Journal of Programmed Reading,* No. 6, undated.

7. McNeil, J. D. Programmed instruction versus usual classroom procedures in teaching boys to read. *American Educational Research Journal,* 1964, 1, 113–119.

8. Schramm, W. *The research on programmed instruction.* Washington, D.C.: U.S. Office of Education, 1964.

9. Skinner, B. F. The science of learning and the art of teaching, *Harvard Educational Review,* 24, 1954, 86–97.

10. Wingate, R. C. Iowa school reports success using PR in low-ability class. *Journal of Programmed Reading,* No. 4, undated.

23 Neurological Dysfunction and Reading Disability*

Norinne H. Olson
Arthur V. Olson
Patricia H. Duncan

For many years those who are genuinely concerned with the disabled reader have pondered the nature of reading disability. Causes and symptoms have been enumerated in the hope of discovering patterns or syndromes which would enable diagnosticians to classify afflicted individuals. The primary goal of such investigation has been that of attempting to pin-point the problems in order to administer appropriate remedial techniques which would provide maximum improvement in reading skills.

Among the classifications of factors related to reading disability (physical, emotional-social, intellectual, and educational) there have persisted some anomalies which have evaded diagnosis. Many of these have been grouped into the sub-category of neurological factors. Early interest was shown in the study of neurological dysfunction associated with reading disability in 1925, when Samuel T. Orton began his work with children with specific language disability. He first called the attention of his medical colleagues in neurology and psychiatry to the fact that many otherwise normal children have a specific difficulty in learning to read (11, p. 1). Recent reports have indicated that much controversy exists regarding the implications of neurological factors. Senz has stated:

*From *The Reading Teacher,* vol. 22, November 1968, pp. 157–162. Reprinted with permission of the International Reading Association.

... measurements of brain function are crude and open to more than one interpretation. Arguments still rage as to whether higher intellectual processes are a function of the brain as a whole or of specific parts of it. . . . Communication is difficult in this field because the terminology is inexact and used inconsistently(5,p.217).

The classification "neurological dysfunction" has been employed by the authors to include the following conditions: (a) those in which the brain and nervous system appear to be intact but are not functioning according to normal patterns of organization; and (b) those in which the brain or nervous system has been affected by a lesion occurring at or before birth or in a later period along the developmental continuum. In an effort to focus this investigation along those conditions closely related to the writers' area of endeavor, the scope of the article has been limited primarily to those neurological factors affecting the child of average or above average intelligence. The disabled reader has been referred to in this article according to the definition of Bond and Tinker(1):

> Typically the disabled reader is a child of intellectual capability who has, for a variety of reasons . . . failed to grow in reading. He is not living up to his potential as a learner at least in reading. He is quite likely to be ineffective in all that is expected of him in school. He may reject reading, become a discouraged person, acquire unfortunate adjustment patterns, and become increasingly less able to learn.

Parts of the Brain Involved in the Reading Process

Electroencephalography, a method of recording the electrical activity of the brain, has thrown some light on learning problems, but has not been used to study these problems to a great degree. Burks studied the behavior characteristic of 137 school problem children and compared them with a control group of ninety-four. Those with abnormal EEG tracings displayed greater difficulties in perceptual-academic functions, and when such tests as the *Wechsler Intelligence Scale for Children* were used, had more difficulties with the verbal sub-tests. Recent experiments, still inconclusive, suggest a difference between the EEG's of reading failures and non-failures. The two most common abnormalities in EEG tracings are reported by Knott, Muehl, and Benton(8) in their discussion of the disabled reader. The two particular syndromes mentioned are stated as: (a) slow rhythm from the posterior area when the subject is awake; and (b) the presence of "14 and 6 CPS positive spikes" when the subject is asleep.

McFie(9), reported two case-clinical studies on male retarded readers and indicated the primary significant aspect as poor development in the parieto-occipital area. Eames(3) indicated that this particular area is considered to be of primary importance in the perception of material by the brain.

N. Dale Bryant reported that neurological inefficiency which produces reading disability is almost certainly in the temporal, parietal, and occipital association areas in and around the angular gyrus of the dominant hemisphere, or in the cortical-thalmic-cortical and cortical-cortical connections which serve these areas(5, p. 142).

Katrina de Hirsch, however, denied that precise areas of the brain are responsible for specific performance. Although she acknowledged the fact that in lesions of the angular gyrus the interpretation of printed material is impaired or lost, she immediately included the counter-point that the areas adjacent to the angular gyrus do subserve processes in reading. She further postulated that "... we no longer believe that we deal with separate cortical excitations. Rather we assume the existence of highly complex activities involving the whole brain"(5, p. 219).

Types of Disability Attributed to Neurological Dysfunction

Disabilities involving some neurological dysfunction include alexia, dyslexia, mixed-lateral dominance, and strephosymbolia. Mixed-lateral dominance, although perhaps not considered a dsyfunction, has been included because it represents a deviation from the normal pattern of brain organization.

ALEXIA

According to Fernald(5), alexia is "essentially a disorder in the perception or understanding of letter forms, existing apart from any other language or agnostic disturbances." It has been termed "word blindness" in that the person may see black marks on paper, but does not recognize that they represent words, i.e., specific sounds and ideas(1).

Alexia has usually been associated with a brain lesion, generally in the left hemisphere, which may be either severe or minor. To be more medically specific, alexia is generally believed to result when there is injury or failure of development in the angular and supra-marginal gyri of the brain. The most common causes of the condition appear to be failure of full development, vascular lesions, tumors, and inflammations. If the part affected is on the dominant side of the brain, a group of symptoms known as "Gerstman's syndrome" may occur. This symptom complex includes inability to read (alexia), inability to recognize objects by touch (astereognosis), inability to write (agraphia), confusion of orientation, homonymous hemianopsia (half vision), and inability to do arithmetic. The complete Gerstman's syndrome is likely to appear only in very severe cases. The term "congenital word-blindness" has often been applied to young non-readers and, in the opinion of most authorities, the term is misused at the earlier age levels(1).

DYSLEXIA

A mild form of alexia has often been referred to as dyslexia. It has been used to classify reading defects caused by brain injury or degeneration or those which represent a developmental failure to profit from reading instruction. More specifically, dyslexia has been defined by Money (10) as the inability to read even with adequate teaching. It is a failure which is severe and which is specific to reading. Dyslexia is usually considered quite separate from mental retardation, although the symptomatology in terms of academic successes might appear similar upon initial consideration.

The dyslexic child is not easily detected from the "slow learner" in the early years of schooling, but is not too difficult to detect in upper elementary and secondary grades. Developmental dyslexia usually appears without demonstrable early brain injury. It has been observed to accompany other factors, such as hypothyroidism, which relate significantly to reading disability. Reversals and translocations of letters and words are examples of persistent dyslexic traits, but are not peculiar to dyslexia(10). Oral reading tends to be word-by-word. Repetition and guessing are frequent. Some deviate speech has been observed, such as an unusually soft voice, choppiness, reversal of concepts, and confusion of direction. The handwriting of the dyslexic child often falls into a typical pattern characterized by poorly formed letters, irregular characters, and lack of evenness of style. "Crucial" letters (p, g, b, d, q, u, n, and the printed t and f) as well as entire words may be reversed(10).

MIXED-LATERAL DOMINANCE

Laterality refers to the dominant cortical hemisphere. A right-handed, right-eyed, right-footed individual is said to have unilateral dominance. This implies that the left hemisphere of the brain is totally dominant since each hemisphere of the brain controls the opposite side of the body. When conditions exist in which neither side is totally dominant or in which there is equal dominance (as in ambidexterity), the individual is said to have mixed-lateral dominance.

Harris(6), in comparing 215 children with severe reading disabilities with 345 unselected school children, found that 40 per cent of the reading disability cases showed mixed dominance compared with 18 per cent of the unselected cases. From his study, Harris concluded that "Ability to distinguish between left and right and a clear preference for one hand develop slowly in a significantly larger percentage of reading cases than in unselected children. This suggests the presence of a special kind of slowness in maturation, possibly neurological in nature."

Delacato(2) pursued the lateral dominance factor further. It has been his opinion that the tonic-neck-reflex (combination of averted head, extended arm, and flexed arm) and what it connotes in terms of total neurological organization is a critical factor in the evaluation, treatment, and prevention of language disabilities. He further suggested that parents adjust the sleeping positions of their children to effect unilateral dominance.

This view has been severely criticized by many authorities. Money(10) states:

> The second purpose of reopening the topic of cerebral dominance is to point out that the information the foregoing cases and Zangwill's paper furnish is completely incompatible with current faddist theories of dyslexia on the basis of cerebral dominance[10]. Scientifically speaking, it is far too premature to be applying hypotheses of cerebral dominance to methods of treatment. What these hypotheses need, above all else, is to be tested experimentally, and in controlled observation, for validity.

STREPHOSYMBOLIA

Dr. Samuel T. Orton coined the term "strephosymbolia" (twisted symbols) to describe school children who seemed confused by whole word patterns and the orientation of letters. He explained this condition in terms of hemispheral dominance and postulated that the cells of the nondominant side of the brain form a mirror pattern of the dominant side. When this balance is upset, it produces failure to differentiate between symbols (such as p and q, b and d, etc.). Orton extended his hypothesis to explain mirror writing and mirror reading.

Dr. Paul Dozier developed some principles to be followed in the remediation of strephosymbolia cases. These principles included the following: (a) re-education beginning with the elementary phonics; (b) distinguishing units from similar units; (c) reinforcing visual symbols by associating them with auditory and kinesthetic symbols; and (d) many repetitions in which the stimulus is quantitatively reduced, refined, and reinforced(11).

It appears to the authors that the term "strephosymbolia" has been employed to include or cut across many of the more specific types of neurological dysfunction—namely alexia, dyslexia, and aphasia.

Summary

The conditions of alexia, dyslexia, mixed-lateral dominance, and strephosymbolia are but a representative group of the types of disorders having a neurological basis. They have been found to coexist frequently with more broadly classified neurological categories, such as cerebral palsy which may be accompanied by dyslexia, nystagmus, and/or mixed-lateral dominance (7, pp. 274, 253–255).

The problem that exists with regard to these conditions lies in the inability to properly screen and to diagnose accurately. Diagnosis without prognosis and treatment has been a major criticism of the clinicians who attempt to determine the nature of a disability. The difficulty of correlating disease and disability, as well as individual response to the disability, have been considerations not to be overlooked with regard to neurological dysfunction (5, pp. 117–218).

Although neurological symptoms necessitate caution on the part of the reading clinician, it must not be implied that they be relegated to the category of intangibles. In proper dynamic diagnosis they should be regarded, along with other significant correlates of performance, in the synthesis of a disability profile.

Those concerned with providing children with the maximum reading skills that their capacities will permit should bear in mind this statement of Senz:

> Nature guards her secrets jealously and no magic answers are available. We must continue to plod along, studying our case material, avoiding pretensions to knowledge that do not exist, setting realistic goals for children, and encouraging experimentation (5, p. 218).

REFERENCES

1. Bond, G. L., and Tinker, M. A. *Reading difficulties: their diagnosis and correction.* New York: Appleton, 1957. Pp. 68–69, 99.
2. Delacato, C. H. *The treatment and prevention of reading problems.* Springfield: Charles C Thomas, 1959.
3. Eames, T. H. Some neural and glandular bases of learning. *Journal of Education,* 1960, *142,* 1–36.
4. Fernald, Grace M. *Remedial techniques in basic school subjects.* New York: McGraw-Hill, 1943.
5. Figurel, J. A. (Ed.) Challenge and experiment in reading. *Proceedings of the International Reading Association,* 1962, *7.*
6. Harris, A. Lateral dominance, directional confusion, and reading disability. *Journal of Psychology,* 1957, *44,* 183–294.
7. Kirk, S. A. *The education of exceptional children.* Boston: Houghton Mifflin, 1962.

8. Knott, J. R., Muehl, S., and Benton, A. Electroencephalography in children with reading disabilities. *Electroencephalography and Clinical Neurophysiology,* 1965, *18,* 513–533.
9. McFie, J. Cerebral dominance in cases of reading disability. *Journal of Neurology, Neurosurgery, and Psychiatry,* 1952, *15,* 194–199.
10. Money, J. (Ed.) *Reading disability: progress and research needs in dyslexia.* Baltimore: Johns Hopkins Press, 1962.
11. Orton, June Lyday. (Ed.) *Bulletin of the Orton society, special language disabilities.* Vol. 13. Pomfret, Connecticut: The Orton Society, 1963.

PART IV

READING SKILLS AND GROUPING FOR INDIVIDUAL DIFFERENCES

Articles on phonics are included in this part. A formal phonics method of teaching reading generally teaches that phonetic analysis is the most important word recognition skill and presents more and earlier phonic generalizations than does any other reading method. Phonetic analysis often is defined as the association of phonemes (sounds) and graphemes (symbols). Phonetic analysis generally is taught in an integrated way in the basal reader approach and in a less functional way in a formal phonics program. Other word recognition techniques including those of word form clues, recognizing a word by its total shape or configuration; structural analysis, recognizing a word by its parts such as prefixes, suffixes, base words, or syllables; picture and context clues, obtaining the meaning of an unknown word from its picture or its use in the sentence or paragraph; and dictionary usage, obtaining the meaning or pronunciation of an unknown word by the use of a dictionary or glossary are discussed in other articles.

The history of phonics methods of teaching reading and of phonetic analysis is described in an article by Emans (Selection 24). In his article, Bagford (Selection 25) discusses the values of teaching phonetic analysis in an elementary reading program. Several methods for teaching the word recognition skills of structural analysis are presented by Schell (Selection 26). Emans and Fisher (Selection 27) present a useful article about how to use context or meaning clues as a word recognition technique.

The development of concepts and a meaning vocabulary in

the elementary school is described in one section in this part. O'Leary (Selection 28) and Sutton (Selection 29) present some methods of developing vocabulary. Their articles also illustrate the similarities and differences between words and concepts. Sister Margaretta (Selection 30) discusses how to develop vocabulary by creative writing in her article.

Another section contains articles dealing with the development of the various comprehension or understanding skills needed for effective reading. Literal or factual comprehension and inferential or higher-type comprehension skills are discussed, and some suggestions are given for developing comprehension abilities in the elementary school. Critical reading, the evaluating of what is read in terms of some criteria, is discussed, and some suggestions for developing critical reading ability in elementary-school children are presented. Cushenberry (Selection 31) illustrates a number of effective ways to improve comprehension. The use and value of the new and important cloze procedure for improving reading comprehension is discussed by Schneyer (Selection 32) in his article. The late Russell (Selection 33) presents a thought-provoking article in his area of specialization, the development of critical reading ability.

Ediger (Selection 34) discusses the special reading skills needed to read science materials effectively, while Kravitz (Selection 35) illustrates the special skills needed to read social studies effectively. A research study discussing the use of the Survey Q3R study technique is discussed in an article by Sister Mary Donald (Selection 36). The Joplin Plan and its values and limitations are described in an article by Miller (Selection 37). Powell (Selection 38) also presents his assessment of the Joplin Plan. Wilson (Selection 39) lists a number of criteria which should be considered by a teacher when she is formulating groups for elementary reading instruction.

The following questions may guide the reading of the articles included in Part IV:

What is the difference between a formal phonics program and integrated phonetic analysis?

Which is the most important of the various word recognition techniques?

Should a word recognition technique be used alone or in combination with several other word recognition skills?

What are the most effective ways of building vocabulary at the elementary level?

Of what does higher-type comprehension ability consist?

What are the special skills needed for effective reading in the various content fields?

What is the Survey Q3R study technique?

Does the Joplin Plan of interclass grouping result in better reading achievement in the intermediate grades than does a traditional program?

24 History of Phonics*

Robert Emans

The teachers' room slowly becomes saturated with cigarette smoke. The instant coffee tastes bitter and less enjoyable. Invariably, the topic of conversation turns to reading. Miss Smith, possessing thirty years of teaching experience, expounds her view that the staff has heard before many times! "I can remember when no one dared to teach phonics; now it has come back. It just goes to show that if you teach long enough the old ways return." Miss Young, a student teacher from Nearby College, listens intently hoping to learn from the more experienced teacher. She knows what Miss Smith is saying is true; that phonics, once in disrepute in some education circles, is now considered to be an important aspect of the reading program. However, she also knows that what she sees in Miss Smith's room is different from what she learned about phonic instruction back at Nearby College.

History could help Miss Young in her confusion; it does show that phonics has a way of disappearing and returning to reading programs. However, history also shows that phonic instruction, although included today, is very different from what it used to be in the memory of Miss

*From *Elementary English,* vol. 45, May 1968, pp. 602–608. Reprinted with the permission of the National Council of Teachers of English and Robert Emans.

Smith. Although over-simplified, this historical resumé will show the tendency of reading programs to reject phonics only to return phonics *in some other form* at a later date.

The literature concerning phonics is extensive. Heilman (15, pp. 213–14) writes "Phonics is the most written-about topic in the area of teaching reading and, possibly, the least understood." Detailed accounts of the literature concerning phonics and related areas are found in a number of references (4, 31).

Early Approaches

In the earliest days children probably first learned to read by having someone read to them over and over again until they wished to try to read for themselves. Then the adult told the child the words he could not recognize. Of course, such an approach gave the child no method by which he could figure out words for himself.

The first attempt to teach independence in reading was probably an alphabet-spelling approach which may go back to the time of the Greeks and Romans, or before. The well known *New England Primer* of 1690 in this country used it. In this approach children first were taught the names of the letters of the alphabet. Then, as each new word was presented, they were taught to spell it. Of course, the sounds of the letter names bore little resemblance to the sounds the letter names represented in the word content. Nevertheless, people, especially some advocating computerized instruction, are supporting this century-old approach today.

As far back as 1534, Ickelsamer advocated the teaching of sounds rather than letters. In 1570 John Hart illustrated Ickelsamer's criticism by pointing out that the spelling of *t-h-r* resulted in the child saying te-ache-er or teacher. The versatile genius Benjamin Franklin revised Ickelsamer's and Hart's concepts in teaching letter sounds and in 1768 published a device for teaching the sounds of the letters of the alphabet in *Scheme for a New Alphabet and Reformed Mode of Spelling*. However, it was not until the time of the American Revolution that a letter-sound approach was put into practice and then not for the reasons previously proposed.

Near the end of the eighteenth century Noah Webster developed a scheme of phonics, not as a means for teaching reading, but to establish a standardized American speech which would reflect the new nation's concern for communication in a democracy. In the preface of the *American Spelling Book* (38, p. 1), popularly known as "The Blue-Back Speller," Webster stated his purpose for his phonic procedures.

To disfuse a uniformity and purity of language in America—to destroy the provincial prejudices that originate in trifling differences of dialect, and produce reciprocal ridicule—to promote the interest of literature and harmony of the United States—is the most ardent wish of the Author; and it is his highest ambition to deserve the approbation and encouragement of his countrymen.

Thus the original reason for the wide adoption of a phonic method of teaching reading was not to teach reading *per se,* but rather to develop a uniform American dialect.

Reaction against Phonics

The predominance of phonic instruction in America went nearly unchallenged for forty years until the 1840's when Americans such as Horace Mann visited the schools in Prussia and Switzerland and liked what they saw. There, through the influence of Pestalozzi, who advocated teaching reading by presenting an object or a picture together with a word, educators began seriously to question the merits of the phonic methods they were using. In 1658 Comenius had already authored his book, *Orbis Sensualium Pictur* (The World of Sense Objects Pictured), in which he had advocated teaching the meanings of words rather than their sounds. Samuel Worcester, the American author of *Primer of the English Language* in 1828 reiterated Comenius' words when he wrote,

> It is not, perhaps, important that a child should know the letters before he begins to read. He may first learn to read words by seeing them, hearing them pronounced, and having their meanings illustrated, and afterwards, he may learn to analyze them or name the letters of which they are composed (31, p.86).

A pioneering study by Cattel in 1885 supported the new ideas for teaching whole words. He showed that in a given unit of time only a few unrelated letter sounds could be recognized, but in the same amount of time it was possible to recognize words containing up to four times as many letters. Of this period Smith states, "This was the only period in American history in which the so-called word method was ever advocated by editors and authors as a general method of teaching reading" (32, p. 191).

Reaction against Word Method

The word method was in vogue for approximately forty-five years until about 1890, when phonics was brought back with a renewed emphasis, as it once again was thought to have merit. However, the phonics instruction introduced at this time was very different from the phonic instruction abandoned a half century before. While the earlier phonic method had drilled the child on sounds of individual letters, the phonic method of this era shifted to an emphasis on groups of letters, often called word families. Reading was again reduced to a number of mechanical drills, each of which focused attention on a unit smaller than a word, such as *ill, am, ick, ate, old, ack.* Children were drilled on more than a hundred phonetic elements before whole words or real sentences were introduced. The context, when introduced, was subservient to the phonic elements, *e.g.,* Kate ate a date.

Reaction against Phonics; Word Method Re-introduced

The extreme emphasis on phonics at the turn of the century brought about, once more, a reaction against phonics during the 1920's. Unfortunately, there was no climate for reform—only expulsion. The new stress on reading silently and the increased volume of scientific research gave impetus to the reaction. As reported by Gray(11,p.918), Hamilton and Judd concluded that the general characteristics of a word were the most used clues, but when a word was strange or different, distinction within the word becomes necessary.

In 1911 in England, Gill(10) reported a study testing a sentence method against a phonics method for reading speed. He found the sentence method superior. Other studies cast doubt on the value of intensive phonic instruction(8,30). Garrison and Heard(7) found that while instruction in phonics was helpful in the recognition and pronunciation of words, pupils who had not had phonic training were superior in comprehension and in smoothness of reading. Smith summarizes this era when she states, "With the new emphasis on meanings and severe criticism of the method of teaching phonics, the whole area of phonics teaching fell into disrepute. . . . Phonics was practically abandoned throughout the country"(32,p.193).

Phonics Re-introduced

Gradually, with dissatisfaction with the word method, more sophisticated research studies, and the advent of new approaches, phonics made a comeback once again in the 1930's. A strict adherence to the word method was found to be unrealistic in that it was found to be difficult to learn all words by sight. Total application of the word method did not diminish the trouble children experienced learning to read. Phonics was re-examined because it was thought that the difficulty children in former years had had in learning to read might not have been the fault of phonics after all(32,p.193).

A number of studies supported the teaching of phonics. Winch(39) in England tested the alphabet, the word approach, and two phonic approaches. His conclusions favored phonics. Tiffin and McKinnis(35) correlated phonic ability with silent reading ability and found a considerable association between the two skills. In a study widely quoted by both opponents and supporters of phonics, Agnew(2) found that phonics increased independence in word recognition, encouraged correct pronunciation, and improved oral reading, but did not affect comprehension; as a whole the study seemed to favor phonic instruction. On the college level, Rogers(27) showed that poor phonic ability was associated with inaccurate comprehension and generally with decreased proficiency in reading. Gates and Russell(9) compared the general reading ability of children given no phonics, moderate phonics, and much phonics. They concluded that moderate amounts of phonics were best. Using somewhat more longitudinal procedures, Sexton and Herron(30) concluded that phonics instruction was of very little help during the first part of reading instruction but was of great value in the second grade.

The new procedures of teaching phonics, developed during the late thirties and forties, differed from the procedures used previously; the alphabet spelling method, the teaching of letter sounds, or the teaching of word families. Formerly, drill was given on parts of words before the child encountered them in whole words. This drill on isolated exercises, or a synthetic approach, gave way to a new approach often called the analytic approach. These terms differentiated the approaches—one being the building up of words from their parts; the other the taking apart of a word in order to recognize it.

In the newer approach, the word was observed as a whole, then the parts were seen as components of the whole. This practice supported the previous research by Hamilton and Judd indicating that people tend to recognize the larger visual shapes of a word first and examine the details only when the larger configuration cannot be readily identified(27). The process started with real words which children already spoke—words which interested them. Words which gave difficulty in daily reading were compared with words children already knew. Most teachers still use this approach, which removed phonics from the criticisms that children memorized phonic elements in exercises isolated from reading itself(32, p. 199). Hildreth(16, p. 341) summarizes the advantages of the analytical approach:

1. Young children are interested primarily in the meanings words have for them . . .
2. Whole-word sounding encourages children's self-discovery of letter-sound relationships and arouses children's interest in words . . .
3. The analytic method avoids blending problems, the chief stumbling block with other methods . . .
4. The whole-word method provides a maximum amount of practice in "read-

ing through" words, the phonics skill most needed when the pupil deals with new words in context independently.

5. Whole-word sounding contributes directly to learning words so that they become familiar sight words.

A number of studies supported this newer approach. House(17) conducted a study in the middle grades and concluded that word analysis skills were best learned when the functional use of what was taught could be demonstrated by the instruction itself. Tate, Herber, and Zeman(34) found that phonics taught in connection with children's needs in attacking words was superior both to isolated phonics and to no phonics. Studies by Gunderson(12) and Tiffin and McKinnis(35) came to similar conclusions.

Little interest in phonics and few studies grew out of the 1940's, possibly because the public was concerned with other matters. However, in the 1950's, perhaps partly in consequence of Rudolf Flesch's(6) book, *Why Johnny Can't Read,* people began to think again about the place and objectives of phonics in a total reading program(28, p. 303). A flurry of research studies was reported. Studies by Triggs(37), Mulder(24), and Luser(22) all supported the belief that phonics and phonic instruction are beneficial to the reader. A number of other studies did not produce such definite positive results. At the University of Stockholm, Naeslund(25) studied eighteen pairs of twins. He found no difference between the methods used with twins of normal and superior intelligence, but concluded that phonics was especially effective for teaching the less-gifted child. Comparing the effects of lessons using visual, phonic, and kinesthetic procedures, Mills(23) concluded that no one method is best for all. Similarly, Witty and Sizemore(40) found that the nature and amount of phonics instruction was still very much in question and that, for most children, the basal reading programs provided adequate instruction in phonics, although some children needed supplementary practice. Durrell, Nicholson, Olson, Ravel, and Linehan(5) concluded that a lack of knowledge of letter names and sounds produces reading failure. However, Helen M. Robinson(26) commented that their conclusions could have been distorted by their research methods.

More recently, Porter in 1960 reported that his studies, using a procedure of omitting words in context, showed that children need phonic clues 77 percent of the time in order to get the correct word(33, p. 232). Love(21) concluded that isolation of phonics with a special workbook and drill produced no greater gains than emphasis on whole words with incidental phonics. Similarly, Ibeling(18) found adding phonic workbooks to the basal reading programs of grades 2, 4, and 6 did not increase reading vocabulary or comprehension significantly. Sabaroff(29) concluded that phonics taught systematically may be superior for low achievers, while functional phonics is superior for average and high achievers.

Phonic Instruction Today

What about phonic instruction today? Kolson and Kaluger(20,p. 10) point out, "Parents find it hard to believe that phonics is being taught because their son or daughter is not subjected to the hiss and grunt of isolated phonic instruction to which the parents were accustomed." Various surveys show that phonics is taught in most schools today. However, Spache(33,p.229) notes that only about fifteen percent of the teachers use phonic drill isolated from actual reading. Russell(28) surveyed 220 teachers in 33 states attending summer school and found that most teachers teach phonics and believe in them, but favor their emphasis in second or third grade, not first grade. Austin and Morrison(3,p.28) surveyed the opinion of twenty-eight reading authorities who generally agreed that phonics is one of the essential skills that help children identify printed words. They also stated, "Each of the basal reading series currently in use in the schools included in this study introduces phonic elements and teaches certain phonic principles and their application"(3,p.30). On the other hand, Harris(14,p.325) points out, "None of them (modern phonic programs) relies mainly on phonic sounding and blending, as the older phonic systems did. Instead they attempt to provide comprehensive, varied word attack skills which include attention to meaning, configuration clues, structural analysis, and phonics." Tinker and McCullough(36,p.325) concluded, "All contemporary authors who have a background of research as well as a broad experience in the field advise a combined approach for instruction in word recognition." However, there is still much controversy. Austin and Morrison(3,p.28) summarize the state of phonics today when they say,

> The question, then, as to the importance of phonics or to its utilization in the classroom cannot be considered controversial. Reading authorities agree on its importance, and school officials attest its universal adoption. Any bona fide controversy must be elsewhere, and in this instance it is to be found in the approaches used to teach phonics and in the program of instruction which accompanies each approach.

The current studies show that teachers are ill prepared to teach phonics. Austin and Morrison(3,p.34) note, "Many teachers, whether using a basal reading or a sounding approach, are not well versed in an understanding of phonic principles themselves. Consequently, instruction may be expected to be inferior." Aaron(1) sought to determine how much teachers and prospective teachers knew about phonics. He gave a sixty item test to 293 students. Only 2 percent got more than fifty right, and only 27 percent more than forty. Experienced teachers scored better than inexperienced teachers, but surprisingly, lower grade teachers knew no more than upper grade teachers. Aaron concluded that courses in teacher education should give more attention, not only to techniques of teaching phonics, but to the principles underlying phonic generalizations.

Summary

This summary of the literature has shown that historically there has been much controversy centered on the teaching of phonics. As a result there has been a tendency to discard phonics instruction at times, only to reintroduce it again later. However, each time that phonics has been returned to the classroom, it usually has been revised into something quite different from what it was when it was discarded. Although phonic instruction is being given today, it is very different from what it was in the past.

REFERENCES

1. Aaron, I. E., "What Teachers and Prospective Teachers Know about Phonics Generalizations," *Journal of Educational Research,* 53 (1960) 323–330.
2. Agnew, D. C., *The Effect of Varied Amounts of Phonetic Training on Primary Reading.* Durham, North Carolina: Duke University Press, 1939.
3. Austin, Mary C. and C. Morrison, *The First R, the Harvard Report on Reading in Elementary Schools.* New York: Macmillan, 1963.
4. Cordts, Anna D., *Phonics for the Reading Teacher.* New York: Holt, Rinehart and Winston, 1965.
5. Durrell, D. C., Alice Nicholson, V. Olson, Sylvia R. Ravel, and Elinor B. Linehan. "Success in First Grade Reading," *Journal of Education,* 140 (1958) 1–48.
6. Flesch, R., *Why Johnny Can't Read and What You Can Do about It.* New York: Harper, 1955.
7. Garrison, S. and M. Heard, "An Experimental Study of the Value of Phonics," *Peabody Journal of Education,* 9 (1931) 9–14.
8. Gates, A. I., "Studies of Phonetic Training in Beginning Reading," *Journal of Educational Psychology,* 18 (1927) 217–226.
9. Gates, A. I. and D. H. Russell, "Types of Materials, Vocabulary Burden, Word Analysis, and Other Factors in Beginning Reading," *Elementary School Journal,* 39 (1938) 27–35 and 119–128.
10. Gill, E. J., "Methods of Teaching Reading," *Journal of Experimental Pedagogy,* 1 (1911–1912) 243–248.
11. Gray, W. S., "Reading," W. S. Monroe (Ed.), *Encyclopedia of Educational Research.* New York: Macmillan, 1941.
12. Gunderson, Agnes G., "Simplified Phonics," *Elementary School Journal,* 39 (1939) 593–608.
13. Hamilton, F., *The Perceptual Factors in Reading.* New York: Columbia University, 1907.
14. Harris, A. J., *How To Increase Reading Ability* (4th ed.). New York: McKay, 1961.

15. Heilman, A. W., *Principles and Practices of Teaching Reading*. Columbus, Ohio: Merrill, 1961.
16. Hildreth, Gertrude, *Teaching Reading*. New York: Holt, Rinehart and Winston, 1958.
17. House, R. W., "The Effect of a Program of Initial Instruction on the Pronunciation Skills at the Fourth Grade Level as Evidence in Skills Growth," *Journal of Experimental Education*, 10 (1941) 54–56.
18. Ibeling, F. W., "Supplementary Phonics Instruction and Reading and Spelling Ability," *Elementary School Journal*, 62 (1961) 152–156.
19. Judd, C. H., and others, *Reading: Its Nature and Development*. Chicago: University of Chicago Press, 1918.
20. Kolson, C. J. and G. Kaluger, *Clinical Aspects of Remedial Reading*. Springfield, Illinois: Charles C Thomas, 1963.
21. Love, H. D., "An Experimental Phonics Program versus a Controlled Integral Reading Program," *Journal of Developmental Reading*, 4 (1961) 280–282.
22. Luser, Carolyn, Eileen Stanton, and C. I. Doyle, "Effect of an Audiovisual Phonics Aid in the Intermediate Grades," *Journal of Educational Psychology*, 49 (1958) 28–30.
23. Mills, R. E., "An Evaluation of Techniques for Teaching Word Recognition, *Elementary School Journal*, 56 (1956) 221–225.
24. Mulder, R. L. and J. Curtin, "Vocal Phonetic Ability and Silent Reading Achievement," *Elementary School Journal*, 56 (1955) 212–213.
25. Naeslund, J., *Methods of Teaching Primary Reading: A Co-twin Control Experiment*. University of Stockholm, 1955.
26. Robinson, Helen M., "News and Comments," *Elementary School Journal*, 50 (1959) 419–426.
27. Rogers, M. V., "Phonic Ability as Related to Certain Aspects of Reading at the College Level," *Journal of Experimental Education*, 6 (1938) 381–395.
28. Russell, D. H., *Children Learn To Read*. Boston: Ginn, 1961.
29. Sabaroff, Rose, "A Comparative Investigation of the Two Methods of Teaching Phonics in a Modern Reading Program: A Pilot Study," *Journal of Experimental Education*, 31 (1963) 249–256.
30. Sexton, E. K. and J. S. Herron, "The Newark Phonics Experiment," *Elementary School Journal*, 28 (1928) 690–701.
31. Smith, Nila B., *American Reading Instruction*. Newark, Delaware: International Reading Association, 1965.
32. Smith, Nila B., *Reading Instruction for Today's Children*, Englewood Cliffs, New Jersey: Prentice-Hall, 1963.
33. Spache, G. D., *Toward Better Reading*. Champaign, Illinois: Garrard Publishing Co., 1963.
34. Tate, H. J., Theresa M. Herbert, and Josephine K. Zeman, "Nonphonic Primary Reading," *Elementary School Journal*, 40 (1940) 529–537.
35. Tiffin, J. and Mary McKinnis, "Phonic Ability: Its Measurement and Relation to Reading Ability," *School and Society*, 51 (1940) 190–192.
36. Tinker, M. A., and Constance M. McCullough, *Teaching Elementary Reading*. (2nd ed.) New York: Appleton, 1962.
37. Triggs, F. O., "The Development of Measured Word Recognition Skills, Grade

Four through the College Freshman Year," *Educational and Psychological Measurement,* 12 (1952) 345–349.

38. Webster, N., *The American Spelling Book.* Boston: Isaiah Thomas and Ebenezer Andrews, 1798.

39. Winch, W. H., "Teaching Beginners To Read in England: Its Methods, Results and Psychological Bases," *Journal of Educational Research Monographs,* 1925.

40. Witty, P. A. and R. A. Sizemore, "Phonics in the Reading Program: A Review and an Evaluation, *Elementary English,* 32 (1955) 355–371.

25 | The Role of Phonics in Teaching Reading*

Jack Bagford

In the past, there has been much controversy among teachers concerning the value of phonics to the teaching of reading. Some have argued that phonics has limited usefulness because of the relatively unphonetic character of the English language; others have felt that such knowledge is not only a useful but necessary part of the reading program. Fortunately, there are now some limited agreements about the use of phonics in the teaching of reading.

There is no longer any serious doubt about whether phonics content should be included in the reading program; teachers and reading specialists almost universally accept it as an indispensable tool for teaching children to read. Disagreements concerning phonics are still very much in evidence, but they have now centered largely on questions of (a) how phonics should be presented, (b) what content should be included, and (c) when should it be emphasized. Though space will not permit a penetrating analysis of these questions, an attempt will be made to raise some basic issues regarding the manner in which these questions may be answered and to provide reading teachers with guidelines for action until results of research and practice answer them more adequately.

*From *Reading and Realism,* IRA Conference Proceedings, 1969, pp. 82–87. Reprinted with permission of Jack Bagford and the International Reading Association.

How Should Phonics Be Taught

Historically, there have been several different approaches to the teaching of phonics. In recent decades it has been customary to categorize them into two main types, analytic approaches and synthetic approaches.

The *analytic approaches* to teaching phonics are those approaches in which the teacher first teaches a limited number of sight words, possibly 75 to 100, and then teaches the reader to utilize these known words to infer letter-sound associations for unknown words. In presenting phonics analytically, a teacher might teach a number of sight words, including, for example, *bat, bill,* and *bug.* Then by *analyzing* the words and noting that they all begin with the same sound, the students learn the letter-sound association for *b.* Subsequently, when unknown words such as *basket, bitter,* and *bundle* occur in his reading, the student will know the *b* sound and will thus have a clue to help him identify the words.

The *synthetic approaches* to teaching phonics are those approaches in which the teacher first teaches the sounds which certain letters represent and then teaches the pupil to combine (or synthesize) the sounds into words. Following one of the synthetic approaches, a teacher would first present the sounds represented by the printed form of the letters: for example, *p* usually sounds like *puh; a* sounds like *a;* and *t* sounds like *tuh.* When the sounds are blended, the word is *pat.* Later on, when the student meets words like *pen* and *pig,* he will know that they begin with the *p* sound and thus he will have a clue to their identification.

Since the early 1930's, those who favored analytic approaches have been in the majority, but there has been continuous support for the synthetic approaches. Recently, since linguistic scholars have focused attention on "breaking the code" as the prime emphasis for early reading instruction, the synthetic approaches have gained remarkably in their popularity. Beginning with the Boston studies in the mid-fifties(7) and continuing with the Sparks-Fay study(11), the Bear study(3), the Bliesmer-Yarborough study(4), and the USOE First and Second Grades Studies(8), evidence has been presented to support the contention that synthetic approaches provide a more rapid start in reading than analytic approaches do.

Chall(5) recently presented a convincing case for those reading programs which make use of the synthetic approaches. Under a grant from the Carnegie Foundation, she has made a searching analysis of the major research findings related to problems of beginning reading instruction. One of her major conclusions was that "code emphasis" approaches (synthetic approaches) proved superior, at least in the primary grades, to "meaning emphasis" approaches (analytic approaches).

There does appear to be some question about whether early gains made by synthetic approaches can be maintained as the children progress through the reading program (11). Further longitudinal research is needed on this very important point, but one would think that intermediate grade teachers and curriculum workers could find ways of maintaining reading gains achieved by primary grade teachers, almost regardless of the manner in which the gains were achieved.

This assumption, however, may be entirely contrary to fact. Children taught by synthetic methods may over-learn some word-analysis habits which later militate against reading growth; they may learn to concentrate so intently on word analysis that attention to meaning is impeded; they may acquire habits that slow down the reading rate and thus make it difficult to comprehend rapidly; they may grow to believe that reading is a process of drill on seemingly meaningless sounds and thus grow to dislike reading. If in their zeal for phonics mastery, primary grade teachers have overemphasized habits that will need to be unlearned at a later date, then it does seem probable that children taught by the more moderate or the more analytic approach would become the better readers.

With present knowledge teachers still must rely somewhat on their own judgment about what is best. It is comforting to note that children do learn to read by any of several methods. At this point in time a reasonable course seems to be (a) teach letter-sound associations relatively early in the reading program with a synthetic emphasis while at the same time considering interest and comprehension as prime goals and prime guides for teaching procedures, and (b) after the child has progressed sufficiently in his word recognition ability, shift the emphasis rather rapidly to comprehension while at the same time trying to foster high interest in reading.

What Phonic Content Should Be Taught

Through the years much information has been compiled concerning speech sounds and their written representations. It is a generally accepted fact that some of the information is helpful in teaching reading and some of it is not. In fact, this matter is implied by the way phonics is defined. *Phonetics* is generally defined as the science of speech sounds, while *phonics* is defined as that portion of phonetics which is applicable in teaching children to read. For the purpose of teaching reading, it is neither feasible nor desirable to try to teach all that is known about phonetics.

One of the basic reasons for including any phonetic knowledge in a reading program is to improve the efficiency of the teaching process. To accomplish this good, programs should concentrate on content which occurs frequently in reading, is easy to teach, and is relatively regular in its application.

Studies by Clymer(6), Fry(10), Bailey(2), and Emans(9) have investigated the question of "what content" by making use of one or more of the preceding criteria in judging the value of selected phonic content. They have found that at least some of the phonic content that is usually included in reading programs is not adequately justified by these criteria. These studies need to be expanded and amplified into other pertinent areas, but they do provide some substantial data which should prove extremely helpful as teachers concern themselves with problems of what phonics content *should* and *should not* be included in the reading program.

Some Basic Considerations

In determining the proper role of phonics in a reading program one needs to consider underlying factors which relate to this role. Some of the basic considerations follow.

Children differ in their ability to benefit from a sound-oriented approach to the teaching of reading. It seems plausible to assume that some children learn better from a method which emphasizes a whole-word approach to word recognition while others probably learn better from a method which emphasizes sound-symbol correspondence. To put it another way, some children probably learn better through visual means while others learn better through auditory means. Generally speaking, teaching materials are designed with the underlying assumption that all children learn equally well with all modalities. This assumption may or may not be correct. Thus it seems logical to advise that whenever a child is experiencing difficulty with learning to read, the teacher should investigate the possibility that he may be emphasizing the least effective modality for the child in question.

Research studies that arrive at generalizations about which method works best for *large* groups of children miss a very basic point; i.e., methods which produce significantly higher mean scores for the total group do not necessarily work best for each individual student in the group. Certain individuals may profit more from a method which has been shown to produce significantly lower mean scores than another. Teachers should recognize this possibility and adjust their teaching accordingly.

It seems likely that some words are more easily learned by a phonic method than by a sight method, while others are more easily learned by the sight method. High frequency, but irregularly sounded, words probably are more efficiently taught by a sight method while phonetically regular words and words which contain easily learned sounds probably are better taught by a phonic method. Learning the word recognition skills is a step in a developmental process, one of the goals of which is to know a large number of words by sight. Accomplishing this goal by the most efficient method is important. Sometimes the most efficient method is determined by the nature of the word itself.

A given child may be able to utilize a sound-oriented approach better at one age than another. The concept of reading readiness suggests that there is an optimum time in the developmental process for a child to learn any given skill. Presumably, attempts to teach a skill prior to this optimum time will prove unsuccessful and may even cause emotional or psychological problems which seriously retard normal growth. Also, it is assumed that if instruction is postponed until later than this optimum time, the skill involved is not as readily learned as it would have been at the optimum time.

In a like manner, each child may have an optimum time in his total development for learning phonics content. For some phonic readiness may be achieved relatively early in school while others may take considerably longer. In presenting phonics content, teachers should consider the natural growth patterns of the pupils.

How the teacher feels about the teaching procedure which he is following seems to make a difference in the effectiveness of the teaching method. If children can learn to read by any of several approaches, which apparently they can, then how the teacher feels about the method may well be one of the most important factors in determining its success. If the teacher is philosophically committed to the method he is using, then he is likely to do a good job of teaching reading regardless of how good or how bad the method might be. When selecting a particular phonics program or determining degree of emphasis on content or methodology, one of the key factors to be considered should be what the teachers think about it.

Interest may not be directly related to method. It is doubtful that one method is inherently more interesting than another. Enthusiastic teachers can take very dull content and make an interesting lesson out of it. Others can take what seems to be very interesting material and create pure drudgery for children. Whether a method is interesting is probably less related to method than it is to other factors related to the teaching-learning situation.

Two factors which influence pupil interest are variety of presentation and appropriateness of teaching level. If presentations are varied within a method, interest is not likely to be lacking. Likewise, if a child is given a learning challenge, but at a level where he has a relatively good chance for success, he will seldom lose interest. The important point related to phonics is that approaches probably should not be accepted or rejected because of interest or lack of it. Rather, *effective* approaches should be selected for use and then adjustments made in the teaching situation to maintain a high interest level.

Guidelines for the Reading Teacher

In teaching phonics, the major task which confronts today's reading teacher is how to maintain a proper balance between attention to phonics and attention to other important reading goals. The myriad of research results and the verbal wranglings of reading "experts" are likely to confuse the average teacher about the proper course of action as he performs the daily tasks of teaching reading. The following are suggested as broad guidelines to follow as teachers attempt to determine the role of phonics in the teaching of reading.

Phonics content is taught so that children have a tool to identify words which are known in the spoken form but not in the printed form. All decisions concerning the use of phonics should reflect this purpose. Teachers should regularly ask themselves whether the phonic content being taught and the methods being employed in teaching it contribute to the accomplishment of this major purpose. If not, the teacher should adjust accordingly.

Phonics is but one aspect of word recognition; word recognition is but one goal of the reading program. Phonics is best used in conjunction with other word recognition skills. As a child learns to read, he gradually learns several ways to identify words. Ideally, he learns them in such a manner so that he can coordinate and combine their use as he attacks unknown words. The ability to use sound-symbol relationships is one of the more important reading skills, but it is just one and should be so considered.

The second aspect of this guideline has to do with the relationship of word recognition skills to the total reading program. Word identification techniques should be taught in a manner that facilitates, not hampers, the attainment of other important reading goals. Intensive attention to phonics can seriously impair progress toward goals of speed, interest, and meaning; teachers need to recognize this possibility so that emphasis can be adjusted to best serve the total reading program.

The teacher is the key person in determining the success of a reading program. Whether children learn better by one method than another is largely determined by the skill and enthusiasm of the teacher. In recent years, research has consistently shown that the quality of the teacher in the classroom is the most important variable relating to how well the pupils in a class learn to read. Effective functioning in such a key role requires that a teacher know as much as possible about (a) phonics and research related to phonics, (b) the total reading process, and (c) the pupils' reading abilities and needs.

Acting in terms of the preceding guidelines leads one directly to the next. *Teachers should take an active part in determining the role of phonics in the reading program.* On the whole, modern-day teachers are well-trained, competent people who are capable of determining the reading needs of pupils and adjusting the program to meet these needs. Caring for individual differences is a constant job, and only teachers are in a position to know these needs well enough to adjust instructional procedures to meet them; teachers should be encouraged to do so.

This guideline means, for example, that teachers should adjust content and method for children who are slow learners or fast learners; for children who have speech and hearing problems; and for those who learn better through visual means than through auditory means. It means that teachers need to recognize and adjust for the fact that some phonic content is learned by all pupils without any direct teaching.

It is recognized that adjusting for individual differences is an age-old problem that has no easy solutions. Nevertheless, with the wide variety of high quality materials available to today's teachers, intensive efforts toward recognizing differences and providing for them can produce rich benefits for the pupils.

Relatively speaking, phonics should be taught fairly early in the reading program. Basically, the two major goals of a reading program are *word recognition* and *comprehension.* These goals can hardly be separated, but for instructional purposes it is probably better to place the heavy emphasis on one and then the other. Early in the process of learning to read, word recognition (including phonics) should receive major attention; and as progress is made, the emphasis should be shifted to comprehension.

Summary

Phonics has an extremely important role to play in the teaching of reading. In this paper it is assumed that phonic analysis is best used in conjunction with other word-identification techniques for the purpose of unlocking words which are known in their spoken form but unknown in their written form. It is known that the pupils can learn to read by any of a number of methods. Thus teachers, rather than method, are the most important variable in the teaching process. Teachers are encouraged to know research relating to methods and materials and to utilize their knowledge in adjusting their procedures to the individual needs in their own classrooms. Guidelines for making these adjustments are provided.

REFERENCES

1. Bagford, Jack. *Phonics: Its Role in Teaching Reading.* Iowa City: Sernoll, 1967.
2. Bailey, Mildred Hart. "The Utility of Phonic Generalizations in Grades One through Six," *Reading Teacher,* 20 (February 1967), 413–418.

3. Bear, David, "Phonics for First Grade: A Comparison of Two Methods," *Elementary School Journal,* 59 (April 1959), 394–402.

4. Bliesmer, Emery P., and Betty H. Yarborough. "A Comparison of Ten Different Beginning Reading Programs in First Grade," *Phi Delta Kappan,* 46 (June 1965), 500–504.

5. Chall, Jeanne. *Learning To Read: The Great Debate.* New York: McGraw-Hill, 1967.

6. Clymer, Theodore. "The Utility of Phonics Generalizations in the Primary Grades," *Reading Teacher,* 16 (February 1963), 252–258.

7. Durrell, Donald D., (Ed.). "Success in First Grade Reading," *Journal of Education,* Boston University, (February 1958), 1–48.

8. Dykstra, Robert. *Continuation of the Coordinating Center for First-Grade Reading Instruction Programs.* USOE. Project Number 6–1651. Minneapolis: University of Minnesota, 1967.

9. Emans, Robert. "The Usefulness of Phonic Generalizations above the Primary Level," *Reading Teacher,* 20 (February 1967), 419–425.

10. Fry, Edward. "A Frequency Approach to Phonics," *Elementary English,* 41 (November 1964), 759–765.

11. Sparks, Paul E., and Leo C. Fay. "An Evaluation of Two Methods of Teaching Reading," *Elementary School Journal,* 57 (April 1957), 386–390.

26 | Teaching Structural Analysis*

Leo M. Schell

To teach children how to figure out the pronunciation and/or meaning of an unrecognized word through the use of phonic and structural analysis is one important goal of reading instruction. Yet Clymer(2) has shown that many phonic generalizations lack either validity or frequency of application and that consideration should be given to some possible revisions in the commonly taught content of phonic analysis. Recently, Winkley(13) has raised some similar disturbing questions about the worth of certain generalizations about accenting. It therefore seems a propitious time to examine some of the problems concerning the content of structural analysis as found in both professional methods textbooks and basal reading series.

The Meaning of Affixes

Methods textbooks typically list prefixes and suffixes which the elementary school pupil should know. Usually, it is not clear whether

*From *The Reading Teacher,* vol. 21, November 1967, pp. 133–137. Reprinted with permission of Leo M. Schell and the International Reading Association.

it is the pronunciation or meaning or both which pupils should know. If it is the meaning which is intended, some problems arise.

Few prefixes are valuable for meaning. Four prefixes commonly recommended to be taught—and their meanings—are:

> con- . . . together, with, very
> ex- . . . out of, from, beyond, without
> pre- . . . before in time
> re- . . . backwards, again

Yet, consider the plight of the intermediate grade pupil trying to apply what he has been taught to any of these words commonly found in elementary school textbooks: *conserve, exclaim, present,* and *resin.*

The obvious problem is that these prefixes have meaning to an elementary school child only when there is a known base word. Even though in Latin these prefixes were attached to base words, over the years these bases have lost their independent standing and the prefixes have become known as "absorbed prefixes." In such words, knowledge of the meaning of the prefix is virtually worthless.

Suffixes present difficulties in two ways. Many suffixes have multiple meanings; e.g., -ment may mean act, condition, or concrete instance. To use the suffix to help derive the word's meaning, the reader must (a) recall these three meanings, (b) choose the appropriate one, and (c) apply this meaning to the base form—a prodigious task for most elementary school pupils. Surely, there must be a *more efficient* procedure.

Suffixes are most valuable to the reader when they are affixed to a known base word; e.g., *development.* But, in some cases it does the reader little good to detach the suffix in order to locate the base word because the base changes forms when a suffix is added, e.g., *admission* and *deceptive.* In such instances, recognition and knowledge of the meaning of the suffix seem of little value in determining the meaning of an unrecognized word.

Inaccurate Instruction

Not only are there difficulties inherent in the construction and meaning of affixed words, but the accuracy of the content taught is sometimes questionable. Instructional techniques frequently fail to distinguish between reading and spelling. For example, one prominent reading specialist writes, "When a word ends in *y* following a consonant, *y* is usually changed to *i* when adding an ending as in *cried, ponies, tinier, happily*" (10). This rule goes from the base to the inflected form, a spelling sequence. The reading sequence should go from the inflected form to the base. Perhaps it isn't too confusing to children, but it seems to indicate some lack of understanding by those engaged in teaching teachers.

It appears that sometimes it is not clear whether pronunciation or syllabication comes first. The senior author of one of the best selling basal series writes in his professional text, "Lead pupils to note that the vowel sound (in *"paper"*) is long and therefore, the first syllable is probably *"pa"*(5). Similarly, another basal series author writes in her professional text, "When two vowels come together and each keeps its own sound, they form separate syllables, as *pi-o-neer"* (7).

Both of these principles imply that the pupil must pronounce the word before he can syllabicate it. But, if he can already pronounce the word, why should he need to syllabicate it? Furthermore, the latter generalization is a tautology: the dependent and independent clauses say the same thing, just in different words. The definition of a syllable is such that this statement does not really tell one anything; it only masquerades as information.

Unfortunately, most principles of syllabic division are based on the vocabulary entry in the dictionary rather than on the respelling, a procedure excellent for composition but questionable for reading. Troup outlines the historical process by which the present system evolved and points out that

> The way a word is pronounced has nothing whatsoever to do with the way it is divided at the end of a line in writing. . . . Over the years, educators set up a kind of a phonics system based on a mechanical practice that was never intended to relate to speech. In any dictionary, for example, you will find the word *vision* divided *vi-sion* in the entry and respelled the only way it can be pronounced in English, the first syllable being *vizh*(11, p. 142).

Pupils are told that affixes form separate syllables and then asked to divide and pronounce words such as *building* which everyone pronounces in context as *bil-ding* rather than *bild-ing*. It is surprising there is not a complete generation of skeptics, unwilling to accept what is told them. Maybe teachers are lucky students do not take instruction too seriously!

Directions for how to use structural analysis to unlock an unrecognized word may be inefficient even if not inaccurate. One fourth grade basal workbook tells pupils to syllabicate the word and then look for affixes (8). Since affixes are predominantly monosyllabic, it seems easiest to locate known affixes first. This leaves only the base word to be syllabicated.

Practice exercises in workbooks, basal series, etc. leave much to be desired. One fifth grade workbook presents this principle, "If a word ends in *le* preceded by a consonant, the consonant is included in the last syllable," and then asks the pupil to apply it to the word *single* (9). A widely used methods text uses *don-key* as appropriate practice for the rule about dividing syllables between medial consonants (1). These words may follow the respective generalizations, but they would be of little help in pronouncing an unknown word.

Valuable Principles?

It may be a waste of pupils' time to teach them certain structural principles. One methods text recommends teaching this accenting generalization: "In multisyllabic words, the first or second syllable has either a primary or secondary accent (su'per-vi'sor, re-spon'si-bil'i-ty)"(6). If the reader syllabicates correctly and then accents incorrectly, is he at much of a disadvantage? The purpose for learning accenting principles is to allow the reader to recreate the sound of a word he already knows, to activate its auditory memory. Should the reader give the first rather than the second syllable a primary accent, it hardly seems that this minor deviation will hinder the desired recreation. Having children learn this principle seems to be the educational equivalent of "overkill."

From Here, Where?

The foregoing discussion was not intended to be a comprehensive survey of all the problems associated with the content and methodology of structural analysis. It was meant only to highlight, to call attention to, certain facets of the topic which deserve critical scrutiny. Some suggestions for dealing with these problems seem warranted.

That pupils should be made aware of the limited applicability of the meaning of prefixes seems an obvious first step. But, if it has ever been previously suggested, it has never been practiced systematically. Intermediate grade pupils should have a realistic perception of what they can—and cannot—do with their learnings. To help them attain this goal, after introducing and practicing on prefix meanings, it would be wise to present and discuss some common exceptions, e.g., *disaster, illusion,* and *uncouth.*

In dealing with the meaning of suffixes, perhaps it would be more efficient to stress the grammatical function of the suffixed word in the sentence than to teach the meaning of individual suffixes. For example, rather than teach that -al means "pertaining to" and that therefore *musical* means "pertaining to music," have pupils examine the location of "musical" in the sentence and note its relation to other words. In "We went to a musical comedy," the grammatical function of the word is an obvious cue to the grammatically informed that music had a dominant role in the play.

To rectify inaccurate instruction, there must be more precise understanding of how structural analysis aids in unlocking unrecognized words. Possibly better than teaching a set of separate and independent rules (tactics), concentration should be on a general technique (strategy) applicable to various situations. The first three steps of such an approach could be:

1. Visually locate and isolate any recognized affixes.
2. If the base word is not recognized, syllabicate it.
3. Determine the vowel sound in each syllable.

This approach begins with the affixed form and goes to the base form, a realistic reading procedure. It also treats syllabication as an integral part of phonics, which is its correct role.

It seems probable that linguists with their emphasis on the subordination of writing to speaking may provide a more functional set of principles governing syllabic division than those now used. Teachers need to know how best to handle the syllabication of words such as *connect* and how to cope with the problem of neutral (schwa) sounds in unaccented syllables.

The most practical way to teach accenting generalizations would seem to be to coordinate them with dictionary work rather than to present and practice them in isolation. This approach not only gives pupils independence with unrecognized words in their listening vocabulary, but also helps them pronounce words not already in their listening vocabulary—the two functions of accenting. "Two birds with one stone."

There must be studies using the techniques of Clymer(2) and Winkley (13) to provide information about as yet uninvestigated areas of structural analysis and to extend their ideas to other material and grade levels. However, twiddling collective thumbs until someone produces this information hardly seems the proper attitude. Teachers need to be selective in what they teach and how they teach it. They should feel free to omit a principle that has little applicability or to revise suggested procedures so they are correct and accurate. A teacher is primarily a decision maker and should not be shackled to suggestions in teachers' manuals.

And finally, we must consider the possibility that our total approach to the teaching of syllabication is wrong. I am not really convinced that calculating the percentage of utility of a rule and then using only those which meet some criteria—or possibly revising the rules to make them more useful—is much of an answer. Especially for below-average intelligence youngsters and definitely for retarded readers. Glass(3,4) and Wardhaugh(12) have penetratingly questioned some of our traditional assumptions about how we should teach children to syllabicate words. Glass can find no evidence that adults or children apply known principles of syllabication in sounding out an unrecognized multisyllabic word. He maintains that readers respond to clusters of letters rather than looking for places to divide a word according to certain principles. (To understand his contention, look at these two words, *phenylpuruvic, oligaphrenia.* Did you apply syllabication principles? Or did you look for pronounceable clusters of letters?) He outlines a program labeled "perceptual conditioning" which he says has been used with numerous children with gratifying success. The idea merits serious consideration. The prevailing attitude seems to be "Which rules are most valid?" and "How can we help children better learn these rules?" Perhaps we should ask, "Are there ways other than rules which can be equally efficacious?"

There seems to be sufficient evidence that some of the content of structural analysis is incorrect and seldom applicable and that some current methodology may be inefficient and questionable. All teachers must be aware of these shortcomings and must search for more accurate content and better methods of instruction.

REFERENCES

1. Bond, G. L., and Wagner, Eva. *Teaching the child to read.* New York: Macmillan, 1966, p. 167.
2. Clymer, T. The utility of phonic generalizations in the primary grades. *The Reading Teacher,* January 1963, 16, 252–258.
3. Glass, Gerald G. The strange world of syllabication. *Elementary School Journal,* 67 (May 1967), 403–405.
4. Glass, Gerald G. The teaching of word analysis through perceptual conditioning. *Reading and Inquiry,* J. Allen Figurel, editor, Newark, Del.: International Reading Association, 1965, 410–413.
5. Gray, W. S. *On their own in reading.* Chicago: Scott, Foresman, 1960, p. 128.
6. Harris, A. J. *Effective teaching of reading.* New York: McKay, 1962, p. 369.
7. Hester, Kathleen. *Teaching every child to read.* New York: Harper & Row, 1964, p. 149.
8. Russell, D. H., and McCullough, Constance M. *My do and learn book to accompany roads to everywhere.* Boston: Ginn, 1961, p. 23.
9. Russell, D. H., and McCullough, Constance M. *My do and learn book to accompany trails to treasure.* Boston: Ginn, 1961, p. 13.
10. Smith, Nila Banton. *Reading instruction for today's children.* Englewood Cliffs, N.J.: Prentice-Hall, 1963, p. 225.
11. Troup, Mildred. Controversial issues related to published instructional materials. Controversial issues in reading and promising solutions. *Supplementary Educational Monographs,* No. 91, 1961, 135–144.
12. Wardhaugh, Ronald. Syl-lab-i-ca-tion. *Elementary English,* 43 (Nov. 66), 785–788.
13. Winkley, Carol K. Which accent generalizations are worth teaching? *The Reading Teacher,* December 1966, 20, 219–224.

27 | # Teaching the Use of Context Clues*

Robert Emans
Gladys Mary Fisher

The Problem

The purpose of this study was to develop a series of exercises for teaching the use of context clues in word recognition. Used along with phonetic and structural analysis, context clues provide one of the best means for achieving the recognition of a word. Finding that unlocking of a previously unknown word makes sense in context, provides a check as to the pronunciation of the word. Although context clues can also be used for determining the meaning of a word, the concern of this study was the use of context clues as a word recognition device. As Miles A. Tinker states, "Context clues are derived from the meanings of those words in the sentence already known to the child. These meanings are used to obtain the pronunciation of the one or two new words in the sentence."[1]

Authorities such as Nila B. Smith,[2] Arthur W. Heilman,[3] Emmet A.

*From *Elementary English,* vol. 44, March 1967, pp. 243–246. Reprinted with the permission of National Council of Teachers of English, Robert Emans, and Gladys Mary Fisher.
[1] Miles A. Tinker, *Teaching Elementary Reading.* New York: Appleton, 1952, p. 92.
[2] Nila Banton Smith, *Reading Instruction for Today's Children.* Englewood Cliffs, New Jersey: Prentice-Hall, 1963, p. 470.
[3] Arthur W. Heilman, *Principles and Practices of Teaching Reading.* Columbus, Ohio: Merrill, 1961, p. 182.

Betts,[4] Homer Carter,[5] and Dorothy McGinnis, and many others agree to the importance of context clues in identifying words. William S. Gray said, "Context clues are perhaps the most important single aid to word perception."[6]

Not only is there wide acceptance of the importance of context clues, but there is also wide acceptance of the value of teaching their use. For example, Miles Tinker and Constance McCullough write, "Few children will be able to make all the use they might of these clues without such training."[7] Smith believes context clues require ". . . more than incidental attention if children learn to make the most of this skill."[8] And Kathleen Hester agrees: "Systematic guidance is necessary to help him (the child) to learn this important technique for recognizing words."[9]

In spite of the importance of context clues in word recognition and the need for explicitly guiding children in their use, little research has been conducted in this area. Smith states "Not many studies have been made in regard to children's use of context clues as a word identification technique."[10] McCullough makes this point dramatically when she states that the process of using context clues still remains "an area of considerable ignorance among us."[11] Nevertheless, a few studies have been conducted. McCullough has identified four types of clues which aid in the recognition of words as being experience, comparison or contrast, familiar expression, and definition.[12] Paul McKee found that the average child in fourth grade can use context clues to identify the meaning of an unrecognized word in his textbooks about once in three times.[13] H. Alan Robinson found that context clues alone were not sufficient for successful recognition by average fourth-grade children although he thought that children would probably profit from instruction in the use of context clues.[14]

---

[4] Emmet A. Betts, *Foundations of Reading Instruction.* Chicago: American Book, 1946, p. 229.
[5] Homer L. J. Carter and Dorothy J. McGinnis, *Teaching Individuals To Read.* Boston: Heath, 1962, p. 84.
[6] William S. Gray, *On Their Own in Reading.* Chicago: Scott, Foresman, 1960, p. 25.
[7] Miles A. Tinker and Constance M. McCullough, *Teaching Elementary Reading.* New York: Appleton, 1962, p. 150.
[8] Smith, *loc. cit.,* p. 541.
[9] Kathleen B. Hester, *Teaching Every Child To Read.* New York: Harper and Row, 1964, p. 138.
[10] Smith, *loc. cit.,* p. 182.
[11] Constance McCullough, "Context Aids in Reading," *The Reading Teacher,* 11 (April, 1958), 229.
[12] Constance McCullough, "Context Aids in Reading," *Elementary English Review,* 20 (April, 1943), 140–43.
[13] Paul McKee, *The Teaching of Reading.* Boston: Houghton Mifflin, 1948, p. 73.
[14] H. Alan Robinson, "A Study of the Technique of Word Identification," *The Reading Teacher,* 16 (January, 1963), 238–42.

The Background

How can children learn to take advantage of context clues in word recognition? Because of the lack of research in this area, twenty-one teachers and administrators at Fort Atkinson, Wisconsin, decided they would try to develop a series of exercises for helping children develop this skill. Participants included special reading teachers, elementary teachers, teachers in special content fields, and administrators.

A survey of the literature indicates that many authorities believe context clues are best used when combined with other means of word recognition including word configuration and phonetic analysis. For example, Tinker and McCullough state ". . . context clues should be combined with such aids as word form, phonetics, and even use of the dictionary."[15] Bond and Wagner believe, "Context clues are practically always used in combination with other methods of word recognition . . ."[16] Robert Karlin goes so far as to say that "Context clues should not be used separately to unlock unknown words, and the teacher does well to prepare exercises that utilize at least two word-recognition techniques simultaneously."[17]

Many exercises combine context clues with other word attack skills. However, no hierarchy of difficulty among the various forms was found. This is an important gap in our knowledge since it is almost always desirable to start with easy exercises and proceed with continually more difficult ones. It has been difficult, therefore, to develop a systematic, sequential program for teaching context clues.

The Testing Situation

Because of this need the participants devised six exercises to determine the relative difficulty of six different techniques found in the literature. To assure compatibility among the exercises, revisions of various forms of the already standardized test, *Gates Reading Survey,*[18] were used. In Form I, the key word was omitted and a correct response was to be chosen from four choices supplied. In Form II, the beginning and ending letter of each word was given with the others omitted. In Form III, just the beginning letter was given. In Form IV, only the vowels were omitted from the key words. In Form V, the complete word was omitted and the line for

[15] Tinker and McCullough, *loc. cit.,* p. 150.
[16] Guy L. Bond and Eva Bond Wagner, *Teaching the Child To Read.* New York: Macmillan, 1960, p. 172.
[17] Robert Karlin, *Teaching Reading in High School.* New York: Bobbs-Merrill, 1964, p. 91.
[18] Arthur I. Gates, *Gates Reading Survey.* New York: Bureau of Publications, Teachers College.

each missing word was the same length. In Form VI, the entire word was omitted, but the length of the line was determined by the length of the word.

Various exercises teach the use of context clues in word recognition somewhat indirectly. Instead of varying the context in helping to recognize a word, the exercises vary the amount of configuration and phonic clues provided. The exercises require the child to search his listening-speaking vocabularies to find the word that is suitable for the context and, also, consistent with other word attack clues including phonics and word form. The thinking is that meeting success in this fashion will prepare the reader to use a similar approach with an unknown word.

The Findings

These exercises were administered in eleven schools by the twenty-one participating teachers. The schools included a parochial school and a college campus training school, as well as nine public schools. The tests were given in all grades from three to ten. There was a range of from 50 to 150 pupils in each grade. A total of 781 subjects were given all six forms of the test. The order of administration for the tests was altered so that not all would take the tests in the same order in case any learning would occur from one or more of the tests. All of the tests were administered by participating teachers or under the supervision of a participating teacher.

The tests were partially scored at a meeting of the teachers to determine what answers were acceptable. Responses were considered correct if they made sense in light of the context, even though they might be misspelled or have an incorrectly inflected ending, or have an incorrect verb tense except where letters or words given limited the response. In the case of Form IV, an answer was considered correct if fifty percent or more of the vowels were correct. Individual participating teachers then scored each test, computed raw scores, and determined the rank of the six tests for each subject. After this, the frequency of each rank for the forms of the tests was computed for the entire group. The frequency of the ranks were compared using the Chi Square Test.

The Findings

The results showed, all significant at the .001 level, that:

1. Form IV, consonants given, was easier than Forms I, II, III, V, VI.
2. Form I, four word choices given, was easier than Forms II, III, V, VI.

3. Form II, beginning and ending letters given, was easier than Forms III, V, VI.
4. Form VI, length of word given, was easier than Forms III, V.
5. Form III, beginning letter given, was easier than Form V.
6. Form V, no clue given, was the most difficult.

It is interesting to note that Form III, with only the initial letter given, is the second most difficult type of exercise. This type is one of the most frequently mentioned exercises found in the literature. The importance of this study is verified since it shows a need for identifying easier exercises.

The results indicate that, in general, the more clues a reader has the easier it is to unlock an unknown word. In Form IV, where only the vowels were omitted, the subject was given phonetic and configuration clues, as well as context clues, to aid him in determining the correct response. This proved to be the easiest form of the test. On the other hand, Form V, which was the most difficult form of the test, provided the subject with no clues at all other than context. Furthermore, in Form V, a number of responses made sense in context, and were correct which bears out the hypotheses that context clues must be used in conjunction with other word attack techniques if the appropriate response is to be made.

Analyzing the other forms of the test to determine the relationship between the number of clues given and the relative difficulty of the task showed a positive relationship in most cases. In Form I (in which the subject was given multiple choices to complete the items) phonetic and configuration clues, and possibly some structural analysis clues were available to help the subject make the correct responses. However, the limitations of the subject's own vocabulary may have prevented him from making the correct response in some cases. Even though he may have been able to sound out all of the words, if he did not know the meaning of any of them, the clues would not be helpful. Nevertheless, Forms I and IV did supply more clues than any of the other forms and would certainly seem to indicate that the teaching of the use of context clues would be most effective if additional word attack clues were included.

Form II included phonetic clues with the beginning and ending letters given and with a rank of third easiest fits into the pattern described— fewer clues make word attack more difficult. Then the rank of Form III, with only the initial letter given, and Form V, with no clues other than context, continue in the same pattern.

The rank of Form VI indicated that the length of the line would give more of a clue than giving the initial letter, as in Form III. However, in scoring, no notice was taken as to whether the response was short on a short line, or long on a long line as long as the sentence made sense.

TABLE 1

Summary Chart of Findings Pertaining to Democratic Data and Difficulty in Context Clue Aids

Demographic Data	Spearman r^a	Kendall $_s^b$	Probability
Sex	1.0	—	.01
Intelligence Quotient	1.0	—	.01
Comprehension Level	—	117.5	.05
Vocabulary Level	—	153.5	.01
Grade Level	—	149.5	.01

[a] Spearmen Rank Correlation Coefficient
[b] Kendall Coefficient of Concordance

What difference does sex, intelligence, comprehension, vocabulary, and grade level make in the rank of difficulty of the tests? Did IQ score make a difference as to which test was easier? To discover the answer to these questions, the pupils' test scores were compared in respect to various demographic variables. Table 1 shows the results obtained by this analysis.

These data showed that readers regardless of sex, intelligence, comprehension, vocabulary, and grade level use the same clues in unlocking words. The same sequence of difficulty in exercises could, therefore, be used for all children in respect to the various variables studied.

This study demonstrated not one, but two, important conclusions. The first showed that a group of practitioners could plan and execute an experiment which had highly statistically significant and important findings. The second showed that it was possible to identify a hierarchy of easy to difficult exercises for orienting the child towards the use of context clues. These exercises can be put to practical use for teaching context clues in the classroom.

28 | Vocabulary Presentation and Enrichment*

Helen F. O'Leary

The purpose of this article is to list and describe briefly some suggestions for introducing vocabulary which the writer has found effective. Some of these methods will be familiar, and others may seem very elaborate and time consuming. Yet, trying to get words introduced too quickly and too casually is one of the common reasons why children receive a very vague and inadequate impression. Under this plan "new" words continue to remain in that category, and too often children fail to hear or realize what the teacher has presented. However, attaching importance to and cultivating enthusiasm for word presentation can go a long way in transforming a boring and dull lesson into a fascinating and thought-provoking session.

Suggestions

1. Choose four or five magazine pictures which may suggest or may describe one adjective such as *enthusiastic, downcast, curious, happy, active,* or *daring.* Display the set of pictures without captions and elicit from the

*From *Elementary English,* vol. 41, October 1964, pp. 613–615. Reprinted with the permission of the National Council of Teachers of English and Helen F. O'Leary, Associate Professor, University of Massachusetts.

group through discussion and questioning the desired word. Naturally the use of synonyms will be encouraged and through them not only can refinement in meaning be developed, but gradually the specific word will be reached.

2. Tell a story or relate an anecdote of some famous person who typifies the meaning of an abstract word. Everyone gives attention to a clever storyteller, and, moreover, when children are far removed from the reading circle, the word picture will still linger in their minds. They will remember the meaning of the *devotion* of Dr. Tom Dooley, the *versatility* of Paul Revere, the *ambition* of Booker T. Washington, the *persistence* of Louis Pasteur, and the *humanity* of Clara Barton.

3. At the intermediate grade level the teacher may form a research committee of able students who can be assigned words in advance of the lesson. The students may illustrate meanings, use words in context, relate word histories, give dictionary and glossary meanings, explain the meaning by phonetic or structural analysis, or show what people are most apt to use the assigned words. An activity like this is not only beneficial to the pupil but definitely valuable for the teacher.

4. Make a chart which demonstrates the use of a word in several simple sentences such as:

   His illness created many very *anxious* days of waiting.

   The commander was *anxious* to win a victory.

   The men were *anxious* to return to their homes.

   The families at home were *anxious* to know if their loved ones were safe.

   Then, discuss the sentences and ask for synonyms which suggest the same meaning. In this type of introduction children come to realize also that synonyms must be chosen carefully.

5. Encourage listening and critical thinking by giving a riddle and making children responsible for using clues to detect the word. For example, the teacher might say: "It is a most useful food usually served at dinner. It is grown in great quantities in many states, but Maine and the Dakotas are most widely known for its production." (Now, if the child says *banana* or *cotton* the teacher should call attention to unused clues or incorrect use of clues which disprove the answer. "Is cotton a food?" "Are bananas grown in climates like Maine or the Dakotas?") Again in this area participation of pupils may be included in devising appropriate riddles for other new words.

6. Some words lend themselves to diagramming—such as *diagonal, adjacent,* a *plain,* a *plateau,* a *route, perpendicular,* and other mathematical and geographic terms. After the meaning has been illustrated on the chalkboard, check with dictionary, math book, or geography for further illustration or clear-cut definitions.

7. Other words can easily be explained by displaying the actual objects— a *locket,* a *darning needle,* an *abacus,* an *avocado,* a *geometric solid,* or any other object which can be made available. Give children the experience of constructing definitions from observation of the objects at first hand. Follow this step by comparing the children's definitions with dictionary entries. Evaluate the work of the children with them in deciding which entries are clearer and more complete.

8. In the upper grades words may be introduced by contrast, through the use of antonyms. For example:

The man was certainly not cheerful; in fact his whole expression was
_____.

The children did not play quietly; indeed, they could always be heard
shouting _____.

Dictionaries may be used to supply antonyms or illustrations may suggest
contrasting words.

9. Oftentimes in primary grades puppets can carry on a conversation or inquiry about a word. Through a series of short comments or questions the
puppet can reveal ignorance which can be corrected by teachers and
pupils. Since staying long enough with a word is desirable, this technique
affords pleasurable concentration. Variety can be supplied by the use of
stick figures or flannelboard characters.

10. A series of related words can be placed in a simple crossword puzzle in
some characteristic design related to a character or object in the story.
This puzzle done together by the group will attract attention and interest.
Later a copy of the puzzle to work out can be given to the class for a test
of retention and understanding. This can also supply interesting seat work.
In this instance also children might be encouraged to design original crossword puzzles related to various subject-matter areas.

11. Build a picture file from which material can be selected for illustration
and definition. Have the children participate by furnishing the pictures,
suggesting the classifications, filing them alphabetically according to categories, and including cross reference data. Encourage children to use the
file for their own projects and assignments.

12. Present a matching test with five words to be defined in one list and seven
definitions of words in the second list. Discuss the test orally emphasizing
that word forms must be taken into consideration in selecting answers. At
the upper grade levels this caution may be observed by selecting the same
part of speech as the word to be defined. This is good readiness for parts
of speech mastery when the teacher inquires: "What noun can we select
for *persistence?*" or "What verb from List B is a synonym for *attempts?*"
or "What adjective can we substitute for *glorious?*"

13. Dictionary work can also be of service. Oftentimes the glossary definition
can be used as the starting point with reference to the dictionary for wider
and varied meanings. As different synonyms are suggested, develop the
idea of similarity and not equality of meaning. Suggest appropriate uses
for the various meanings by associating them with words they seem to be-
long to or suggest. For example, the *clever* inventor, the *ingenious* device.

14. Some words have interesting histories. The use of the unabridged dictionary gives the teacher the opportunity of increasing children's word
knowledge and also emphasizing the use of the dictionary for revealing
word origins and experiences. When children discover how *blatant, tan-
talize, boycott, bonfire,* and *curfew* came into being, they may be interested in learning the ways that other words became part of our language.

15. Construct a series of simple drawings to show the meaning of compound
words. Let children contribute other illustrations or rebus ideas. Such an
activity encourages creative thinking about word meanings and can be very
rewarding. For example, illustrating a *schoolyard,* a *cowhand,* a *cornfield,*
a *football,* or a *stockyard* may result in meaningful representations and
absorbing seat work activities.

16. Let a series of dashes indicate the number of syllables in a word. Then

supply meanings to see if the right word can be suggested. Give some clues to channel thinking into the right direction. For example, the word may be defined, used in a sentence, exemplified in contrast, illustrated, or associated with objects.

17. Build a list of related words from a new word. For example the word *action* may produce: *act, activity, actor, reactor, reaction, active, inactive, activate, reactivate, actively* and others. Use words in discussion as they are suggested and leave the impression that the supply of related words has not been exhausted.

18. Let words suggest workers, occupations, or locale. For instance, the single word *logging* may suggest a picture of majestic trees, rushing streams, hardy workers, close companionship, blazing campfires, and lonely silences. The teacher may suggest to intermediate grades just a single word but to primary grades she may display an appropriate picture. Such an activity may furnish the basis for a composite story or individual compositions.

19. Encourage children to become resource experts and develop specialized vocabularies related to their specific skills. Thus, the baseball enthusiast can compile a list of words particularly associated with baseball. So the stamp collector, the skilled skier, the airplane lover, the eager fisherman, the budding golfer, the young scientist, and the amateur bowler possess specialized word wealth which will not only enhance the knowledge of others, but will also increase their status in the classroom. Interesting individualized picture dictionaries may be made in connection with this activity. Moreover, this may be a continuous activity where children in the room coming across certain words will refer them to the respective experts.

The above list is by no means exhaustive, but it may serve to illustrate how many various activities may be utilized to get children interested in working with words, in developing more meaningful concepts, in stimulating creative activities, and in attracting and holding attention during the reading periods.

29 | Words versus Concepts*

Rachel S. Sutton

The bounds of verbal categories are set by human beings. They are not built into the human organism, but they are acquired from the culture in which the individual lives. Language is an itemized inventory of reality that reflects the particular kind of psycho-social standardization of word-object and word-idea relationship as well as the characteristic attitudes, values, and ways of thinking that prevail in a given culture.

Characteristic patterns of thought in a particular culture affect the nature of the language that evolves, and the language in turn patterns and limits the type of thinking in which individual members of the culture engage. Words and concepts are the warp and woof of thinking. Their complementary relationships are observed in the learning process, in vocabulary development, and in concept attainment.

In the Learning Process

Words are representational symbolism. Another psychological component involved in language behavior is formal concept acquisition or the

*From *Education,* vol. 83, May 1963, pp. 537–540. Reprinted from the May 1963 issue of *Education.* Copyright 1963 by The Bobbs-Merrill Company, Inc., Indianapolis, Ind.

developmental process whereby a verbal symbol with particular culturally accepted meaning comes to represent a definite conceptual content for the individual.

As the essential properties of concepts are abstracted from diverse contexts, the symbols that designate them are applied more precisely. Their application is generalized to include appropriate situations not previously encompassed and restricted to exclude inappropriate situations previously included.

Much of the child's early naming and labeling activities reflect his own private verbal symbols in a representational sense. He soon learns that sounds are socially standardized symbols that can be used as substitutes for particular objects and their ideational equivalents. A rich, viable vocabulary and clear concepts become the basis of clear communication.

Language is necessary for the abstraction, consolidation, and differentiation of the child's self-concept, and for such complex aspects as self-criticism, aspirational level, competition, assimilation of values and identification with reference groups. It provides a medium for expression of self-assertion, defiance, and negativism that becomes progressively more subtle, indirect, and circumlocutious with increasing age.

Learning is not a matter of building intellectual deposits outside the self, nor does it occur smoothly and evenly. It is a process of developing an optimal synthesis of objective, socially meaningful material and subjective idiosyncratic material.

The synthesis is changing and transitory. A state of balance, integration, and coherence develops which makes it possible for the individual to deal with numerous impressions, feelings, and demands.

The teacher cannot supply the pupil with a state of coherence. It must emerge, develop, and be synthesized within the individual. The teacher has the responsibility to keep the process active in order that learning may be maximized thereby.

Learning is enhanced by increasing the range and depth of a child's sensitization to the world around him. A wealth of raw materials for work and creation, the natural outdoors for exploration and discovery, vivid color and form in school surroundings, and a climate of purposeful inquiry represent ingredients of a stimulating atmosphere for learning.

Broad exposure to many situations, to varied and complex ideas and problems, directly experienced beyond the casual sense level, is an important foundation for the mastery of the symbolic system.

Mere exposure cannot be assumed to enhance learning. A more active educational process is required to support the integration of cognitive experience through stimulating connectives. The connectives of similarities and differences, of time-sequence, of cause-effect relationships, of evidence and judgment help a child deal with an ordered world in terms of logic and a perception of reality.

The environment offers the stimulus and places value upon the action, but learning, specifically the cognitive process, does not begin until the learner is sufficiently mature to make the required discrimination-differentiation and coordination-integration necessary for concept formation. The teacher guides the partly formed but freely expressed ideas of young minds through a disciplined intellectual process of reading, speaking, and writing, toward increased clarity and complexity of understanding.

Learning increases when the teacher creates settings and opportunities for children to make their own discoveries and arrive at insights independently. An example of this is given from an observation of a first grade.

After reading "The Balloon Man"[1] the teacher asked the children to imagine meeting him and to describe what might have taken place at such a meeting.

Doug told a story about the balloon man at a circus. "The wind tugged at his string so hard that he lost his hold on the balloons and they went up and up into the sky. The acrobats and elephants made a 'pyramid' for the balloon man so that he could catch the string that held his balloons together."

To Doug the word *pyramid* had characteristics of a concept: height, a building-up quality, an image of something larger at the bottom and smaller at the top as it was formed upward, and a function.

In Vocabulary Development

The teacher can foster the cognitive development of the child best when he realizes that the child has learned a variety of concepts as represented by a large vocabulary before he enters school, but that the many gaps which still exist in his verbal response system must be filled in as naturally as possible. This can be done by providing many pertinent experiences and establishing learning conditions which will allow the child to see revelant distinctions in meaning and differential classification of concepts.

The several aspects of vocabulary development are: word recognition, word knowledge including multiple meanings of words, comprehension of passages, thoughtful reaction to ideas expressed, and use and application of ideas. The learner brings to the interpretation of a passage the meanings he has attached previously to specific words. The extent of his meaning vocabulary depends on the richness, variety, and reflective quality of his past experiences.

Words are essential in building the understanding necessary in concept

---

[1] "The Balloon Man," Rose Fyleman, *Sung Under the Silver Umbrella,* Association for Childhood Education, New York, Macmillan, 1958, p. 54.

formation. The teacher may encourage the child to express his ideas in different ways, to choose words that are plain, direct, and uncluttered.

An exercise that is helpful for this purpose is to ask the child to name the first thing he thinks about as a word is called or seen. First-grade children gave these responses to a list of words:

water—wet, hose, flowers, plants, bath
dog—bark, Jip, puppy, little, shaggy
mother—cooks, hat, father, works, pretty
girl—dress, cry, doll, plays, pretty
animal—rabbit, dog, goldfish, toy, bird
ball—bounce, red, fun, play, run

Too often the teacher is more concerned with the form of a child's expression than with his thinking process. Careful differentiation should be made between verbalism and understanding.

The child's language may reveal that he lacks the terminology for concept attainment or that concept formation is complicated by a vocabulary burden of too many ambiguous terms. Careful instruction in word study to extend vocabularies and knowledge of word meanings will improve communication, concept attainment, and the thinking process.

In Concept Attainment

Perceptual experiences depend on personal characteristics, and in like manner the ease with which a concept is acquired is affected by such individual characteristics as chronological age, mental age, and specific experiences of the learner.

Concepts differ in completeness and correctness. They are wide modifications of the percepts and may be formed from a reorganization and rearrangement of an idea. They reflect the objective properties of the object, quality, or relationship and subjective perceptions of the individuals forming the concept.

The working definition of a concept is the network of inferences that are or may be set into play by an act of categorization.[2] Categorizing serves to cut down the diversity of objects and events that must be dealt with uniquely and makes possible the sorting of functionally significant groupings. Virtually all cognitive activity involves and is dependent on the process of categorizing.

Concept attainment is an aspect of what is conventionally called think-

[2] Jerome S. Bruner, J. J. Goodnow, and G. A. Austin, *A Study of Thinking,* New York, Wiley, 1956, pp. 1–12.

ing. Knowledge in itself does not necessarily imply thinking, but thinking is dependent on knowledge. The steps involved in attaining a concept are successive choices, earlier ones of which affect the degrees of freedom possible for later choices. The patterning of choices reflects in varying degrees the demand of the situation.

The teacher aids concept attainment by (a) adding to the student's knowledge, giving him more material for thought, (b) asking questions which stimulate thought, (c) aiding in goal identification, (d) encouraging free expression of ideas, (e) providing exercises in thinking rather than memory and identification and (f) developing an awareness of relationships.

For example, the mind of the young reader is assailed at first by every word in the paragraph. The teacher offers assistance in selecting, repressing, softening, emphasizing, correlating, and organizing the mass of impressions from the printed page in terms of the reader's plan or purpose. The conscious or unconscious sensing of appropriate relationships within sentence elements and structure facilitates a clear grasp of meaning on the part of the reader.

Summary

Analysis of a child's cognitive behavior includes a measure of the depth, breadth, and height of words and concepts he understands and uses. By depth is meant a degree of completeness, by breadth the number of subject areas embraced, and by height the level of purpose for use.

Each individual possesses his own reservoir of meaning which he can associate with the printed symbol and from which he must choose a particular meaning for each situation. Correct expression in speaking and writing means the properly selective use of meaningful units.

Development of vocabulary, recognition and use of many words are necessary for concept attainment. The learner employs energy, stamina, and self-discipline to increase word power and to discover relationships between ideas from many fields of knowledge. He uses imagination to discover, invent, and create for himself. Conceptualization occurs in the emergence of principles and guides for action.

Words and concepts, the raw material of thinking, are many, but the processes are few. Thinking results from a determined course of ideas, symbolic in character, initiated by a problem or task, leading to a conclusion that is tested in the spectative and participative behavior of the learner.

30 Building Vocabulary through Creative Writing*

Sister Margaretta, O.S.B.

The following methods for teaching children creative writing have been successful in foreign language teaching in the elementary grades as well as other levels of foreign language instruction. The key to creative writing in any language is creative thinking and speaking. Words are signs; they are symbols which we employ to express those ideas, emotions and experiences we wish to share with, or communicate to, others. Every word we use has a distinct meaning for each separate use of it. It follows that the more carefully we use words, the more accurate and precise will be the ideas which we will convey to our listeners.

We can help children become creative in thinking and speaking, and ultimately in writing, in various ways. First, we can encourage them to really *see* the things at which they look. Children can be taught to notice carefully and to remember exactly at least one aspect or a few details of everything they see. They can be encouraged to share their experiences and reactions by relating them simply but accurately and in some detail.

If, for example, a child saw a squirrel, he might ordinarily tell about it by saying simply, "It was so cute!" For children everything that is not

* From *Catholic School Journal,* vol. 67, February 1967, p. 40. Reprinted from the February 1967 issue of *Catholic School Journal* with permission of the publisher. This article is copyrighted. © 1967 by CCM Professional Magazines, Inc. All rights reserved.

ugly is "cute," "pretty" or "nice." Perhaps the child could be taught to tell whether the squirrel he saw was wild or tame, frightened or bold, saucy or timid, agile or awkward, cunning or pert, sickly or sleek, gray or red. The child could be encouraged further to tell what the squirrel did and how it did it, using the best choice of words he can command to describe the little creature.

The use of concrete descriptive verbs will help make his report come alive. Instead of saying, "The squirrel went up a tree," he might add whether the animal ran, hopped, tripped, jumped, tumbled, raced, sprang, leaped, bounded or scampered up the tree. How much more clearly and adequately he would express what he saw!

After the choice of colorful adjectives and vivid verbs, the use of very precise adverbs should be encouraged. The fact that the cute squirrel went up a tree might become much more alive to the listener if he knew how the animal acted. Did it act excitedly or calmly, warily or boldly, angrily or mildly, nervously or gently, chatteringly or quietly, quickly or slowly?

Let older children make comparisons in order to describe more vividly and completely. The squirrel scolded like an angry bird. Bird-like, the squirrel seemed to fly from branch to branch.

In helping children write well, it may be profitable to have them play games. In these games, children could describe a person, place or thing as carefully and accurately as their vocabulary allows them, by using the most fitting and apt words. For this, items in the classroom, pictures, persons at hand—anything all the children in the class can see—could be used. If each child, describing an item, used a different descriptive word, the vocabularies of all would be enlarged rapidly.

A new-word-a-day project is a fine idea to help children increase their vocabularies, so they speak and write more creatively. Synonym studies also help them to see different shades of meaning and to use these new words instead of common, trite or over-used words. Both the new word and the synonym studies are most profitable if they introduce the children to only one or to a few new words daily. It is probably best to have only one such project in progress at a time. Some teachers successfully employ small notebooks for new words. In these notebooks, pupils enter the new words they learn, study them and confidently use them in school, at home, anywhere.

For a writing lesson, a teacher might encourage children to look at something and carefully to notice one special or striking detail so well as to be able to describe it carefully, clearly, concisely and concretely in a short descriptive paragraph. Have them share these written assignments with the class. Short descriptions could also be made orally if desired.

Children are natural artists. They are instinctively creative. Hence, encouraging them early to express themselves creatively, will help them to think, speak, and write creatively, not only as children but as adults.

31 Building Effective Comprehension Skills*

Donald C. Cushenbery

In the attempt to help pupils build skills in the area of comprehension, one must understand certain basic tenets. First, getting meaning from the printed page is the end product of the reading act. Children may be well informed with regard to phonetic generalizations, structural generalizations, and other word attack skills; but unless they can use these tools to secure meaning in the different areas of comprehension, the reading act will not be fulfilled. Second, comprehension is a global term which encompasses such abilities as reading for details, grasping the main idea, and differentiating between a fact and an opinion. Third, pupils develop an understanding of comprehension in light of the questions asked by the teacher. If the teacher asks only questions which involve details, the students will gain the impression that effective comprehension consists only of reading for details. Fourth, materials used for constructing skills in this important area must be on the instructional reading level of the pupil. Students who are forced to read from a single text at a given readability level cannot hope to derive a satisfactory degree of understanding from the materials.

*From *Reading and Realism,* IRA Conference Proceedings, 1969, pp. 100–103. Reprinted with permission of Donald C. Cushenbery and the International Reading Association.

The Relationship of Certain Factors
to Comprehension

If one is to help children with comprehension skills, the relationship of certain factors to this body of skills must be understood.

PHYSICAL

Children must be rested, alert, and anxious to learn if an adequate meaning is to be derived. The tired, anxious pupil cannot be expected to remember details. The status of the emotional and physical health of every student must be studied by every teacher.

MENTAL

One must realize that the entire reading act is a mental process. While a high level of intelligence is a distinct advantage to the learner, it does not necessarily insure a high level of comprehension. A clear understanding of each child's level of intelligence must be established.

BACKGROUND OF EXPERIENCE

In order for words to have meaning, the reader must be able to attach some kind of meaning to the words which are read. A child cannot fully comprehend the meaning of the word "hydrant" unless he has seen a picture of the object or the actual object itself. The culturally disadvantaged child is apt to be particularly deficient in this area. To compensate for the lack of actual experience with objects and ideas, the teacher of these pupils must use such tools and techniques as filmstrips, films, and field trips.

WORD RECOGNITION

A prime prerequisite for building effective comprehension skills is a basic understanding of such word perception skills as phonetic analysis, structural analysis, and context clues. One cannot derive the exact meaning of phrases and sentences unless each word can be pronounced. There is little justification for beginning a sophisticated program in the various areas of comprehension until word recognition limitations have been corrected.

PURPOSE OF THE READER

To gain a complete understanding of a given selection, the pupil must be given a purpose for reading. The use of a reading-study formula such as SQ3R will be of invaluable aid in helping a child secure intended meaning from a paragraph or chapter.

The Comprehension Skill Strands

As indicated in the opening section, comprehension must be thought of as a combination of several facets. Direct and sequential training must be given in each of these areas if the student is to be equipped to gain meaning from many different types of material. Each of these aspects is described in the following section.

READING FOR DETAILS

An essential aspect of total proficiency in reading at all age and grade levels is the ability to secure details from many different kinds of reading materials. The steps involved in completing an experiment or an income tax form will necessarily be a relatively slow analytical process which requires careful attention on the part of the reader.

READING TO SECURE MAIN IDEAS

Pupils at all educational levels are frequently asked to read a selection at a fairly rapid rate to secure one main concept or idea. This skill calls for discriminatory reading in which the reader attempts to place a number of small details into a main idea. Practice should be given using paragraphs, chapters, and complete books as the skill is developed.

READING TO DIFFERENTIATE BETWEEN FACT AND OPINION

One of the most neglected and yet one of the most important skill strands is that of reading to decide if a given statement is a fact or an opinion. Pupils should be taught as early as the first grade that a statement may be fanciful or it may be factual. Older pupils must be taught to analyze copyright dates, different versions of stories, and the qualifications of authors. The attitude of the teacher is important in the development of the skill. The teacher who leads the pupil to believe that a given statement is absolutely true because it is in the textbook is doing little to develop skill in the important area of critical thinking and critical reading.

READING TO FOLLOW DIRECTIONS

This skill must be developed adequately at every age level. Everyone is called upon daily to follow directions such as obeying a traffic sign, constructing a do-it-yourself furniture item, or completing an income tax form. Pupils should be trained in listening skills in order that verbal directions may be followed more explicitly. Numerous opportunities should be given for them to read written directions. They should understand that there is a purpose for all directions and that the teacher will not tolerate a "nearly" correct response.

READING MAPS, GRAPHS, AND CHARTS

The skill of interpreting maps, graphs, and charts is frequently taken for granted. These skills must be taught in a sequential manner at all grade levels. These aids serve the important purpose of conveying meaningful information in a short amount of space. The pupil who fails to interpret these items misses much of the story or article and does not have a clear understanding of the total body of concepts which are presented.

READING TO PREDICT OUTCOMES

The ability to predict outcomes is contingent upon the reader's ability to grasp details, his background of experience, and his ability to display a reasonable attention span. Active anticipation on the part of the reader leads him to develop a desire for the complete meaning to be derived from a given selection.

READING TO FOLLOW THE WRITER'S PLAN AND INTENT

Since authors have unique plans for presenting a body of information, a very careful study of the writer's organizational pattern must be made. While most reading material usually contains a brief introduction, a body, and a summary of the total presentation, some writers choose other methods of compiling information. A careful analysis of the total plan will help the reader to assimilate the intended meanings.

READING TO SUMMARIZE AND ORGANIZE

An efficient reader organizes and summarizes material in order to see the relationships among the various details presented in a selection. In a few instances, the summary may be the establishment of a mental concept in which the pupil summarizes a number of brief facts into a meaningful mindset regarding a given topic. Summaries will more often take a written form in which the reader wishes to preserve certain ideas for use on later occasions.

Principles To Follow in Teaching Comprehension Skills

Remember that comprehension is a global term which encompasses more than just reading for details and parroting them back to the teacher.

The sequential teaching and reteaching of all comprehension skills are vital. Pupils do not learn to comprehend by osmosis or because they are efficient word callers. A careful formulation of reading objectives which will insure steady growth in all areas of comprehension must be undertaken.

If comprehension skills are to be adequately developed, the reading materials must be at the child's instructional level. Materials which are too difficult frustrate the reader while materials which are too easy fail to challenge the child. If the child can comprehend at least 75 percent of the silent reading material and can pronounce at least 95 percent of the words orally, one might make the judgment that a given selection is at the instructional level. A more formal analysis of any given material can be made through the use of readability formulas which have been constructed by Flesch, Dale-Chall, and others.

Reading purposes must be developed with pupils in order for satisfactory meaning to be derived. Before reading, the purpose must be established whether the reading is to be done to gain details, main ideas, or a significant generalization. Teachers are guilty of contributing to ineffective comprehension by asking pupils to "read chapter 5 for tomorrow" without additional comments. The importance of establishing questions which form a purpose for reading cannot be overstressed. As pointed out in another part of this presentation, students must be made to understand that effective comprehension consists of more than the mere recall of selected details. Teachers should give instruction and practice in all of the comprehension skill-strand areas.

Pupils must be taught that writers have many different styles of writing, and pupils must determine whether the topics are written from a subjective, fictional, or factual point of view. The reader must decide very early in the exercise what kinds, if any, of information he is seeking and what methods and procedures should be employed. For example, if he decides that the article is of a controversial nature, he should apply critical reading techniques and compare the statements of the material in question with pronouncements found in other sources which have been written in the same subject area.

Steps for Building Effective Comprehension Skills in All Subject Areas

Well-developed, sequential lessons must be planned and executed in all content areas if a high level of comprehension is to be realized. The following steps must be implemented if this objective is constructed properly:

First, the teacher must build readiness for the selection which is to be assigned. During the period, a discussion with the pupils should be held at which time each of them would recall any experiences which he has had regarding the topic. Difficult words, phrases, and concepts should be introduced and explained. Guiding questions by the teacher and the pupils should be compiled with additional questions selected from the textbook or workbook. Many different kinds of books besides the textbook should be available in order to care for the wide range of reading levels which are typically present in a heterogeneous classroom.

Second, the period for silent reading must be scheduled. Observation should be undertaken to locate pupils who have improper silent reading habits such as finger pointing, lip movement, and subvocalization.

Third, a general discussion of the study topic should be undertaken in light of the guiding questions which were established during the readiness period. In some cases oral rereading of certain passages of the selection may be appropriate to clarify and substantiate certain ideas and concepts.

Fourth, meaningful culminating activities in such areas as social studies and science might serve to clinch essential principles which are explained in the written material. A time line might be constructed by the pupils after they have read various selections on the topic "Important Events in American History." The use of audiovisual aids, such as films and filmstrips, may also serve to reinforce important facts.

Evaluation of Comprehension Skills

A knowledge of each pupil's strengths and limitations in the area of comprehension must be established on a continuing basis. The use of a subjective reading inventory or some other informal device may lend valuable information in this important area. Several commercial tests such as the California Achievement Test, Iowa Test of Basic Skills, Diagnostic Reading Scales, Durrell Analysis of Reading Difficulties, or the Gates-McKillop Reading Diagnostic Test may be used profitably in the evaluation procedures. A careful observation should also be made of the reader's oral responses to various types of questions. The instructional program should be based on the demonstrated needs of the pupils as revealed by the results of these tools and techniques.

Summary

Getting meaning from the printed pages is the end product of the reading act. Comprehension is a global term and is composed of many different facts. If comprehension skills are to be developed properly, every teacher must construct lesson plans which will insure that ability in this important area is developed in a sequential manner. Establishing readiness for a given topic scheduling a silent reading period, discussing the topic, and developing appropriate culminating activities will help each pupil understand intended meanings in a given subject area. Various evaluation procedures should be employed to help the teaching structure the proper instructional program in comprehension.

32 Use of the Cloze Procedure for Improving Reading Comprehension*

J. Wesley Schneyer

This investigation was undertaken to explore the effects of the cloze procedure upon the reading comprehension of sixth grade pupils.[1] Although most previous investigations employing the cloze procedure have been conducted with high school (3) or college (1, 4) students, its possible use with elementary school pupils has been suggested (1, 4). Some doubts have been expressed about the effectiveness of the cloze-procedure below the junior high school level because of pupil limitations in word recognition ability(1).

The cloze procedure as a technique for measuring comprehension and readability of reading materials was introduced by Taylor in 1953(5). The term "cloze" is derived from the Gestalt concept of "closure," the tendency to complete a structured whole by filling in a missing gap. A cloze test or practice exercise is constructed by deleting certain words in some regular manner from a verbal passage and substituting underlined blank spaces.

*From *The Reading Teacher,* vol. 19, December 1965, pp. 174–179. Reprinted with permission of J. Wesley Schneyer and the International Reading Association.
[1] Grateful acknowledgement is expressed to Mr. William Buffington, principal, Mr. James Garrity, control group teacher, and Mr. James Habecker, experimental group teacher—all from the Westtown-Thornbury Joint School—for their assistance in carrying out this experiment.

The individual responding to the cloze test or exercise is asked to fill in the word which belongs in each blank space. The comprehension score on the cloze test or exercise consists of the number of correctly filled spaces.

Rankin (4) and Jenkinson (3) have demonstrated that cloze tests have adequate validity for evaluating reading comprehension for most general uses. Using the Cooperative English Test, Reading Comprehension C2, as a criterion of general comprehension, Jenkinson obtained correlations of .78 and .73 between cloze test scores based on literacy materials and the Vocabulary and Level of Comprehension subtests, respectively. Rankin found similarly high correlations between cloze test scores and the Diagnostic Reading Test, Survey Section.

Rankin studied the use of the cloze test to measure different aspects of reading comprehension, such as comprehension of specific facts and comprehension of general relationships between ideas. He found that cloze tests constructed by deleting only nouns and verbs from a reading passage are primarily a measure of factual comprehension; cloze tests constructed by deleting all types of words indiscriminately resulted in a better measure of the comprehension of relationships. He also obtained evidence that cloze test scores based on noun-verb deletions show lower correlations with intelligence test scores than do cloze scores based on deletions of words without consideration of the type of word that is deleted.

Bormuth (2) found that cloze tests were efficient measures of reading comprehension in various content areas with children in Grades 4, 5, and 6. He also reported that the cloze tests used in his study were valid predictors of the readability levels of the reading passages upon which they were based.

Bloomer (1) reported that an experimental group of college students in a remedial reading program using a graded series of cloze exercises made significantly greater improvement on a standardized reading comprehension test than did a control group which followed other remedial procedures.

The null hypotheses tested in the present study were:

1. There are no significant differences in performance on a final reading comprehension test between the mean scores of pupils who use the cloze exercises and pupils who do not.

2. There are no significant relationships between performance on cloze exercises and (a) verbal intelligence, (b) vocabulary, (c) speed, (d) comprehension, and (e) word recognition.

Procedures

A series of 200-word cloze exercises based on material from a recently published basal reading series was prepared by the investigator.

Two types of cloze exercises were prepared at each reader level. One type was based on the deletion of every tenth word regardless of the type of word (hereafter referred to as "10th-word deletion"), resulting in twenty deletions per passage. Each deletion was replaced by an underlined blank space, ten type-written spaces wide. The second type was based on deletion of nouns and verbs only (hereafter referred to as "noun-verb deletions"). In these passages the nouns and verbs were first identified, and then alternate nouns and verbs were deleted until there were twenty deletions in a 200-word passage. The deletions in these passages were also replaced by underlined blank spaces. Three exercises of each type at each reader level were prepared (a total of 57 exercises).

The cloze passages were given to the children in an alternating order at each reader level. That is, the pupil would first be given a 10th-word deletion passage at the first reader level, and the following day would be given a noun-verb deletion passage at the same reader level. The third day the pupil would complete the second 10th-word deletion passage at the first reader level, and the following day the second of the noun-verb deletion passages at this level. In this manner, at the rate of one exercise per day, the students completed the entire set of materials through the sixth reader level.

After each exercise was completed, it was scored by the teacher and returned to the children, either later the same day or on the following day. Each exercise was reviewed and the correct choice for each blank was indicated. The papers were then returned and scores were recorded on a master sheet by the examiner.

The subjects of this investigation were children in two sixth grade classes in an elementary school some twenty-three miles from Philadelphia. There were 32 pupils (19 boys and 13 girls) in the experimental class which used the cloze exercises, and 34 pupils (22 boys and 12 girls) in the control class, which did not use the cloze exercises.

All subjects in both classes took the California Test of Mental Maturity (CTMM), Elementary Level–Short Form (1957), and the Gates Reading Survey (Form I, at the beginning of the experiment and Form II at the end). Both classes also took an informal word recognition test consisting of lists of twenty isolated words at each level from preprimer through senior high.

The children in both classes participated in the regular reading program, using conventional basal readers. As far as could be noted from observation and conferences with the teachers, the reading program for the two classes was quite similar.

Results

The major hypothesis of this investigation was concerned with whether pupils who completed a series of cloze exercises would achieve signifi-

TABLE 1

Initial and Final Raw Score Means and Standard Deviations for Experimental and Control Groups on Gates Reading Survey

Groups	Vocabulary		Speed		Comprehension	
	Initial	Final	Initial	Final	Initial	Final
Experimental, Mean	36.19	10.72	23.25	21.53	30.27	33.00
Experimental, SD (N = 32)	8.16	7.77	6.16	6.98	5.08	5.53
Control, Mean	38.41	43.47	21.91	20.12	31.68	33.29
Control, SD (N = 31)	7.83	7.17	5.44	6.16	5.10	5.50

cantly greater improvement in reading comprehension, as measured by standardized tests, than did pupils who had not completed such exercises. The results of the initial and final administrations of the Gates Reading Survey are shown in Table 1.

The differences between initial and final mean scores indicate that both groups increased in vocabulary and reading comprehension and decreased in reading speed. The first hypothesis was concerned only with changes in reading comprehension. Therefore, only the comprehension scores were tested for significance of differences by analysis of covariance with control of initial scores. The results of this analysis are shown in Table 2.

When the final comprehension test scores were analyzed by analysis of covariance with control of initial scores, the difference between the

TABLE 2

Analysis of Covariance of Final Reading Comprehension Test Scores with Control of Initial Scores

Sources of Variation	Sum of Squares		Sum of Products	Sum of Squares Residuals	Degrees of Freedom	Variance Estimate
	x^2	y^2				
Between groups				8.6	1	8.6
Within groups	1709.4	2007.1	1232.2	1118.9	63	17.76
Total	1713.0	2008.5	1239.2	1127.5	64	
F = .48*						

* For 1 and 63 degrees of freedom an F value of 4.00 is required for significance at the .05 level.

means of the two groups was not significant, and therefore the pupils who had completed the cloze exercises did not show significantly greater improvement in reading comprehension. Thus, the first null hypothesis was accepted.

To test the second hypothesis, of possible relationship with other reading factors, total scores for the 27 10th-word deletion cloze exercises and total scores for the 27 noun-verb deletion cloze exercises were obtained for each pupil in the experimental group. Total cloze scores were then correlated with factors of intelligence and reading as described below.

CLOZE SCORES AND INTELLIGENCE

The Language I.Q.'s on the CTMM for the control group ranged from 88 to 150 (M, 116.6; SD, 14.67). Language I.Q.'s for the experimental group ranged from 98 to 144 (M, 119.6; SD, 12.09). Language I.Q.'s were significantly correlated with 10th-word deletion total scores ($r = .63$, $p < .01$) and with noun-verb deletion total scores ($r = .42$, $p < .02$).

CLOZE SCORES AND READING

Correlations between total cloze scores on 10th-word deletion exercises and the reading factors (as measured by the initial scores on the Gates Reading Survey) were all significant at the .01 level or below (vocabulary, $r = .74$; comprehension, $r = .68$; speed, $r = .63$). Correlations between total cloze scores on the noun-verb deletion exercises and the reading factors were also significant beyond the .01 level (vocabulary, $r = .63$; comprehension, $r = .60$; speed, $r = .60$).

To test whether word recognition ability was related to achievement in the cloze exercises, the performance of students in the experimental class on the word recognition test was compared with their performance on the 10th-word cloze exercises (see Table 3). Word recognition levels of students achieving above the median on the cloze exercises were compared with word recognition levels of students achieving below the median. Word recognition performance at sixth reader level or above was compared with performance at fifth reader level and below. These data indicate that students whose word recognition ability was at sixth reader level or above performed significantly better on the cloze exercises than did students whose word recognition ability was at fifth reader level or below.

Thus, the second null hypothesis was rejected. The performance of the experimental class on 10th-word deletion cloze exercises was found to be significantly related to verbal ability, reading comprehension, speed of comprehension, reading vocabulary, and word recognition.

TABLE 3

Word Recognition Levels and Total Scores on 10th Word Cloze Exercises

Level	Word Recog. 6th Reader and Above	Word Recog. 5th Reader and Below
Above Median, Total Cloze Score	14	2
Below Median, Total Cloze Score	1	12
Total	18	14

Chi square = 12.64; df, 1; level of significance <.001.

Discussion

How may the lack of significant improvement in reading comprehension by the pupils in the experimental group be explained? One obvious explanation is that practice in cloze exercises does not contribute to improvement in comprehension abilities. Yet, it would seem that the skills involved in determining the precise word required for each blank in the cloze exercise, by the very nature of these skills, should result in such improvement. In order to select the specific words for the cloze passage the reader must possess a knowledge of word meanings, must understand the main idea of the passage, must attend to details, and must make inferences and draw conclusions. All of these are important skills involved in reading comprehension.

Since these comprehension skills are just as essential for comprehending a cloze passage as for comprehending any other reading matter, a second explanation for the results of the present experiment is suggested. This explanation may be that merely filling in the cloze blanks and then checking for correct or incorrect answers does not provide the pupil with increased knowledge of comprehension skills as they function in a particular passage.

This situation might be compared with a common procedure for improving reading comprehension in which the pupil reads a passage and then responds to questions calling for knowledge of word meanings, main ideas, important details, and conclusions. By merely checking right or wrong answers a pupil may not learn why a certain group of words contains the main idea and not another group of words, or why a certain conclusion may be drawn from the passage and not another conclusion. *The reasons for the appropriate responses must be verbalized.*

It may be that the crucial factor which is involved in improving comprehension ability on cloze exercises is the reader's awareness of the reasons for the appropriateness of specific words for each blank in the passage. That is, in addition to checking the correctness of each response the pupils should also discuss the reasons for each choice. The clues from the passage context, previous experience, or knowledge of language structure which the reader employs in selecting precise words for each blank should be verbalized.

Further research with cloze exercises is planned in which the pupils will also verbalize their choices for each blank to test the above suggestions.

The correlation of .63 between total cloze scores based on 10th-word deletions and Language I.Q.'s on the CTMM compares favorably with those between standardized reading tests and intelligence tests. The use of cloze exercises may prove more useful with pupils of average or above average ability. A lower correlation between noun-verb deletions scores and Language I.Q.'s is similar to the findings of Rankin(4) and Taylor (5). As Rankin suggests, the noun-verb cloze procedure may provide a measure of comprehension less influenced by intelligence.

The relationship between adequate achievement in word recognition ability and significant performance on the cloze exercises suggests that pupils with word recognition deficiencies are likely to find cloze exercises too difficult, just as such pupils are likely to have trouble with comprehension of conventional reading materials.

REFERENCES

1. Bloomer, Richard H. "The Cloze Procedure as a Remedial Reading Exercise," *Journal of Developmental Reading,* 5 (Spring 1962), 173–181.
2. Bormuth, John R. "Cloze Tests as Measures of Readability and Comprehension Ability." Unpublished Ed.D. dissertation, University of Indiana, 1962.
3. Jenkinson, Marion E. "Selected Processes and Difficulties in Reading Comprehension." Unpublished Ph.D. dissertation, University of Chicago, 1957.
4. Rankin, Earl F., Jr. "An Evaluation of the Cloze Procedure as a Technique for Measuring Reading Comprehension." Unpublished Ph.D. dissertation, University of Michigan, 1957. "The Cloze Procedure—Its Validity and Utility," In Oscar S. Causey and William Eller, Eds. *Starting and Improving College Reading Programs,* Eighth Yearbook of the National Reading Conference, pp. 131–134, Fort Worth: Texas Christian University Press, 1958.
5. Taylor, Wilson L. "Application of 'Cloze' and Entropy Measures to the Study of Contextual Constraint in Samples of Continuous Prose." Unpublished Ph.D. dissertation. University of Illinois, 1954. "Cloze Readability Scores as Indices of Individual Differences in Comprehension and Aptitude." *Journal of Applied Psychology,* Feb. 1957, pp. 19–26.

33 The Prerequisite: Knowing How To Read Critically*

David H. Russell

Censorship usually involves a decision by a person or group about what others should read; ability in critical reading suggests that the individual himself makes the choice. Should the screening be done by the Lord Chamberlin, by the Watch and Ward Society or by the person doing the reading or viewing? The primary concern of NCTE is not with the banning of materials at the source. We must have competence and established procedures in dealing with censorship by individuals or groups in our local districts but our first concern is with the critical abilities of children and youth. We want to help young people to reject for themselves the vulgar, the meretricious, the fallacious. We want students who can decide whether there is communism in *Robin Hood,* pornography in *The Good Earth* or *Drums Along the Mohawk.*

Critical reading does not exist in a vacuum by itself but can be thought of as being closely related to critical thinking. Recent statements of the aims of education and psychological studies of cognition made during the last thirty years both give us leads to a consideration of critical thinking.

The importance of the idea has been expressed in the last bulletin of

---

*From *Elementary English,* vol. 41, October 1963, pp. 579–582. Reprinted with the permission of the National Council of Teachers of English.

the Educational Policies Commission entitled "The Central Purpose of American Education." The writers of the bulletin put it this way: "The pupose which runs through and strengthens all other educational purposes —the common thread of education—is the development of the ability to think." In another place the bulletin discusses ethical character in relation to thinking. "Character is misunderstood if thought of as mere conformity to standards imposed by external authority—(It has) meaning to the extent (it represents) affirmative, thoughtful choices by individuals. The ability to make these choices depends on awareness of values . . . and this awareness of standards or values is an integral part of critical thinking."

This brings us to the question of what we mean by "thinking" and "critical thinking." As currently used the word *thinking* is an omnibus term carrying too heavy a load, such a heavy load that it sometimes becomes meaningless. We say a child is thinking when he builds a bridge with blocks, a housewife when she is following a recipe, a poet when contriving a sonnet. The same confusion exists in defining the type of thinking called "critical thinking." One of my doctoral candidates has recently compiled no less than thirty-five descriptions of critical thinking in educational journals. It is probably time we became critical about the definitions of critical thinking.

If I may be critical of the Educational Policies report on "The Central Purpose" I would say that it tends to regard thinking as one thing. Sometimes as teachers of English we are urged to teach youth to think as if thinking were some single, unitary ability. The research evidence in psychology is against this single-mindedness. Different psychologists use different terms, but it is my own belief that the kinds of thinking we do in school or business or the rest of the world's work can be divided into some six overlapping categories. Elsewhere I have called these: perceptual thinking, associative thinking, concept formation, problem solving, critical thinking, and creative thinking. We see, then, that critical thinking is only one of the kinds of thinking we want children to learn and adults to practice.

What is critical thinking? I believe it can be best described as essentially a three-factor ability. It includes an attitude factor of questioning and suspended judgment, a conative or functional factor which involves use of methods of logical inquiry and problem solving, and a judgment factor of evaluating in terms of some norm or standard or consensus. The attitude factor for example, may be represented by "I'm from Missouri" or "Show me." It means checking on the assumptions of the author—a difficult task, especially in some fiction. The conative or action factor may include selecting significant words and phrases in a statement, identifying emotion and bias, picking out stereotypes and clichés. We can all have fun recognizing an emotional appeal to something sacred like home or mother or identifying what E. E. Cummings calls a "duck-billed platitude." The third judgment factor may include distinguishing the relevant and irrelevant, assessing literary merit, and looking for evidence in any conclusion drawn by speaker or writer.

All these sound like formidable accomplishments which we all need to practice. They appear difficult to us adults so how can they be started with children? We might as well face the facts that critical thinking abilities are difficult and they are slow agrowing. And yet the need to use them is all around us.

May I state four reasons why I believe critical thinking must be stressed from kindergarten through college—why I believe teachers and curriculum committees must give development of abilities in critical thinking a continuous place in the curriculum.

The mass media of communication influence us to think and act alike. Conformity, not individuality, is stressed in our listening and much of our reading. In 1962, the date farmer in Southern California, the lumberman in Washington, and the owner of the cranberry bog in New England read the same columnists, hear the same radio news reports, watch the same TV shows. We know that elementary school children, millions of them, watch television on an average of over 20 hours a week. As one man has said, television is a cookie cutter shaping our minds all in the same mold. Wiser men than I have written about the dangers of conformity in our society. These dangers are particularly great, and insidious, in relation to the impressionable minds of children. The effect of our mass culture is to make little bands of conformists—only the home and the school can help children think for themselves, reject the unworthy, resist the blandishments of the "guy with a bill of goods for sale."

High performance on an intelligence test does not guarantee high scores on a test of critical thinking. Good mental ability does not guarantee strong critical thinking ability. The relationship between general intelligence and critical thinking is positive but not high. Critical thinking abilities are not acquired automatically as a part of general mental growth; specific provision must be made for their development in all curricular areas.

Attitudes are learned. The first of the many components of critical thinking I have mentioned is an attitude of questioning, a suspending of judgment until the facts are all in. Youth do not develop a questioning attitude automatically. Instead, teachers and schools have to work to develop the attitude. I do not believe that teacher and child must always be suspicious. Some of us saw the *New Yorker* cartoon of an instructor and his class. On the chalkboard was written $2 + 2 = 4$. The caption on the cartoon was only one word but the instructor was saying, "However. . ."

The facts in a single book on science or on fictionalized biography may be questioned just as doubts can be expressed about some news story in a newspaper or in the words of the speaker. An attitude of questioning and criticism is sometimes relevant. Such attitudes are learned partly by imitation, for attitudes may be caught as well as taught.

The third component of critical thinking I have described as judgment or evaluative judgment in terms of some norm or standard or consensus implies a background of experiences which sometimes the school must apply. Knowledge and experience are prerequisite to critical thinking in the process in which the thinking is done. We must ask children or adults to be critical thinkers. In these days when many children have never seen a farm, when rural children may never have entered an apartment house, the school must help supply a good background of experiences before problem solving or creative thinking or critical thinking can be attempted. But from the first grade on, let us not stop just with the experience— teacher and group must discuss, contrast, and compare, and then the teacher moves imperceptibly into questioning and judgment. (*Why* are trains and railways losing out these days?)

Here, then are four reasons why school people must take definite steps to develop critical thinking abilities: (1) The whole force of mass culture is toward conformity rather than individuality. (2) Good mental ability does not guarantee some of the specific skills needed in critical thinking. (3) Attitudes of critical thinking can be learned, at least in part, by imitation of the procedures of the teacher and other adults; and (4) The school must often help supply the background of experience, the familiarity and know-how, which is the necessary basis for critical thinking. Each of these reasons, and especially the fourth, relate to the question of self-censorship instead of outside censorship.

Some of you, and especially those of you who work with older adolescents or college students, may think I am pretty optimistic when I recommend beginning work with young children in critical thinking. You know that some students come to high school or even college who have difficulty in reading for literal meaning, much less being critical of what they read or hear. Can the ten-year-old or the fifteen-year-old really exercise the judgment necessary for evaluating the newspapers, films or novels he sees? In partial answer here are nine statements of things we know or believe which have been at least partly verified by research. I give them in rapid-fire order but each can be expanded in your own thinking:

1. Some children have acquired abilities in critical thinking before they enter school. (One five-year-old said to me smilingly, "*All* the TV ads say they have the best breakfast cereal.")

2. Activities in critical thinking begin in the primary grades—not with the "rational" adult. (A first grade recently distinguished fantasy and reality after they heard the story "The Day It Rained Cats and Dogs.")

3. Critical thinking depends less upon specific techniques and more upon attitude and experience. (In the words of Don Marquis, we can detect

the speaker who "strokes a platitude until it purrs like an epigram," but we must be able to discover the platitude.)

4. Part of the attitude factor in critical thinking is the objectivity which comes from the ability to shift perspective—to see one's own behavior and ideas as they may be viewed by others. (This may be part of developing the self concept, especially crucial in the junior high school years.)

5. The experience factor in critical thinking involves considerable participation in the social and linguistic community. A chance to talk things over or explore the effects of action produces a validation by consensus which is prerequisite to making sound judgments.

6. Although probably not so important as attitude or experience, there are hundreds of skills in the conative or operational phase of critical thinking. These include the ability to read for exact details, to relate cause and effect in a speaker's statement, and to detect a propaganda device such as "glittering generality." In relation to Communism the favorite device is name calling. Long ago a political opponent said that FDR was substituting the hammer and sickle for the stars and stripes in the American flag. This device is not dead today.

7. The evaluation phase of critical thinking is closely related to the ability to check one's own thinking against some social norm or consensual validation. This means that the child or youth must know the habits and customs of the group and the school must be aware of possible differences between home and community values.

8. Irrationality in thinking occurs when the challenge to the individual is too severe, when he does not have the resources to meet the questioning of an idea close to the heart of his own personality or philosophy. If we are threatened by a statement or idea it is hard to consider it unemotionally and critically.

9. Critical thinking about materials which may be labeled "lewd" or "obscene" or "pornographic" by certain censors is probably related to the reader's standards or tastes. Many teachers have reported successful efforts to raise their students' tastes in literature and in cinema. If this is accomplished the knowledge and attitude may provide the best bulwark against undesirable material.

These nine principles have been partly validated by research and indicate action for each of us.

I have suggested this morning that, ever so often, we have to dynamite some educational debris out of the way and replace it with the high priorities, the essentials for today. In English and other curricular areas we need greater emphasis on thinking abilities. At least six different thinking abilities can be identified and one of the most important of these is critical thinking. Most of the influences of modern life are against such skill and so the school has a peculiar and unique responsibility for developing it, from the first grade onward. It is not enough to be *against* Communism or sadism or hedonism, we must be *for* the development of skills in critical thinking about any "ism." In one of my children's group-written newspapers recently appeared this epigram, "Many a good story has been ruined by over-verification." Fortunately for us, many a bad story can be ruined by it too when we have the time and skill to check it critically.

In our pluralistic culture, there are many extreme voices. We must be able to resist some of the statements of a Senator Joseph McCarthy, a Texas oil millionaire, or a hard-fighting labor boss. We must be able to decide for ourselves that this writer has something to say but that one is merely filthy. Socrates, facing death, told his accusers that "The unexamined life is not worth living." The ability to examine complex community affairs or personal problems begins in childhood and develops slowly over the years. As a product of our schools we do not want bulging-jawed squirrels crammed with knowledge. We want not sheep but curious, questioning people; not thoughtless conformity, but thoughtful appraisal; not parrotting back but reflecting and judging; not prohibiting but evaluating.

34 Reading in the Elementary School Science Program*

Marlow Ediger

Teachers need to follow certain basic procedures in helping children read content with meaning and understanding in the area of elementary school science. Prior to reading from an elementary school science textbook, pupils should have background experiences which will help them to understand what they are reading as well as provide interest in what is read. If pupils are to read on the topic of Erosion, the teacher needs to provide some learnings for pupils which will help them in their reading. The teacher can show a motion picture film or filmstrip showing different kinds of erosion. Pupils can ask questions about the contents of the film concerning different types of erosion and their effects. The teacher could carefully select pictures from library books or reference books which would help clarify major concepts concerning erosion, such as gully erosion, sheet erosion, wind erosion, water erosion, strip-cropping, terracing, and contour farming. Pupils should also be guided in observing pictures carefully in their science textbooks. If pupils have a chance to discuss the motion picture film, the filmstrips, and the pictures, they will be able through a discussion to ask questions concerning concepts they do not understand

*From *Science Education,* vol. 49, October 1965, pp. 389–390.

and the teacher will notice misunderstandings that pupils have while guiding the discussion.

After pupils have gained background information which is necessary in order to understand what is read from the textbook on erosion, the teacher needs to present the new words from that reading lesson. A teacher who knows his pupils well, especially in the area of reading science content, can readily foresee which words pupils will have difficulty in pronouncing and understanding their meaning. These words should be written on the blackboard in meaningful sentences pertaining to erosion by the teacher. The sentences should be read carefully by the teacher. The teacher needs to emphasize the correct pronunciation of each new word contained in the sentences. Pupils should have an opportunity to pronounce these words, discuss a variety of meanings for these words, and use the words in a variety of meaningful sentences.

By this time, pupils will have asked some questions which they feel are important and would want to have answered. These questions could arise from the use of the film and pictures or from the words that were written on the board. These questions that were considered important by the teacher and pupils would provide an incentive or purpose on the part of pupils to read from their elementary school science textbooks. Reading is not done for the sake of reading, but there is a purpose involved on the part of children while reading, and that is to find answers to important questions. Pupils will not be able to have all their questions answered from reading the text. This provides wonderful opportunities for pupils to read from other sources—library books, reference books, and the science section from a basal reader—to get appropriate information for their questions. Pupils learn to use a variety of sources and to compare statements from sources used while getting information to answer their questions. When pupils are motivated to read, they will have a desire to do more reading and to retain what has been read for a longer period of time compared to pupils who are not motivated to read.

As pupils read from their textbook, they will find new questions or problem areas which are of concern to them such as "Why does sheet erosion occur?" "What can be done to prevent gully erosion?" or "Why does water cause soil to erode?" These questions may also have been asked by children after viewing the motion picture film or filmstrip when background information was provided for pupils. The teacher should always guide pupils to ask questions concerning what is read in science. The teacher can use these questions for additional learning experiences that can be provided for pupils, such as taking pupils on an excursion to areas where different kinds of soil erosion have taken place or the teacher can show a motion picture film or filmstrip which would answer the questions. A soil conservation specialist could be asked to talk to children about questions that have been raised concerning erosion. Experiments performed in the classroom could also help to answer many of these questions.

A variety of rich, purposeful learning experiences for pupils can do much to help pupils gain meaning and understanding from the reading that is done in the area of elementary school science. Motivation to read and interest in reading should be present in pupils.

35 Teaching the Essential Reading Skills in Social Studies*

Alvin Kravitz

Within the past few years teachers have become aware of the need for teaching reading skills in the content areas. One of the major content areas, social studies, requires an approach somewhat different from other subject areas. Let us view the topic from four interrelated, yet different, angles.

Directed Reading Activity

Elementary and secondary teachers who are involved in teaching social studies have found increasing success in presenting their subject matter through the use of a directed reading activity.

Whipple(18) states the format of present day social studies texts is similar to a reading book used for basal instruction. However, the reader's job is quite different. Children need guidance in selecting what to remember and then techniques in how to remember(17).

The New York State Curriculum Guides(8,17) point out the advis-

*From *Forging Ahead in Reading,* IRA Conference Proceedings, 1968, pp. 223–228. Reprinted with permission of Alvin Kravitz and the International Reading Association.

ability of a directed reading activity for basic instructional purposes. Spache (15) indicates the superiority of guided reading in the teaching of social studies.

All too often students are forced to plunge into complex materials with little idea of what to look for or even why they are reading a particular text. The involved structure of social studies texts requires preparation and assistance for the student. Strang (16) suggests that the teacher can guide the student through the use of prepared questions. Let us go a step further and prepare not only the questions for consideration during the lesson but the necessary matter prior to beginning any part of the lesson.

A plan for a directed reading activity in social studies is contained in Five Steps to Reading Success (2):

Step One: Readiness

Arousing pupil interest
Setting a purpose for the reading
Developing a background and a sense of continuity
Creating an awareness of the reading required

Step Two: Concept Development

Discussing the vocabulary and concepts which need clarification
Explaining how context may give a term meaning
Studying pronunciation and spelling when appropriate

Step Three: Silent Reading

Locating specific details
Finding the main idea and supporting details
Seeing a vivid picture through word concepts
Locating information by skimming
Determining accuracy of statements

Step Four: Discussion (Oral or Written)

Checking comprehension
Sharing different points of view

Step Five: Rereading (Silent or Oral)

Checking accuracy
Examining critically

Karlin (5) discusses a directed reading activity with a slight modification. His five-step process includes:

1. Readiness—vocabulary and purpose
2. Silent Reading—refer to question
3. Discussion—relating to silent reading

4. Rereading—for different purposes
5. Application—to the lesson

Gates(3) suggested that we cultivate student interest in each content subject. He believed that social studies texts needed to be reformed because of the too difficult readability, the poor literary quality, and the lack of organization of school materials. Since it is extremely difficult for the classroom teacher to rewrite texts while teaching the students in the classroom, perhaps the next best thing would be to circumvent the problem through the use of a directed reading activity.

Vocabulary

Each subject area has its own vocabulary which is unique. Social studies certainly is no exception to the rule. It is vital for the teacher to develop the vocabulary of the specific lesson within its own context, or comprehension of the total subject will be much less than expected (16). Smith(14) indicates the child's ability to deal with the content area improves as training is given in the vocabulary of that subject. *Reading in Secondary Schools*(8) shows the desirability of vocabulary development through the use of context meaning, word study, and the attainment of word attack skills as a means of improving overall comprehension.

Bamman(1) points out that reading social studies is more difficult than reading narrative material to which the elementary student is accustomed. The vocabulary is not controlled; the student must organize a mass of unrelated facts; the ideas are very complex; and much previous knowledge must be brought forward to assist the student in developing concepts.

Vocabulary is a general term which covers various subdivisions. Bamman(1) has made six headings to include the types of difficult word areas the student may meet in his social studies work.

a. technical terms—
would include words such as feudalism, vassal, primogeniture, guild, and crusade.
b. multisyllabic words—
formidable words are totalitarian, accountability, telecommunication, endowments, and philanthropic.
c. abstract words—
maturation would help the student to understand such words as liberty, justice, equality, democracy, and despotism.
d. general terms—
multiple meanings arise in the use of elevator since the student may not realize we speak of a grain elevator.

e. mathematical terms—
usually included in the use of time designations, area, population statistics, graphs, and charts.

f. concepts—
these words produce mental images which are really abstractions such as "tolerance." A student's view will broaden as he begins the study of human relations. What is tolerance to one child may be intolerance to another.

Jenkinson(4) has an interesting approach to vocabulary development as she uses the term Functional Word Knowledge. She has divided the topic into three areas:

a. function words—
this area includes small words that are often ignored. Some examples of structure words are as follows:
(1) cause and effect—
because, since, so that
(2) suggest condition—
unless, if, although
(3) indicate contrast—
whereas, while
(4) time relationships—
as, before, when, after
(5) parallel ideas—
however, therefore, hence

b. shifts in word meaning—
the use of familiar words in unfamiliar context, i.e.

(1) cabinet minister clergy furniture

(2) iron curtain? cold war? tariff wall?

c. classifying—
since learning often takes place through recognizing similarities and differences, it is essential to use this procedure.
(1) compare similarities and differences—
declaration and proclamation
(2) contrast differences—
a kingdom and a democracy
(3) paired qualities—
kind and gentle; humid and dank

No matter what procedure a teacher may wish to use for the introduction of vocabulary to any lesson it is vital that we understand the value of instruction in this area. If we wish to improve comprehension, we need to broaden our approach to include vocabulary development as a basic tool.

The SQ3R Study Formula

Students need to be taught how to study social studies as well as other subject areas. We often find elementary and secondary pupils who are so disorganized in their approach to the basic procedures that they do not know where or how to begin a study program. Robinson (9) proved the effectiveness of his study formula in his examination of college students' study habits. As a result, we have the SQ3R study formula in use throughout the entire educational strata.

Preston (6) suggests a modified approach for the elementary student beginning at the intermediate level. Strang (16) indicates a more difficult process whereby students at the high school level ask themselves a general question which cuts across the author's organization. We would not expect the same thoroughness or ability from an elementary youngster as we anticipate from a high school student. Since the application of the study method is one of degree dependent upon the grade level of the student, it is worthwhile to consider the following approach as a means of reaching most children.

Here is a sample lesson for the development of the SQ3R Study Formula that may be used from the intermediate level right on to the high school student. The language has been simplified in order that almost any child who reads at the fourth level or above might be able to understand the directions. Naturally, the teacher would direct the beginning lessons in the use of the procedure, but the student could retain the directional sheet for further study and reference.

S—Survey
Q—Question
R—Read
R—Recite
R—Review

STEP I—SURVEY

Look through the whole assignment before you actually read to answer your questions. You should look for all of the following items before you begin to read.

A. *Boldface type*
This is the heavy, dark, large print at the beginning of each chapter, section, and paragraph. Look at the name of the chapter and the section heading.
B. *Pictures with Captions*
The picture and its caption, which is the explanation of the picture, will help to tell about the material you will soon read.

C. *Charts*
A chart will give you much information at a glance. When you read the chart before you read the story, you will have much information to help you understand the paragraphs.

D. *Drawings with Captions*
A drawing is considered the same as a picture when you survey the material before you read. Look at the drawing and its caption to help you understand the chapter or section.

E. *Maps and Diagrams*
A map or diagram will explain many paragraphs of written material if you look at it before you begin to read. A map or diagram may reduce half a page of writing into one small drawing.

F. *Summary*
At the end of most chapters there is a summary. The summary tells very briefly about the information that is in the chapter. After you have read the summary, you will usually have a very good idea of the main topics in the chapter.

G. *Questions*
The author has added questions to his chapter to direct your attention to some of the important ideas. Be sure to look at the questions before you read the selection. This step will help you to be ready for the new thoughts you are about to read.

STEP 2—QUESTION

Use the boldface type to make your question. If the heading of the section is "Great Plains Soil," use these words to make the following questions:

What is Great Plains soil like?
Of what is Great Plains Soil made?
What must farmers consider when using Great Plains soil?

If there is no boldface type to help you make a question, use this question: What does the author expect me to learn about *this* topic from studying this selection?

A. *Study Guide*
1. Fold or rule a sheet of large-sized notebook paper lengthwise, down the middle.
2. Write your question on the left side of the page.
3. Answer your questions on the right side of the page.
4. When you write your answers use only key words to describe the ideas or facts you have decided are most important. *Do not write long answers.*
5. Be sure you have read the paragraph or section after your question and thought about it before you write the answer.

STEP 3—READ

Read the paragraph or section to find the answer to your question. Do not stop to read every word carefully; concentrate on finding the main point. You cannot remember all the facts you find, so you must look for the important ones. There are usually *one or two main points* for each section.

STEP 4—RECITE

After you have finished the assignment, go back over the lesson immediately. Cover the right side of the paper where the answers are written, and ask yourself the questions on the left side of the page.

Answer the question orally. That means you must say the answers *out loud* so that you will know if you have made a mistake.

If you find you cannot answer the questions, look back at the key words which are your answers. Sometimes you will have to go back to the book to restudy the particular part which you did not understand or have forgotten.

Step 4 is very important. When you give yourself an immediate quiz on what you have studied, it is the best possible way to prevent forgetting.

Practice until you can recite the whole study guide without looking back to the key words. Then practice some more. This extra practice is what pays off.

STEP 5—REVIEW

About four weeks later, and also before every examination, go back to your questions and answers again and quiz yourself. Reread only those parts which you have forgotten.

If you have taken steps 1 (Survey), 2 (Question), 3 (Read), and 4 (Recite) faithfully, you will find that you do not have too much to restudy.

Study Skills

Here is an area that encompasses all others previously discussed. In order for a student to apply himself to the full understanding of the material he has read in social studies, he must have basic knowledge of the study skills pertaining to his subject area.

Spache(15) states most students only receive training in reading of a basal reading type which often concludes by the fourth or sixth grade.

This has been the situation until quite recently. The influx of federal aid money has encouraged many school districts to begin advanced training and even developmental programs at the secondary level. The writer would certainly agree with Spache(15) and Strang(16) that advanced reading training should be provided by all teachers for effective reading in the content fields.

Smith(14) has pointed out that study skills improve in a specific content area if they are pulled out and given special attention. She has indicated how teachers may help children if they are taught to recognize the major patterns found in elementary textbooks which deal with content areas. The necessary skills defined for social studies are indicated by Smith(14): reading pictures; reading maps, globes, atlases; reading for cause and effect content; reading for comparison; reading for sequence; reading to locate dates with events; and reading critically to determine different viewpoints, facts mixed with opinion, and when propaganda is used.

Smith's(13, 14) basic grouping of skills common to all areas appears wide enough to include many authors in the field of reading study skills. Five major areas are listed for classification purposes: selection and evaluation, organization, location of information, following directions, and specialized skills.

Other authors have listed those skills necessary for learning social studies. Spache(15) has three categories which include (a) locating information, (b) organizing information, and (c) retaining and using information. Russell's(12) emphasis for the social studies area is applied to the ability to locate information in reference books. Bamman's(1) suggested skills fall into the general pattern of information skills. Robinson(10) applied the major areas as established by Smith with a slight variation in the EDL Study Skills Library. Here the same concepts are involved, but they are classified under the headings of interpretation, evaluation, organization, and reference (locating information) with the theme of following directions throughout all the lessons. *A Teacher's Guide to Curriculum Planning*(7) has extensive listings of skills which should be covered by the teacher as instruction is given to students in the social studies curriculum.

Robinson's(11) pilot study attempted to determine the reading skills fourth grade pupils actually used as they tried to solve problems in social studies. Although many study skills were put into practice properly, it is interesting to note those skills in which deficiencies existed or application was not made by the student. This small group of intermediate students did not make maximum use of retaining details, comparing information, grasping unstated main ideas, remembering relevant details, making inferences, or using the table of contents, headings or guides, pictorial aids, and the index. The author of the pilot study suggests the teacher should be aware of the student's reading skills, analyze the skills necessary to carry out an assignment, and teach those skills required to carry out the assignment.

Karlin(5) has prepared a checklist of study skills based upon the classifications suggested by Smith(13,14). It would be most helpful for the teacher to use this format in planning a program of instruction in study skills for the student.

Checklist of Study Skills (5)

I. Selection and Evaluation
   Can the student do the following?
   a. recognize the significance of the content
   b. recognize important details
   c. identify unrelated details
   d. find the main idea of a paragraph
   e. find the main idea of larger selections
   f. locate topic sentences
   g. locate answers to specific questions
   h. develop independent purposes for reading
   i. realize the author's purpose
   j. determine the accuracy and relevancy of information

II. Organization
   Can the student do the following?
   a. take notes
   b. determine relationship between paragraphs
   c. follow time sequences
   d. outline single paragraphs
   e. outline sections of a chapter
   f. outline an entire chapter
   g. summarize single paragraphs
   h. summarize larger units of material

III. Location of Information
   Can the student do the following?
   a. find information through a table of contents
   b. locate information through the index
   c. use a library card catalog to locate materials
   d. use the *Reader's Guide to Periodical Literature* to locate sources
      of information.
   e. use an almanac to obtain data
   f. understand and use various appendices
   g. use glossaries
   h. use encyclopedias to locate information

IV. Following Directions
   Can the student do the following?

    a. see the relation between the purposes and the directions
    b. follow one-step directions
    c. follow steps in sequence
  V. Specialized Skills
    Can the student do the following?
    a. understand the significance of pictorial aids
    b. read and interpret graphs
    c. read and interpret tables
    d. read and interpret charts
    e. read and interpret maps
    f. read and interpret cartoons
    g. read and interpret diagrams
    h. read and interpret pictures

Conclusion

Many factors are involved in teaching the essential reading skills in social studies. Teachers of this content area need to apply diverse methods and techniques in order that students may become more skilled as they read subject matter material. It would be useful to consider the overall approach which includes the directed reading activity, vocabulary development, a workable study formula, and applicable study skills for a worthwhile and effective program at the elementary and secondary level.

REFERENCES

1. Bamman, Henry A., Ursula Hogan, and Charles E. Green. *Reading Instruction in the Secondary Schools.* New York: McKay, 1961, 135–154.
2. *Five Steps to Reading Success in Science, Social Studies and Mathematics.* New York: Metropolitan School Study Council, Teachers College, Columbia University, 1960, 8–9.
3. Gates, Arthur I. "The Nature and Function of Reading in the Content Areas," *New Frontiers in Reading,* in J. Allen Figurel (Ed.), International Reading Association Conference Proceedings (Scholastic Magazines, New York) 5, 1960, 152.
4. Jenkinson, Marion D. "Increasing Reading Power in Social Studies," in *Corrective Reading in the High School Classroom,* in H. Alan Robinson and Sidney J. Rauch (Eds.), Perspectives in Reading No. 6, International Reading Association, Newark, Delaware, 1966, 75–87.
5. Karlin, Robert. *Teaching Reading in High School.* New York: Bobbs-Merrill, 1964, 140–141, 236.
6. Preston, Ralph C. "Sequence in Reading in the Content Areas in Social Studies," in *Sequential Development of Reading Abilities,* in Helen M. Robin-

son (Ed.), (Supplementary Educational Monographs, No. 90) December 1960, University of Chicago Press, 128.

7. *Reading—Grades 7-8-9-. A Teacher's Guide to Curriculum Planning.* Board of Education of the City of New York Curriculum Bulletin, 1957–58, Series No. 11.

8. *Reading in Secondary Schools.* The University of the State of New York. Albany, New York: The State Education Department, Bureau of Secondary Curriculum Development, 1965, 44–47.

9. Robinson, Francis P. *Effective Study.* New York: Harper, 1961.

10. Robinson, H. Alan, Stanford E. Taylor, and Helen Frackenpohl. *Teacher's Guide EDL Study Skills Library.* Huntington, New York: Educational Developmental Laboratories, 1962, 4–5.

11. Robinson, H. Alan. "Reading Skills Employed in Solving Social Studies Problems," *The Reading Teacher,* January 1965. International Reading Association, 263–269.

12. Russell, David H. *Children Learn To Read.* New York: Ginn, 1961, 339.

13. Smith, Nila Banton. "The Development of Basic Reading Techniques," *A Report of the Fifth Annual Conference on Reading.* University of Pittsburgh, 1949, 46–60.

14. Smith, Nila Banton. *Reading Instruction for Today's Children.* Englewood Cliffs, New Jersey: Prentice-Hall, 1963, 312, 348–349.

15. Spache, George D. *Toward Better Reading.* Champaign, Illinois: Garrard Publishing Company, 1963, 273–275; Chap. 18, 334–347.

16. Strang, Ruth, Constance M. McCullough, and Arthur E. Traxler. *The Improvement of Reading.* New York: McGraw-Hill, 1961, Chap. 6, 142–156.

17. *The Teaching of Reading.* The University of the State of New York, The State Education Department, Bureau of Elementary Curriculum Development, Albany, New York, 1963, 58–59.

18. Whipple, Gertrude. "Sequence in Reading in the Content Areas," in *Sequential Development of Reading Abilities,* in Helen M. Robinson (Ed.), Supplementary Educational Monographs, No. 90, December 1960. Chicago, Illinois: University of Chicago Press, 128.

36 The SQ3R Method in Grade Seven*

Sister Mary Donald, S.S.N.D.

The purpose of this study was to determine the effect of using the SQ3R method of study to increase reading and social studies achievements in Grade Seven. The study was limited to two equivalent groups of 31 seventh-grade pupils of a southern Minnesota parochial school.

The term SQ3R as used in this study was derived by Francis P. Robinson[1] from the first letters of the steps in the study process he developed: *S*urvey, *Q*uestion, *R*ead, *R*ecite, and *R*eview. The method is based on sound principles for effective learning and presents a high-level study skill for school work. The experiment was limited to one type of study. However, this included related study factors such as finding main ideas and details, using signal words and sectional headings in a book, developing a technical vocabulary, seeing relationships, taking notes, and interpreting graphs, pictures, and maps.

* From *Journal of Reading,* vol. 11, October 1967, pp. 33–35, 43. Reprinted with permission of Sister Mary Donald and the International Reading Association.
[1] Francis P. Robinson, *Effective Study* (New York: Harper & Row, 1946).

Procedure

The students participating in this experiment were divided into two groups, equated on the basis of mental age, intelligence quotient, reading, geography, and history scores. *The Coordinated Scales of Attainment,* an achievement battery test composed of nine areas including reading, history, and geography, was used to secure data for equating the groups. Mean differences were found to be insignificant.

During the course of the year, the SQ3R method was used in teaching social studies to the experimental group. The control group followed the traditional method of teaching assignments and pupil study—that is, group work, oral and written reports, silent and oral reading of content and answering of questions were the usual procedure of class work. No organized method beyond the textbook unit of study was presented to the students. Visual aids such as films, charts, and pictures were used to help develop understandings. Frequent check-up tests were given to ascertain the grasping of factual concepts.

During the period of investigation, the experimental group was given developmental lessons in the SQ3R method of study according to specific sequential steps as part of the regular reading instruction. Special guidance was given to pupils of the experimental group in surveying a lesson, setting up questions preliminary to reading, reading for a purpose, reciting or writing answers, and reviewing the matter studied. They were taught to survey the material by an intelligent skimming of chapter heads, subheads, pictures, maps, diagrams, and unit questions. This stimulated the students to think about what they already knew from previous study and experience and aroused their curiosity.

The next step was to convert headings into challenging questions which increased interest, resulting in better comprehension of the author's ideas. After questions were set up, the paragraphs were read for comprehension of the main ideas and details. Following the reading, the answers to the prepared questions were then recited or written. Different written techniques—including outlining, summaries, informal answers, and main idea statements—were used for variety. After each section of the lesson was studied in this way, the chapter was reviewed by sections with special effort made to recall the main ideas, details, and their relationships. Notes were reviewed before the next class period. This plan of assignments made study easy and led to more purposeful reading.

In order to keep the interest of the children high, several motivational devices were utilized as the experiment progressed. Posters were made to foster a better understanding of the concepts; articles in periodicals which stressed the need and success of the method were read to the children; notebooks were kept; and an occasional questionnaire on the value of the method and the attitude of the pupils toward it was given. The control group was motivated by an increased desire to achieve high grades, to increase their knowledge, and to complete the required material of the curriculum.

Certain variables were controlled: the same definite time for teaching and study was arranged each day; the same materials, curriculum, and reference books were used by both groups. As far as possible, teacher efficiency and enthusiasm were equalized.

Tests were used to evaluate learning outcomes in the experimental and control groups. At the end of each semester, tests constructed by me in geography and history were designed to evaluate the mastery of social studies concepts. This test had been previously validated for difficulty and discrimination[2] on a sample of 116 seventh-graders of the same school system not participating in the experiment. At the end of the year another form of the *Coordinated Scales of Attainment* was given. The initial scores of the control and experimental groups were compared with the final scores of both groups. Measures of central tendency and variability as well as the t-ratio to test significant difference of the mean scores were applied to the results of each group.

Results

Analysis of data from the study indicated that on the standardized tests gain was made by both the control and experimental groups from the initial to the final testing, but the gain did not indicate a statistically significant difference. The mean scores of the experimental group showed growth in reading from 7.66 to 8.64; geography 7.76 to 8.20; history 7.36 to 9.10. The control group's scores in reading showed a gain of 7.50 to 8.30; geography 7.28 to 8.04; history 7.02 to 8.47. The results of the standardized tests could disagree because of a difference between the subject matter taught in the school system and the material contained in the standardized items.

On the teacher-constructed tests of January and May which were prepared by the two teachers, there was a statistically significant difference between the means of the control and experimental group in favor of the experimental. On the January testing the difference in geography between the two groups was 5.73 and in history 10.86. The May testing indicated a difference of 6.69 in geography and 7.08 in history. These tests relied more heavily on judgment and critical evaluation. Both testings indicated significant difference at the .01 level of confidence, which implies that the

---

[2] John E. Stecklein, *How To Make an Item Analysis,* Bulletin on Classroom Testing (University of Minnesota: Bureau of Institutional Research, 1960).

gain made by one pupil out of every one hundred could be due to mere chance. From this one might deduce that the teaching of SQ3R was a contributing factor to the large gains made by the experimental group.

Conclusions

Within the limits of this study, the pupils at the junior high school level benefitted from the organized study method introduced in the SQ3R approach. The use of this method resulted in a significant difference in the factual type of knowledge of content material.

Test scores showed that this method developed better powers of organization, association, and critical thinking. Test scores did not indicate a significant difference on general reading ability, but the difference of the means showed a marginal gain in favor of the experimental group.

Teacher observations indicated that the SQ3R method resulted in the development of study skills and gave security in independent attack when confronting content material.

37 The Joplin Plan— Is It Effective for Intermediate- Grade Reading Instruction?*

Wilma H. Miller

The Joplin Plan—or inter-class grouping—is fairly widely used in today's intermediate grades. Has it really proven to be effective in meeting the reading needs of intermediate-grade pupils, or is it used because teachers feel that it enables them to more easily meet the reading needs of their pupils? This article reviews the origin of inter-class grouping and evaluates some of the most relevant research studies that have been conducted about its effectiveness. In the light of this evidence, a recommendation about its potential value can then be made.

The Origin of Inter-Class Grouping

Certainly inter-class grouping has a long history of use although the name "Joplin Plan" is quite new. One of the early attempts at inter-class grouping was the monitorial system originating in England in which teachers taught a hundred students at a time while smaller groups were taught by tutors. In the United States one of the first school systems to use an

*From *Elementary English,* vol. 46, November 1969, pp. 951–954. Reprinted by permission of the National Council of Teachers of English.

inter-grade grouping plan was in Detroit, Michigan. In this school system, inter-class grouping was called "vertical grouping," and pupils from different grades having comparable intelligence were grouped for instruction. Another early method of inter-class grouping was found in the San Francisco "circling plan" of 1930. In this plan students in the fourth, fifth, and sixth grades were placed in different reading classes on the basis of their reading ability. However the plan was discontinued in 1946 because it had not proven its unqualified effectiveness(1).

However, the greatest interest in inter-class grouping has occurred since 1952 when it was begun in Joplin, Missouri. It was called the Joplin Plan and was initiated by Cecil Floyd in the fourth, fifth, and sixth grades of one elementary school in this city during the 1952–1953 school year. Apparently, the teachers involved were pleased with the plan for it was later carried on in several other of Joplin's elementary schools. It gained nationwide attention in a *Saturday Evening Post* article by Roul Tunley entitled "Johnny Can Read in Joplin." In this article Tunley said that the use of the Joplin Plan would enable every elementary-grade child to make reading progress and to learn to love reading(5). The same month this article appeared, Russia launched its first space satellite which encouraged critics of the American education to ask why levels of academic achievement were not higher than they were. This event probably motivated a number of schools to try the new and apparently highly successful Joplin Plan of grouping.

A Description of the Joplin Plan

In implementing this plan, the principal and intermediate-grade teachers meet in Joplin near the end of each school year to assign pupils to one of the various reading levels that will be formed for the following year. The assignments are made mainly on the basis of group reading achievement tests given near the end of each school year. The grade level score is given the most weight in each assignment. However, some consideration also is given to each child's score on a group intelligence test and to the teacher's evaluation of each child's emotional adjustment and academic achievement in other areas. Pupils who are new in the Joplin system are given a reading achievement test and an informal reading inventory.

The groups are said to be flexible, and the teachers are encouraged to move the children to other reading levels if it is thought to be in their best interest. This plan of inter-class grouping seems to work best in larger elementary school buildings in which four to six intermediate grades can participate and in which six separate reading levels can be established—the third through the eighth reading levels.

In the Joplin Plan, the reading materials are mainly basal reader series with each building principal keeping an accurate list of the basal readers in his school so that these materials may be circulated to other buildings which are participating in the plan. However, basal reader workbooks are not used since it is felt that teacher-prepared worksheets are more valuable. In addition, a twenty minute recreational reading period is scheduled in the opposite half of the day from the one in which the regular reading instruction is found. At this time free reading is done individually at each child's instructional level and using materials that interest him.

In Joplin, standardized reading and achievement tests, teacher observation, and an informal reading inventory are used to evaluate each pupil. A special report card is used to evaluate the reading instruction conducted in Joplin. It contains the four major headings of oral reading, silent reading, word study skills, and recreational reading.

Research Studies Evaluating the Effectiveness of the Joplin Plan

Before the appearance of the 1957 *Saturday Evening Post* article, only one research study had evaluated the effectiveness of the Joplin Plan which used a control group in its experimental design. Since the *Post* article appeared, a number of research studies have been completed with nine of these studies employing the control group. In examining these nine studies, two were found which favored inter-class grouping, one was found which favored intra-class grouping in a self-contained classroom, and the remaining studies discovered that inter- and intra-grouping were about equally effective (1).

The differences in the findings of these nine studies probably were due to the variables involved in each study such as the sample size, the experimental design, each teacher's effectiveness and enthusiasm, and the evaluative instruments used. The Hawthorne Effect or the novelty effect might have produced the superior achievement in the two studies that favored inter-class grouping.

Several of these studies found differences in favor of inter-class grouping during the initial stages of the experiment, but the differences were not long term. For example, William Moorhouse discovered significant differences for inter-class grouping at the end of one semester of his experiment. However, after making additional comparisons at the end of three and five semesters, Moorhouse stated that the reading gain of pupils using the Joplin Plan was not better than that of pupils learning to read in graded classes (3). In all, the studies which continued for two or more years did not find that inter-class grouping resulted in significant gains in reading achievement, while the two studies which did discover significant differences in inter-class grouping lasted for only one year (1).

The sixteen reports of inter-class grouping which were based upon authority judgment (comparison of actual achievement with expected achievement) found advantages in the use of inter-class grouping. Apparently, the authors felt that inter-class grouping stimulated good reading achievement, enabled the pupils to achieve a good emotional and social adjustment, and enabled teachers to provide instruction more easily since the range of reading ability was reduced. Obviously, none of these reports is based upon statistical analyses so their value is lessened (4).

All authority judgment reports indicated that the majority of the teachers, pupils, and parents involved favored inter-class grouping. However, one research study found that when the subjects were allowed to remain anonymous, two-thirds of those in the lower reading level indicated that they would transfer to higher reading levels if given the chance (2).

An Evaluation of the Joplin Plan

Undoubtedly the most important advantage of the Joplin Plan is the teacher's attitude when employing it. If she is convinced that it makes her job of teaching reading more effective and easier, she may do a better job of teaching reading. However, it does not reduce the reading ability range completely since there are still many differences in the reading abilities of the children at each level.

The evaluative devices used to group children for the Joplin Plan most certainly are not infallible for such placement. Standardized survey tests normally measure only two aspects of reading ability—those of word meaning and paragraph reading. In a survey test these two areas also generally overestimate the actual reading level of a pupil by approximately two grade levels. In addition, survey tests do not measure other aspects of reading which should be carefully considered in placing a child in a reading group. Often some aspects of inferential comprehension, critical and creative reading, and the child's attitude toward reading are not measured in such tests. Teacher judgment of a child's reading ability sometimes is influenced by factors such as his behavior and general attitude toward school.

In using inter-class grouping, some teachers may be likely to forget that there still are differences in the reading ability of each group. There are components of reading in which a child achieves better than he does in other areas since reading is a highly complex process. Even the most efficient reader has areas in which he needs to make additional progress.

The basal reader approach as it is used in Joplin probably is not the best approach for intermediate-grade reading instruction. The basal readers are supplemented by daily free reading in Joplin, but some of the better readers probably do not need to use basal readers every day. They probably need additional instruction and practice in content area reading as well as a more extensive program of individualized reading.

The intermediate-grade teacher may not know each child as thoroughly as she would if he were in a self-contained classroom. Reading also may be considered apart from the total curriculum while using the Joplin Plan. It often is not integrated with instruction in the content areas such as social studies and science. Since this is the case, the reading skills learned are not reinforced as they should be.

When inter-class grouping is used, a child in the lower reading levels will have no one to emulate and no one to provide class leadership for him. On the other hand, the better reader may not develop the understanding that is necessary for life in a democratic society. In addition, parents will want to know into what reading level their child has been placed and may subsequently put pressure upon teachers and administrators to place him in a higher reading level.

In conclusion, since the majority of the reviewed research studies found no long-term achievement advantage to the use of the Joplin Plan, and since it contains so many potentially detrimental factors, it is not recommended for use in intermediate-grade reading instruction.

REFERENCES

1. Cushenbery, Donald C. "The Joplin Plan and Cross Grade Grouping," *Perspectives in Reading Number 9: Organizing for Individual Differences.* Newark, Delaware: International Reading Association, 1967–68, 33–45.
2. Kierstead, Reginald. "A Comparison and Evaluation of Two Methods of Organization for the Teaching of Reading," *Journal of Educational Research,* LVI (February, 1963), 317–321.
3. Moorhouse, William P. "Inter-Class Grouping for Reading Instruction," *Elementary School Journal,* LXIV (February, 1964), 280–286.
4. Ramsey, Wallace. *Perspectives in Reading Number 9: Organizing for Individual Differences.* Newark, Delaware: International Reading Association, 1967.
5. Tunley, Roul. "Johnny Can Read in Joplin," *Saturday Evening Post,* CCXXX (October, 1957), 108–110.

38 The Joplin Plan: An Evaluation*

William R. Powell

School personnel have long attempted to meet children's needs through various organizational patterns. In 1847, John Philbrick organized the first graded elementary school in Quincy, Massachusetts. Since then public schools have experimented with various plans for grouping in attempts to improve instruction. Shane has listed thirty-two types of grouping plans that have been used in classrooms in the United States(1).

The Joplin plan is one such plan. Basically it is a device for grouping children in the intermediate grades homogeneously on an interclass basis. The plan embodies the following successive steps: measuring the achievement and needs of children in the intermediate grades, organizing the children into relatively homogeneous groups independent of their grade classification, scheduling reading classes at the same hour during the day, and dispersing pupils to reading classes where the instruction is adapted to their needs(2).

Nation-wide Attention

Although the Joplin plan is not new, few educators or laymen had heard about it before 1957. In 1954 Floyd described the plan in a profes-

*From *Elementary School Journal,* vol. 64, April 1964, pp. 387–392.

sional journal(3). In 1957 the *Saturday Evening Post* described the plan for a lay audience(4), and in 1958 the *Reader's Digest*(4) reprinted a condensed version of the *Post* article. These publications gave the Joplin plan national recognition as well as its current name. The Joplin plan was then news. But there was still no objective proof for the results claimed by the proponents of this organizational design. About all it had to offer was sudden popularity.

In the month that the *Post* article appeared, the USSR launched Sputnik, the first space satellite. Sputnik had an immediate effect on education in the United States. Suddenly critics cried out that something was amiss in the schools, and the charges sent educators scurrying for panaceas. New methods and new teaching techniques were quickly adopted. Many plans that had not been validated rose to prominence. It was in this climate that some school systems adopted the Joplin plan to solve their reading problems.

There is still no empirical data to support claims for the superiority of this grouping plan. According to Morgan and Stucker(5), many school systems that use this plan report superior results in the middle grades, although there appears to be no published statistical research to validate the statements.

An evaluation of the Joplin plan seemed timely and necessary. There is a perennial interest in patterns of grouping pupils for instructional purposes. The opinions and claims of teachers who have used the Joplin plan are overwhelmingly favorable in spite of the lack of significant investigations of the plan.

The purpose of the study was to compare the reading achievement of intermediate-grade pupils who were taught reading under two different patterns of organization: the Joplin plan and the self-contained classroom. Ten hypotheses were proposed stating that there were no significant differences between the two groups in reading achievement for boys and girls, for boys only, for girls only, for high reading achievers, for low reading achievers, in spelling, in arithmetic, in social studies, in science and in study skills.

Sample and Procedure

Two public elementary schools in Indianapolis, Indiana were selected for this study. School A has had the Joplin plan since January, 1958. At the time of this evaluation, the plan had been operating there for about three and a half years. School B had self-contained classrooms.

Two groups of fourth-, fifth-, and sixth-grade pupils of School A and School B were included in this study. The pupils had been enrolled continuously in their respective schools since entering the fourth grade. The pupils in School A were given reading instruction under the organizational design of the Joplin plan; the pupils in School B were given instruction by reading in their self-contained classroom by their regular homeroom teacher. There were 164 pupils from School A and 207 pupils from School B.

School A and School B had a common boundary line. The socioeconomic level of the two school populations as measured by the Minnesota Scale of Paternal Occupations, was not significantly different. About 70 percent of the pupils in each of the two schools were classified in Class 5, the semi-skilled group, and Class 6, the slightly skilled group. Chi-square was applied to the two distributions and found to be 9.48. This value gives a probability of about .15, and the null hypothesis of no difference was sustained.

The two schools had about the same rates of promotion and attendance and about the same per cent of transfer pupils. Class size and time spent in reading in the two schools were approximately equal. The two school environments were similar. The schools were also compared on the basis of the availability of materials the extent of recreational reading by the pupils, and the extent of library participation by the pupils.

At the onset of the experimental program, the pupils in the two schools were approximately equal in reading achievements and in mental ability. The two groups were not far from the average city norms for these variables.

The teachers in School A and School B had about the same level of experience and training. The two schools had the same proportions of experienced and inexperienced teachers. The teaching staffs for the grades used in this study were compared on their understanding of reading problems. The test, The Elementary Grades: Teaching Tasks in Reading, was administered to all teachers of the classes used in this study. When a t test was applied to the means obtained from the teachers' scores, a t ratio of .98 was obtained. The null hypothesis of no difference was sustained.

The Henmon-Nelson Tests of Mental Ability: Revised Edition, Form B, were used to measure the mental ability of all the pupils included in the study. The Developmental Reading Tests, Intermediate Grades, Form R-A, by Bond, Clymer, and Hoyt were used to measure the reading achievement of the pupils in the intermediate grades. The Stanford Achievement Tests, Elementary and Intermediate Battery, Forms K and KM, were used to measure the achievement of the pupils in the content areas: spelling, arithmetic, social studies, science, and study skills.

At the end of October, 1961, the Henmon-Nelson Tests of Mental Ability and the Developmental Reading Tests were administered to all the pupils in their own classrooms by the investigator. In November, 1961, the Stanford Achievement Tests were administered to the pupils by their respective classroom teachers under ordinary classroom conditions. All tests were scored by, or under the direct supervision of, the investigator.

Coefficients of correlation were computed between the intelligence, mental age, chronological age, reading, spelling, and arithmetic scores to determine which variable had the greatest effect on reading achievement.

Means and standard deviations were computed for each of the ten distributions used in this study. A series of critical ratios were calculated for each of the ten hypotheses on mental age and achievement, using successively reading achievement for boys and girls, achievement for boys only, for girls only, for high achievers in reading, for low achievers in reading, spelling, arithmetic, social studies, science, and study skills.

High achieving pupils were defined as the upper third of the distribution in reading achievement. Low achieving pupils were defined as the lower third of the distribution in reading achievement.

In every instance the criterion of classification was between School A and School B. The 1 percent level of significance was used for rejecting the null hypothesis; the 5 percent level represented regions of doubt.

Findings

There were no significant differences between the test performance of the pupils in School A and School B in reading achievement.

There were no significant differences between the test performance of the boys or the girls in School A and School B in reading achievement.

There was a possible difference between the test performance of the superior readers of School A and School B in reading achievement. This difference would be at approximately the 5 percent level of confidence and would favor the superior readers of School B.

In reading achievement there were no significant differences between the test performance of the inferior readers of School A and those of School B.

In spelling achievement there were no significant differences between the test performance of the pupils in School A and School B.

In arithmetic there were no significant differences between the test performance of the pupils in School A and School B.

In social studies achievement there were no significant differences between the test performance of the pupils in Grades 5 and 6 in School A and School B. The tests used to measure achievement in social studies, science, and study skills were not administered to the pupils in Grade 4.

In science achievement there were significant differences between the test performance of the pupils in Grades 5 and 6 of School A and School B. The difference was significant at the 1 percent level of confidence in favor of the pupils in School B.

In study skills there were no significant differences between the test performance of the pupils in Grades 5 and 6 of School A and School B.

Conclusions

In this study definite attempts were made to equate the two schools that used different patterns of organization for reading instruction. The statistical treatment of the data collected indicated that the same results could be obtained with other random samples. The two schools were compared on important variables known to have an effect on reading achievement. The only limitation of this study was the degree to which these factors were comparable in the two schools.

In the light of the evidence obtained, the following conclusions were drawn:

1. The Joplin plan of organization for reading instruction produced no significant differences in reading achievement when reading achievement under that plan was compared with reading achievement in a comparable self-contained classroom situation. This finding applied to the reading achievement of the entire group, to boys separately, to girls separately, to high reading achievers, and to low reading achievers. There was some evidence in the study to suggest that the self-contained classroom possibly produced higher reading achievement for the superior readers than the Joplin plan did.

2. The Joplin plan of reading instruction did not produce any significant differences in performance in the content areas when achievement in those areas was compared with achievement in a self-contained classroom. Any difference that might favor the pupils in School B in science achievement could be attributed to the amount of time and the emphasis given science instruction in that school, not to the organizational design.

3. The Joplin plan of reading instruction as used in this study did encourage wider reading of recreational materials among elementary-school pupils. This effect may not be inherent in the Joplin plan. The finding may indicate that pupils will read more and more varied materials if periods for recreational reading are provided, if recreational reading is encouraged by the classroom teacher, and if the necessary reading materials are in the classroom.

4. An experimental program, such as the Joplin plan, can produce higher teacher interest and enthusiasm for the teaching of reading or possibly any content area. However, the type of organization and the teacher's enthusiasm may be less important than the type of learning activities that take place in a classroom. The results of this study suggest that it takes more than physical grouping arrangements to affect reading achievement.

5. To produce a significant difference in the amount of reading the pupils do, the materials for recreational reading must be in the classroom. This is true even if a public library is near, or even next to, a public school. The easier the access to reading material, the more pupils will read.

6. Regardless of school organization, reading performance for pupils in intermediate grades was not commensurate with their ability or grade level. In both schools, pupil performance upon entering the intermediate grades was approximately normal as indicated by standardized measures. However, during the intermediate grades pupil performance in both schools did not keep pace with the normal grade placement. With the large number of pupils included in this study, it would appear that a decrease in pupil performance would not happen by chance; there must be a reason for this drop in performance. No hypothesis was suggested for the decrease, but it is noteworthy that the decrease is statistically significant.

7. The consistency of the critical ratios in favor of School B, even though School A had a greater volume of pupil reading and greater teacher interest, implies that the Joplin plan, when considered in totality, was less effective than the self-contained classroom approach.

Recommendations

On the basis of the evidence produced by this study, the following recommendations for further investigation and discussion are made:

Studies similar to the present one should be conducted using samples from various populations, especially socioeconomic levels other than the one used in this study.

Studies similar to the present one should be conducted, but another definition of superior and inferior readers should be used.

Experiments should be undertaken to test the effect of accessibility of reading materials on the amount of reading accomplished. Studies should be made comparing the amount of reading children do when they have a classroom collection with the amount they do when they must rely on collections in public libraries near the school.

Studies should be undertaken to determine the validity of the type of instruction actually given to pupils in the intermediate grades.

Studies should be initiated to discover whether there is a significant decrease in reading performance in the intermediate grades and if there is a significant decrease to discover the reasons for it.

REFERENCES

1. Harold G. Shane. "Grouping in the Elementary School," *Phi Delta Kappan,* XII (April, 1960), 313–19.
2. William S. Gray. "The Teaching of Reading" in *Encyclopedia of Educational Research,* p. 1118. New York: Macmillan, 1960 (third edition).

3. Cecil Floyd. "Meeting Children's Reading Needs in the Middle Grades: A Preliminary Report," *Elementary School Journal,* IV (October, 1954), 99–103.
4. Roul Tunley. "Johnny *Can* Read in Joplin" *Saturday Evening Post,* CCXXX (October, 1957), 27+; also in the *Reader's Digest* LXXII (January, 1958), 41–44.
5. Elmer F. Morgan, Jr., and Gerald R. Stucker. "The Joplin Plan versus a Traditional Method," *Journal of Educational Psychology* LI (April, 1960), 69–73.

39 | Criteria for Effective Grouping*

Richard C. Wilson

Few issues in reading have gained more attention or have been embroiled in more controversy than grouping practices—perhaps because there are infinite reasons and ways to group children.

Grouping is more an organizational pattern than a method of teaching. Once a group is formed, regardless of the basis or criteria, what takes place is of more significance than the number, the interest, the age, the sex, the abilities, or grade placement of group members. Grouping is not a substitute for effective teaching. When groups are formed for a definite purpose to facilitate instruction, they are justifiable; otherwise, there are no defensible reasons for forming a special group.

Interclass and Intraclass Groups

Reading ability as measured by standardized tests or teacher judgment is the common basis for interclass and intraclass grouping. Interclass grouping may be vertical. The vertical, or across-grade plan, allows pupils

*From *Forging Ahead in Reading,* IRA Conference Proceedings, 1968, pp. 275–277. Reprinted with permission of the International Reading Association.

from two or more grade levels to meet as a unit for reading. This arrangement is typical of the Joplin plan. Sometimes ability groups are formed
within a specific grade level. This is a horizontal plan. For example, a
school with five sections of fourth grade may decide to arrange all pupils
in terms of total scores on a reading achievement test. The pupils are then
sectioned; one teacher is assigned the top fifth; another, the next; and so
on. Except for a formal reading period, the children function in a regular
heterogeneous or mixed classroom.

The grouping arrangement should not be confused with methodology.
Method is independent of grouping. Once a group meets, the teacher may
use any number of procedures for direct or indirect instruction.

Interclass grouping is most common in departmentalized elementary
and secondary schools. This arrangement lends itself well to a highly
structured and scheduled program.

Grouping Fallacies

In many typical interclass or departmentalized reading groups the
instruction provides little or no variation in materials or procedures. The
assumed homogeneity often precludes any emphasis upon individual
requirements and needs.

Intraclass grouping is a common elementary school practice, especially where teachers employ a basal reader type program. The usual
arrangement is three groups. The groups, labeled in a variety of ways,
are established to narrow the range of reading abilities in order to facilitate
teaching. Again, homogeneity is frequently based upon a single criterion—
total reading achievement measured by formal testing or teacher judgment. Variations in interest, rate, comprehension, vocabulary recognition,
and word concepts are rarely, if ever, a serious consideration.

The three-reading-group arrangement utilizes basal texts in about
three ways: (a) The same text may be used for all groups, but the pacing
varies, some groups may be reading at different rates and thereby the
story topics taught vary among the groups at a given time. (b) The same
text may be used for each group with pacing controlled for all, no group
in this instance changes stories until all change. (c) Each group may have
a different basal text and sometimes the texts are of different levels of
readability. The pacing under these circumstances may vary.

Once intraclass groups are formed, the composition seldom changes.
For many children, "Once a blue bird, always a blue bird!" Intraclass
grouping in a traditional setting, like interclass grouping, does little to
meet individual needs based on variables other than general ability.

Because standardized reading tests measure more than a single reading
skill, it is unreasonable to expect a high degree of homogeneity where

children are grouped according to a composite score. Yet, it is the rule rather than the exception to group on this criterion.

The values of grouping should not be lost because of limitations. Flexible grouping to meet a common, immediate need is widely recognized as a sound educational practice. Diagnostic teaching is the prerequisite. Obviously, grouping especially for a specific need cannot be done until common needs are determined. Why group for any reason if the grouping is planned to teach what the membership already knows? To do so is a needless waste. If a word skill, such as inflected endings, is to be taught, it makes sense to learn who needs the instruction rather than to teach everyone something needed only by a few.

Washburne (5) recognized the basic trouble inherent in any inflexible grouping plan when he wrote, "The difficulty with any attempt at grouping is that each child has his own characteristic profile of abilities and maturities." What is germane to grouping for one moment may be passé at another. An often overlooked danger in grouping is the tendency to see a child in a group as a member rather than as an individual. Wilhelm may have had this tendency in mind when he wrote, "Maybe the greatest hazard in this whole grouping business is that it causes some teachers to search constantly for similarity" (6).

Values

The limitations and pitfalls of grouping should not overshadow the worth and need for the grouping that facilitates and fosters learning and teaching. There are definite values in grouping that should not be forgotten. Here are some examples:

1. Many children participate more actively within small groups than within larger ones. The "auditorium" effect is lessened.
2. Often children need to be with others who have an interest in the same books or other reading materials.
3. The small group frequently facilitates interaction between teacher and pupils.
4. The exchange and sharing of materials is accomplished with greater ease within a small group.
5. Small group instruction minimizes the waste inherent in teaching a larger group for no greater reason than to regimentize teaching and keep all students reading the same materials at the same time (7).

Because of simple physics, sex, and the diversity of abilities, interests, instructional levels, personalities, social factors, and ages, groups should not be based on a single monolithic design. Grouping practices should serve all the variables to meet individual reading needs. The ability group should not be "the" group. No special group should be "the" group. As a matter of fact, it is worthy to consider McKim and Caskey's reminder, "All reading experiences do not call for groups"(4).

Guidelines

Here are some guidelines for grouping that may prove valuable at some appropriate time:

1. Every group should be flexible and subject to change. A stagnant group is as bad as no group.
2. Grouping should meet an immediate recognizable need.
3. Groups should be dissolved when their purposes have been met.
4. There should be no more groups operating simultaneously than can be judiciously handled.
5. Girls and boys sometimes like to be together for reading. On occasion they enjoy being separate. This is a good reason to group by sex sometimes.
6. Because the topic may be more important than "togetherness" on a reading test, grouping because of similar interests has merit.
7. For purposes of discussion, review, and some oral rereading, it makes sense to group when each member has different material about different topics. Bookclubs encourage the practice; children like it, too.
8. No member of a group should feel overwhelmed by the tasks set for the group.
9. Groups should operate with some degree of leadership. They should not shift aimlessly without some direction.
10. Grouping for reading should not isolate reading skills from content. Children should think of reading as a tool for learning rather than as a subject. Reading is a part of every subject.
11. Labeling groups should be for simple short-term identification. The use of such terms as fast, average, and slow should be avoided. Such labels unnecessarily stigmatize and erode a child's self-respect.
12. When possible, provide an opportunity for children to participate in developing group plans and activities; personal involvement fosters interest and good working relationships.
13. Anticipate obstacles and prepare the membership for certain difficult tasks. Discuss possible solutions.
14. Keep in contact with groups working independently. Help when needed; transfer members to other groups when goals are met.

Keep in mind that good grouping practices, like good teaching, do not foster conformity and uniformity, but differences. "In fact," Gray wrote, "good teaching at any level increases the range in reading ability from the poorest to the best"(2).

REFERENCES

1. Burton, William H., Clara Belle Baker, and Grace F. Kemp. *Reading in Child Development.* Indianapolis: Bobbs-Merrill, 1959.
2. Gray, William S. University of Pennsylvania Bulletin—Forty-second Annual Schoolmen's Week Proceeding, September 1955.
3. Hildreth, Gertrude. *Teaching Reading.* New York: Holt, Rinehart and Winston, 1958.
4. McKim, Margaret G. and Helen Caskey. *Guiding Growth in Reading.* New York: Macmillan, 1963, 152.
5. Washburne, Carleton W. "Adjusting the Program to the Child," *Educational Leadership,* December 1953, 38–147.
6. Wilhelm, Fred T. "Grouping within the Elementary Classroom," *NEA Journal,* 58, September 1959, 19–21.
7. Wilson, Richard C. *Individualized Reading: A Practical Approach.* Dubuque, Iowa: William C. Brown Co., 1965, 29.

PART V

DIAGNOSIS AND REMEDIATION OF READING DIFFICULTIES

This part includes articles on the evaluating of reading progress by the use of standardized survey reading tests and diagnostic reading tests. A survey reading test is given to a group of children and a measure of their overall reading ability in the areas of word knowledge and paragraph comprehension is obtained. On the other hand, a standardized diagnostic reading test usually is given individually and a measure of a student's specific reading weaknesses is found. The individual reading inventory is an informal test designed to give a measure of a student's various reading levels and specific reading needs.

McDonald (Selection 40) discusses some limitations in using standardized reading tests. In one article Criscuolo (Selection 41) cautions about over-reliance on the use of standardized reading test scores. Botel (Selection 42) discusses how to determine a student's independent, instructional, and frustration reading levels from the use of an individual reading inventory.

Several articles in this part contain suggestions for working with the culturally disadvantaged child in an elementary classroom. One selection contains many suggestions for working with a disabled reader in the elementary classroom in a program of corrective reading instruction.

Carlton and Moore (Selection 43) discuss how disadvantaged children can be helped in reading by the use of the self-directive dramatization. Miller (Selection 44) presents a reading program for disadvantaged children making use of the language-experience approach, special readers for the disadvantaged, and the individualized reading plan. Many extremely useful principles of corrective and remedial reading instruction are given by Bond and Tinker (Selection 45).

The following questions can be used to set purposes for reading the articles contained in Part V:

Do standardized survey reading tests give an accurate evaluation of a student's actual reading ability?

In what ways is an individual reading inventory superior to a standardized survey reading test?

What is the self-directive dramatization?

What are the titles of the special basal readers for use with culturally disadvantaged children?

How is remedial reading instruction different from developmental reading instruction?

40 Some Pitfalls in Evaluating Progress in Reading Instruction*

Arthur S. McDonald

In the past few years, dramatic results have been claimed for one after another "new method" of teaching reading. In the January, 1963, *Phi Delta Kappan,* the editor warned that most of these results had not been evaluated for possible contamination by the "Hawthorne effect." In point of fact, a number of pitfalls have been overlooked by many researchers in assessing reading instruction.

From the beginning of formalized reading instruction, various kinds of appraisal have been carried on to ascertain progress of an individual and/or a group. Research studies aimed at assessing the effectiveness of different kinds of reading instructional programs have also been conducted.

My own review of published studies in the past ten years shows that the three most commonly used methods for evaluating progress in reading programs are:

1. Determining reading gains by comparison of pre- and post-test scores on alternate test forms of both standardized and informal tests, and finding difference in test performance from that expected (e.g., "Johnny gained six months in reading test performance during a six-week reading program").

*From *Phi Delta Kappan,* vol. 45, April 1964, pp. 336–338.

2. Comparing test gains with the national average yearly gains made with those made in the local reading program.

3. Comparing test-retest results of the remedial group with test-retest performance of a control group.

Of these three methods, the first one is most commonly used in classroom and reading clinic descriptive reports. The third is most usual in published reports of research studies.

Sources of Error

In recent years, several writers have pointed out the dangers inherent in these methods. Among pitfalls are these:

1. Failure to correct for regression to the mean. (Most remedial students are selected on the basis of low initial reading test scores. On a second testing, persons so selected are likely to make higher test scores whether or not they have *actually* improved in reading ability.)

2. Treating reading grade scores as empirically obtained indications of month-by-month progress. In reality, reading grade scores are extrapolated from one grade level to another. (Spache has pointed out that experiments using repeated testing indicate that reading growth is not evenly distributed throughout the year but occurs in an initial spurt during the first few weeks or months of the year.)[1]

3. Interpretation of test scores on the assumption that the tests used provide reliable and valid measures of the most important aspects of reading.

4. Spurious scores obtained from the use of a single test over wide educational (or performance) levels. (For instance, on one commonly used type of reading test a non-reader can miss all the questions and earn a reading grade score of 1.6. If another level of this test were used with the same child, his score would be approximately third reading grade level.)

5. Use, for checking reading comprehension, of test questions which can be answered by most children from their background knowledge (i.e., without even reading the selection).

6. Errors in interpretation because of use of inappropriate norms, failure to allow for inter-form differences in equivalence, etc.

7. Failure to select a really comparable control group.

Other Sources of Error

Even a carefully designed study, however, one carried out with comparable experimental and control groups under conditions providing for

[1] George D. Spache, *Toward Better Reading.* Champaign: Gerrard Press, 1963.

control of many important variables (including student and teacher motivation), may still be vitiated by errors. These errors may arise, in part, because too little attention is paid to reading as a *form of behavior* and, in part, because of errors *inherent in the experimental model itself.*

Thus, in the absence of special precautions, the results obtained by use of comparable-groups methods are likely to be confounded by "Hawthorne" and "placebo" effects.

Cook has defined the Hawthorne effect as ". . . a phenomenon characterized by an awareness on the part of the subjects of special treatment created by artificial experimental conditions."[2]

As partial explanation of this consequence, Orne has shown that "as far as the subject is able, he will behave in an experimental context in a manner designed to play the role of a 'good subject.'"[3] In other words, the student in either an experimental or control group will try to validate the experiment as he understands it.

A special form of the Hawthorne effect accompanies the use of apparatus, equipment, drugs, special instructional material, ritual, "secret methods," etc. This is called "placebo response."

Following Fischer and Dlin,[4] a "placebo" may be defined as a chemical, mechanical, electronic, or psychological agent or treatment employed, with or without ritual, but always with the suggestion or implication of its powerful and helpful properties. The "placebo response" is that effect of the agent or treatment which cannot be due to the agent or treatment itself but which must be due to some other aspect of the situation.

Thus the placebo effect may be related to the attitude (enthusiasm, belief, optimism, etc.) of the administrator, to the administrator, to the atmosphere (security, insecurity, competitiveness, challenge, etc.), to the treatment situation itself, to the expectancy of *both* the subjects and the experimenter.

Often overlooked in assessment studies, in fact, is the considerable research evidence available that the subject's expectations, the cues provided by the environment and the attitudes and expectations of the instructor or experimenter, may significantly alter the effectiveness of the treatment used and the consequences of the study.

As an example, college students who believed they were getting dexedrine (and who *were* receiving dexedrine) had typical energizer-like reactions in both mood and psycho-motor performance, while students who received dexedrine (but *believed* they were getting a barbiturate) showed

[2] Desmond L. Cook, "The Hawthorne Effect in Educational Research," *Phi Delta Kappan,* 44, 1962, p. 118.

[3] Martin T. Orne, "On the Social Psychology of the Psychological Experiment: With Particular Reference to Demand Characteristics and Their Implications," *American Psychologist,* 17, 1962, p. 778.

[4] J. K. Fischer and B. M. Dlin, "The Dynamics of Placebo Therapy: A Clinical Study," *American Journal of Medical Science,* 232, 1956, pp. 504–512.

a tendency toward barbiturate-like reactions. It should be noted that the percentage of such typical *student* responses, however, dropped markedly when the *experimenters* knew what drug was being administered.[5]

In another experiment college students were *not* aware that decaffeinated and regular coffee were administered (to the entire group) at different times, but were told that tests were being made to check certain effects of caffeine. The same effects were reported in a similar way for *both* kinds of beverage. When the subjects were told, however, that decaffeinated coffee was being used "just to prove that it was the caffeine that produced the changes" (but *both* regular and decaffeinated coffee were administered as before to all students), *all* effects being measured returned to pretest conditions.[6] (It is interesting to note that an earlier variation of this experiment, using milk, has often been cited in popular articles as proving that caffeine does not keep one awake.)

Considerable research has shown that the *mere act* of using special treatment or instructional devices, material, drugs, etc., strongly increases their effect. Furthermore, the *intra*individual variation in response to Hawthorne and placebo effects has been shown to be as great as the *inter*individual variation of such responses. The Hawthorne and placebo effects produced depend not only on the particular agent or ritual used and the method of administration but also on the circumstances under which these are used and how the effects are measured. Thus the expectations of the subject, the experimenter, and the nature of the situation in which an agent is administered, a device used, or a course of remediation carried out are important determiners of the effects. Vague means of measuring outcomes, tests with low reliability, and heavy reliance on subjective evaluation strongly favor contamination of results with placebo and Hawthorne responses.

Thus unwanted Hawthorne and placebo contamination is particularly likely in reading programs where the instructors rely heavily on special instrumentation (and themselves believe in the unique beneficial effects of the instruments), or believe strongly in the "powerful" effects of a novel method of instruction, or have found a completely new means of instruction which they believe cannot be measured by existing assessment instruments.

The greater the stress, anxiety, or hope surrounding the circumstances of the treatment or experiment, the greater the desire of the subject to improve, the higher the enthusiastic belief of the experimenter or instructor in the agent and technique used, the greater the tendency for Hawthorne and placebo responses to appear.

[5] Jonathan O. Cole, "The Influence of Drugs on the Individual," in Seymour M. Farber and Roger H. L. Wilson (eds.), *Control of the Mind.* New York: McGraw-Hill, 1961, pp. 110–120.
[6] L. D. Goodfellow, "Significant Incidental Factors in the Measurement of Auditory Sensitivity," *Journal of General Psychology,* 35, 1946, pp. 33–41.

Investigations have shown that completely inert substances, useless agents, or exhortations (such as "read faster, comprehend more"), when used with the understanding that they would produce certain effects, did indeed cause such effects to appear in 20 to 60 percent of the subjects. Lehmann reported that "giving a placebo capsule in a well-controlled, double-blind experimental procedure produced test-retest differences which were larger and of greater significance than the administration of effective doses of psycho-active drugs.[7]

Experimenter Must Be 'Blind'

Nash has pointed out the importance of measures taken by the experimenter to increase his "blindness" concerning the subjects in the experiment and the absolute necessity of his paying close attention to his own desires regarding the outcome of the experiment so that he can erect safeguards against the operation of bias or placebo effects arising from experimenter or subject expectancy. He concludes that systematic errors due to suggestion can be reduced if the conditions affecting suggestion and expectancy are kept approximately the same for control and experimental subjects.[8]

Thus in any study of the effects of initial instruction or corrective or remedial treatment, it is absolutely necessary to assess the Hawthorne and placebo reactions. To show that a certain kind of program or type of reading instruction produces more than a nonspecific Hawthorne or placebo response, it must be shown that its effects are stronger, last longer, and are qualitatively different from those produced by placebo agents (as defined in this article) or by the Hawthorne effect, or that the program affects different kinds of subjects than do placebo and Hawthorne reactions.

In this connection, Spache has warned that by dramatic use of novel methods or impressive equipment "it is possible to produce for a brief space of time what appears to be more than normal progress by remedial techniques or methods that are completely contradictory or even irrelevant to the causes of the reading retardation."[9]

My review of relevant research published in the last ten years shows that more than 80 percent of the studies dealing with evaluation of progress in reading programs of various types at all levels of instruction from ele-

[7] Heinze E. Lehmann, "The Place and Purpose of Objective Methods in Psychopharmacology," in Leonard Uhr and James G. Miller (eds.), *Drugs and Behavior.* New York: Wiley, 1960, pp. 107–127.
[8] Harvey Nash, "The Design and Conduct of Experiments on the Psychological Effects of Drugs," in Leonard Uhr and James G. Miller (eds.), *Drugs and Behavior.* New York: Wiley, 1960, pp. 128–156.
[9] Spache, *op. cit.*

mentary to college suffer from serious (but apparently unsuspected or un-assessed) contamination due to the Hawthorne and placebo effects.

Implications

Improved evaluation of reading progress requires:

1. Careful delineation of objectives in *operational* terms. (What kinds of reading problems can we help with testable techniques and materials? What kinds of reading problems remain unaffected by our current procedures or show only Hawthorne and placebo reactions?)

2. Appropriate generalization from the experimental or clinical situation to the daily teaching situation *elsewhere.*

3. Controlling for Hawthorne and placebo contamination. (Cook cites suggestions that the placebo treatment be used to control the Hawthorne effect. For example, avoid singling out experimental and control groups. Use some form of special instrumentation, specially scheduled time and instructional material, stamped "Experimental Edition," with all students. This approach must contain safeguards against teacher expectancy.)[10]

4. What conditions and procedures in commonly used remedial programs are especially favorable for the occurrence of Hawthorne and placebo responses? What are the most common responses of the nature encountered?

[10] Cook, *op. cit.*

41 | Reading Test Scores Don't Tell the Whole Story*

Nicholas P. Criscuolo

Reading test results usually are judged solely on the basis of scores. If the median last year was lower than this year, the reading program is hailed a success. If the reverse occurs, the program is labeled a failure.

To get the full meaning—and the most for the school district's money—from reading tests, results should be used not only to measure how the program is faring compared with last year, but also to develop a more effective reading program. Four factors that affect results often get overlooked:

1. Pupil Mobility

This usually is a problem in Northern urban school districts that have had an influx of children from deprived areas of the South and from Puerto Rico. Many of the experiences of these children do not parallel those of youngsters who have been living in cities for a long time. The disadvantaged children often perform poorly on tests mainly because of drawbacks

*From *Nation's Schools,* vol. 79, no. 5, May 1967, p. 24. Reprinted with permission of *Nation's Schools,* May 1967. Copyright 1967, McGraw-Hill, Inc., Chicago. All rights reserved.

in environment, not in native ability. Language barriers often add further complications.

When two sections that usually comprise a standardized reading test— word knowledge and paragraph meaning—are compared, test scores for the word section frequently are lower among the disadvantaged. The section often contains words such as barbecue or balcony. City-bred youngsters know what they mean, while their deprived classmates, who may be able to read the word, will fail the test because they do not understand.

Improvement   Teachers should do everything possible to enrich the youngster's background before a test. This will help a pupil relate middle-class values often expressed in basal readers and expand word knowledge at the same time.

2. Following Directions

The correlation between socioeconomic level and reading ability is high. As a rule, the lower the social class, the higher the percentage of youngsters who are penalized on the final score because they do not follow directions. Taking a reading test is a structured situation, and children must listen carefully as the teacher gives directions. Listening is too much of a challenge to many children in lower social levels. Within their home environment, parents argue, TV sets blare, and babies wail. They learn to tune out and avoid listening to most of what's going on around them.

Improvement   Teachers should study carefully manuals that accompany basic reading texts. They contain many suggestions for activities and games to improve listening skills, as well as the ability to follow directions. Tape-recorded directions also can stimulate pupils to listen and, in some cases, perform better at other learning tasks.

3. Choosing the Right Test

Test selection requires sophistication and orientation to testing procedures. For this reason, selecting an appropriate test should be a joint effort of a committee comprised of members of the administrative and supervisory staffs. The crucial question should be: Is this test right for *our* school?

Improvement   Before selecting a reading test to administer on a city-wide basis, examine it carefully for content of skills tested, standardization for the population, validity, reliability and statistical procedures used.

4. Purpose of Tests

Too often a reading test is given by the teacher, corrected, reviewed by the school principal, recorded on the child's test record—and forgotten. When this happens, obviously, there is no point to giving tests.

Improvement   To discover a pupil's strengths and weaknesses, the teacher should analyze test items failed and passed. He should use this information for improving course content. Finally, those children who make a poor showing on tests should be referred to the district reading specialist for a more thorough diagnosis of their reading difficulties.

42 | Ascertaining Instructional Levels*

Morton Botel

Are these truths self-evident?

1. Each pupil is unique, and his reading program must be tailored to this uniqueness.
2. The reading program includes library books, readers, subject matter textbooks, and newspapers.
3. If so, it follows that each pupil must be reading materials in which he is fluent in oral reading and in which his comprehension of vocabulary, details, and main ideas is very high.

Interestingly enough, we find many teachers, supervisors, and school systems who affirm these ideas in written and oral statements of beliefs but whose programs do not reflect such verbal affirmations. For example, in these same schools we find pupils whose oral reading can be characterized as dysfluent and whose comprehension is fuzzy or worse in one or more of the reading-media forms mentioned above. In too many instances such crippling performance is evident in all reading media. It is also true at the other extreme that pupils may be using materials which offer no challenge.

*From *Forging Ahead in Reading,* IRA Conference Proceedings, 1968, pp. 171–174. Reprinted with permission of Morton Botel and the International Reading Association.

Either extreme illustrates how a school, in practice, tries to fit the pupil to a nonfitting book rather than to fit the book to the pupil.

Our rationale for fitting books to the pupil is based on both psychological and linguistic evidence. From a psychological point of view we have evidence that the most efficient learning takes place where pupils are highly motivated, where their self-esteem is enhanced, and where they have rather full comprehension of what they are doing. For those who are overplaced in reading, such lack of success leads to discouragement, loss of dignity or ego support, withdrawal, and often to hostility. At the opposite extreme, to the underplaced the lack of challenge offers inadequate opportunity for involvement, and the effect is to dampen the enthusiasm of these able pupils.

From a linguistic point of view we know that pupils who are dysfluent will find it difficult to make the proper connection between the melodies of oral language and the incomplete representation of these language structures in writing. Some of the fundamental meaning in language, as we know from our studies in linguistics, as expressed through the intonational structures of stress, pitch, and juncture. If we encumber the poor reader with written material which he cannot decode easily from the point of view of word recognition and attack, how can we expect him to provide for himself these missing intonational features?

Given this psychological and linguistic rationale as the basis for matching pupils with readable books, we need to adopt or invent procedures for accomplishing this purpose for each pupil at every grade level in every subject. It has been my experience that this goal will not be achieved generally in a school unless it is spelled out as a matter of policy and implemented in well-defined ways.

In general these procedures are all variations of the informal reading inventory which usually defines the limits of three reading levels for each pupil as summarized in the following chart:

| | Performance in Context | |
| | Oral | Silent |
Levels	Fluency	Comprehension
Independent	99–100%	95–100%
Instructional	95– 98%	75– 94%
Frustration or Overplacement	less than 95%	less than 75%

Some significant schoolwide procedures which are concerned with ascertaining and placing pupils at their instructional levels are: (a) informal teacher appraisal, (b) check-out procedures, and (c) the Informal Reading Inventory and placement tests.

Informal Teacher Appraisal

There is no doubt in my mind that informal teacher appraisal in every subject and in every grade is the ideal approach to the continuous problem of ascertaining instructional levels. Every time a pupil reads aloud and answers a question or completes an activity sheet independently the teacher can determine whether the criteria indicated in the preceding chart are being met. If not, the sensitive teacher can immediately provide such needed help in overcoming the problems leading to lack of fluency or inadequate comprehension as the following:

a. The use of an easier book in a series,
b. More preparation before the pupil is asked to work independently,
c. The substitutions of easy, wide reading experiences for a time, and
d. The substitution of other more appropriate media for the frustrating book.

Check-out Procedures

Many of the school systems I have served have instituted check-out procedures by which reading specialists, master teachers, or principals share with the teacher the responsibility of advancing pupils when they have "mastered" a book in a structured series according to the IRI criteria chartered earlier.

Sometimes this check-out is done in the classroom; sometimes it is done in the principal's office. Sometimes the teacher and class listen in as each pupil reads; sometimes the pupil reads only to the collaborating specialist. To check his oral reading fluency a pupil may be asked to reread familiar stories in the back of his "completed" reader; sometimes he may be asked to read orally at sight in the next reader.

As a check on extent of comprehension, nothing seems to us a more valid criterion or more reliable a measure than the average performance of a pupil on the pages of the workbook he has completed *independently*. Additional comprehension checks may be obtained by asking the pupil questions about stories he has just read or by asking him to summarize briefly the most important ideas or events in a paragraph, a page, or a story.

I have used a variation of this check-out procedure as a basic element in evaluations and surveys I have conducted for schools. These schools are asked to keep a record of the percentage of accuracy of each pupil on five pages of the reading workbook he is using and to record the percentage of accuracy of the oral sight reading of each pupil on 100 running words in the next story in his reader.

Pupils failing to achieve a score of at least 75% in average comprehension *and* at least 95% in oral reading are regarded as probably overplaced.

Reading Fluency and Comprehension Survey

Directions: 1. *Under Oral Reading Fluency* record the percent of words in 100 running words in a new story which the pupils read correctly. Errors are words which pupils mispronounce, refuse to pronounce within five seconds, omit, or insert.

2. *Under Comprehension* record the percent of accuracy on each of five successive pages in the pupil's workbook which he has completed independently.

Pupil	Percent of Oral Reading Fluency	Percent of Comprehension					
		1	2	3	4	5	Average

In some schools, particularly in so-called culturally disadvantaged areas, I have found instances in some classes in which almost every pupil is over-placed in basal readers and in textbooks in the subject areas.

A simple and useful variation of the check-out which I recommend to parents and librarians is this: after a pupil has chosen a book from the library or for purchase, he should be given the "five-finger" check. You do this by marking off or noting a 100-word sequence of words that looks typical of the book and have the pupil read it aloud at sight. If you count more than five errors, the book is probably too difficult and the child should be guided to a more appropriate book.

Reading Inventories

Anyone may develop reading inventories by using pages from structured or scaled reading materials as described in many sources (1,2,4,5). Others may be obtained from reading clinics and some publishers (3,7). Reading inventories vary in length, comprehensiveness, and practicality for the classroom teacher. All, however, provide an estimate of the instructional levels of pupils. Our own Botel Reading Inventory (3) — a measure easy to administer and interpret and considerate of the time pressures of the teacher of 25 or more pupils — was developed with the classroom teacher in mind.

In any event, and this is most important, we must regard the results on these reading inventories as starting points. Nothing can take the place of the continuous informal teacher appraisal after the first estimate has been made by the use of the reading inventory. Only if we follow this procedure are we assured high validity and reliability of our appraisals. Continuous appraisal provides the most meaningful validity in that it is based directly upon the materials and methods we are using and provides high reliability in that our pace and even our level can be modified if a pattern of unsatisfactory fluency or comprehension develops.

The significance which we have come to attach to ascertaining instructional levels and to effective placement of pupils using such methods as described in this paper is probably best expressed by the fact that we believe the eleventh commandment is: Thou shalt not overplace pupils.

REFERENCES

1. Betts, Emmett A. *Foundations of Reading Instruction.* New York: American Book, 1957, 438–485.
2. Botel, Morton. *How To Teach Reading.* Chicago: Follett, 1959, 15–24.
3. Botel, Morton. *The Botel Reading Inventory.* Chicago: Follett, 1961.
4. Harris, Albert J. *How To Increase Reading Ability.* New York: Longmans, Green & Co., (Fourth edition) 1961, 152, 161.
5. Johnson, Marjorie and Roy Kress. *Informal Reading Inventories.* Newark, Delaware: International Reading Association, 1965.
6. Karlin, Robert. *Teaching Reading in High School.* Indianapolis: Bobbs-Merrill, 1964, 73–78.
7. McCracken, Robert. *The Standard Inventory.* Bellingham, Washington: Western Washington State College, 1966.

43 | Culturally Disadvantaged Children Can Be Helped*

Lessie Carlton
Robert H. Moore

People often assume that culturally disadvantaged children cannot make normal progress in school unless conditions in their homes are improved. We believe that this assumption is false, that the school can bring about normal learning progress by providing effective learning experiences, developing a favorable classroom climate, and fostering positive self-concepts.

To determine the validity of this belief, we conducted a study (and a recent corroborative follow-up) in which teachers of culturally disadvantaged elementary children used self-selection and self-directive dramatization of stories by pupils to teach reading.

Classes in each of the first four grades of a school in a very old area of Joliet, Illinois, made up the experimental group. Of the total school population of about 500 children, 85 percent were Negro and 5 percent Puerto Rican and Mexican. Children moved in and out of the community often and very few school records were available. The economic level of the community was low, and pupils frequently came to school crying be-

*From *National Education Association Journal,* September 1966, pp. 13–14. The study reported herein was supported as Cooperative Research Project S-190 by the Cooperative Research Program of the U.S. Office of Education.

cause of cold and hunger. Since the school had no lunch program, many children remained hungry all day.

We found most of the children to be emotionally unstable. They talked incessantly, but rarely to anyone in particular. If a pencil fell on the floor, they would often shout "Thief!" and accuse someone of taking it. They hit each other. They tattled. They moved continuously.

Although we recognized the possibility of obtaining inaccurate results, we administered reading achievement and mental maturity tests to all the children in both the experimental and the control groups. A large percentage in both groups had low intelligence-quotient scores, and the majority were much below their grade level in reading achievement.

Three women and one man taught the experimental groups. All four had studied the techniques of self-directive dramatization, and two had taken part in a similar study with classes made up largely of middle-class white children. One teacher had taught two years in a school which used basal reading books and three reading groups. Another was a beginning teacher.

The teachers of the control group had more experience teaching the culturally disadvantaged than the teachers of the experimental group and had been in their present positions longer but they had not studied techniques of self-directive dramatization. During the study, they gave reading instruction chiefly through the traditional use of a basal reader and mainly in formal whole-class or small-group instruction. No special teachers worked with either the experimental of the control group.

Matches for each pupil in the experimental group were selected from other classes in the same school and from classes in another elementary school with a population of similar racial makeup and socioeconomic level.

To provide for the needs and desires of all the children in the experimental group, books on many different reading levels were made available in the classroom. As a preliminary step to self-directive dramatization, the children selected their own stories and read alone. Gradually they began to work in pairs and in small groups and to take turns reading to each other.

The groups were formed according to each child's preference for a story to read and dramatize. After the children in a particular group had read the story cooperatively, they agreed upon which character each would portray in the complete dramatization. Generally the groups selected different stories and stories on different reading levels. The groups all read their stories at the same time but took turns in dramatizing them. The dramatizations were spontaneous and completely unrehearsed.

Self-directive dramatization was employed in this study not only to find out what gains children would make in reading but also to see if pupils' self-concepts would change. We assumed that a change from a negative to a positive self-concept would contribute to progress in reading.

On the supposition that a child's behavior reflects his concept of himself, we made up a checklist of thirty-one questions dealing with different behaviors. Before the beginning of self-directive dramatization, teachers of the experimental group observed each child in relation to these questions and recorded the observations. At the end of the year, teachers checked the questions again to see what gains each child had made.

Typical checklist questions were:

1. Does the pupil refuse to do things because he thinks he does not do them well enough?
2. Does he try to have the attention of the teacher at all times?
3. Does he often fail to finish what he starts?
4. Does he do things to attract attention—make faces, talk loudly, try to "steal the show"?
5. Does he show signs of being jealous (of a child's new clothes or praise given another pupil, for example)?

The number of checks before and after the use of self-directive dramatization in the classroom led to the inference that desirable changes did occur in the self-concept of the pupils. The following are the number of checks for the children of each grade before and after the self-directive dramatization.

	Grade 1	Grade 2	Grade 3	Grade 4
Before	519	480	318	558
After	204	82	104	105

After participating in self-directive dramatization, many of the children were able to sit together without hitting each other. Intermittently, they still talked at the same time, but not excitedly and unceasingly. They were also a bit more willing to take turns. In various ways, they showed that they felt more kindly not only toward their classmates but toward the adults who worked with them. One child wrote this letter to us:

"You are kind to us. Our teacher is kind to us. You bring us books that we like. Be careful on the highway when you come back to see us."

Children who had refused to have anything to do with reading at the beginning of the school year now often preferred reading to going outside to play, especially if they could find someone to sit near them and listen to them read. This was a great change from the early part of the school year when a boy threatened one of the investigators with his fists for offering to help him read.

Now, too, the children talked with visitors or strangers who came to the school. They smiled occasionally and had lost much of their look of fear, hostility, or suspicion.

In all four experimental groups, the mean gains in reading exceeded those of the control groups. In addition, the gains of all the experimental groups were greater than would be considered "normal" for the length of time involved. For example, the first graders in the experimental group gained more than one year in reading over a period of about three-and-one-half months. The gains for the other grades were made over a seven-and-one-half month period.

The first two columns of the table below show the mean reading grade scores for each grade of the experimental group before and after the experiment; the last two columns show the mean gains of the experimental and control groups.

Mean for Each Grade of Experimental Group		Gain of Experimental Group	Gain of Control Group
Before	After		
Gr. 1 0.58	1.71	1.13	0.24
Gr. 2 1.26	3.13	1.87	1.25
Gr. 3 2.17	3.35	1.18	0.79
Gr. 4 3.39	4.24	0.85	0.43

The results of the reading tests seem to confirm our belief that culturally disadvantaged children can learn if good teachers supplied with appropriate materials employ the best possible methods of teaching.

Among these methods, self-directed dramatization seems to be particularly effective for a number of reasons. On the basis of the study, we feel that it can contribute to the improvement of self-concept of pupils and can help develop their skills in reading. It provides pupils with a chance to express themselves in the guise of somebody else and gives them a chance for physical activity—almost a necessity because these deprived youngsters are inclined to be excitable, restless, and unable to concentrate on desk work for any length of time.

In short, our study suggests that the technique of self-selection and self-directive dramatization of stories may prove to be a major means of upgrading the educational level and improving the personal and social adjustment of culturally disadvantaged pupils.

44 A Reading Program for Disadvantaged Children*

Wilma H. Miller

Excellent academic programs for culturally disadvantaged children have been the topic of considerable research and discussion during the past several years. The best teaching strategies and ideal teacher characteristics have been proposed by a number of specialists in the area of cultural deprivation. This article will briefly review some research directly related to teaching primary-grade reading to culturally disadvantaged children and propose a number of ways of teaching reading that may best insure reading success for the children.

Characteristics of Culturally Disadvantaged Children

The culturally disadvantaged child has a number of special characteristics that must be considered when planning a primary-grade reading program for him. Such a child usually comes from a home which is impoverished of physical stimuli for concept building, has little parent-child interaction, and may not have standard or correct language which he can

*From *Illinois Schools Journal,* vol. 49, Summer 1969, pp. 111–116.

imitate. The lack of physical stimuli and the opportunity to engage in many first-hand and vicarious experiences can lead to a lack of the experiences necessary to effectively interpret the reading material which is encountered in the primary grades. The culturally deprived child's intellectual development is undoubtedly influenced by the lack of parent-child interaction and interest in his home. Many parents of the disadvantaged typically employ a restricted language style which uses few complex sentences, few elaborated verb forms, few adjectives and adverbs, and an imprecise vocabulary. The style of language the disadvantaged child learns at home does not effectively enable him to interpret primary-grade reading materials or to understand the elaborated language used by his teachers.

In summary, the culturally disadvantaged child usually enters the primary grades very poorly equipped to deal with reading instruction. Typically such a child falls further and further behind as he progresses through the elementary grades.

Teaching Strategies and Teacher Characteristics Beneficial to Culturally Disadvantaged Children

In general, teaching strategies which enable a culturally disadvantaged child to participate actively in the learning process are considered to be the most effective. Such a child generally learns best when he is able to do something. The deprived child also needs as many concrete learning experiences as possible and must be able to see the relevance of school learning if he is to be able to profit from it.

Of crucial importance to the success of a disadvantaged child in school is the teacher's attitude toward working with him. A teacher should never attempt to work with disadvantaged children unless she can completely accept each child for what he is at the present and provide a classroom climate and learning opportunities which will enable the child to achieve success. A teacher of the disadvantaged must genuinely be able to respect a deprived child and see his potential ability.

A Reading Program for Culturally Disadvantaged Children in the Primary Grades

In the past few years several proposals for primary-grade reading programs for disadvantaged children have been made. One attempt to improve reading instruction for culturally disadvantaged children has been in the preparation of materials which resemble basal reader materials in methodology. However, these specially prepared materials are unique in that they provide reading materials which are said to utilize the experiences and the language patterns of urban disadvantaged children. These materials are designed to present stories which relate to the child and his own experience so that he will have less difficulty interpreting them. He is thought to identify readily with the children in these stories. In examining them, however, one does not find that urban inner-city life is portrayed realistically. Neither does one find the incorrect usage nor imprecise vocabulary that is commonly used by deprived children.

These specially prepared materials are the *Bank Street Readers*[1] written by the staff of the Bank Street College of Education in New York City, the *City Schools Reading Program*[2] written by the staff of the Detroit Public Schools, and the *Chandler Language-Experience Readers*[3] which use the urban San Francisco area as a setting. A form of the basal reader method is used in primary grades with these materials. Briefly, this method makes use of vocabulary presentation, development of experiential background, guided silent reading, and purposeful oral reading, to extend skills and abilities, and to enrich experiences. The various word recognition and comprehension skills are presented in about the same manner as is done in the basal reader materials.

These special materials for culturally disadvantaged children certainly are not the only way to meet their primary-grade reading needs. These materials may be useful for deprived children, but they need many other reading experiences if they are to achieve success in reading.

The language-experience approach to reading can be of great benefit to disadvantaged children, particularly in beginning reading instruction or in the later primary grades with disabled readers. The language-experience approach was refined and publicized in San Diego County, California, by R. Van Allen, now of the University of Arizona. According to Allen, it can best by crystallized by the following statement:

What I can think about, I can talk about.
What I can say, I can write.
What I can write, I can read.
I can read what I can write and what other people can write for me to read.[4]

The language-experience approach uses child-dictated or child-written experience charts or stories as the major materials for reading instruction. However, culturally deprived children must have many worthwhile experi-

[1] (New York: Macmillan, 1965–1966).
[2] (Chicago: Follett, 1962–1966).
[3] (San Francisco: Chandler Publishing Company, 1964–1966).
[4] Presented at the Conference on Beginning Reading Instruction, United States Office of Education, Washington, D. C., November 1962.

ences under the direction of the school if they are to have anything interesting to talk or write about. Such experiences can be visits to places of interest in the community such as the grocery store, the dairy, or the museum. Primary-grade classrooms must also be extremely well equipped and have interest centers to compensate for the lack of physical stimuli found in many disadvantaged homes.

After engaging in an experience such as a school trip to the zoo, first-grade children can dictate an experience chart in the group setting to the teacher who then transcribes it on to the chalkboard or a sheet of chart paper. This group-composed experience chart can then be mimeographed and a copy given to each child to take home to read to his family. In addition, an individual child can dictate an experience story to his teacher who then writes it down for him. She later types the story on a primary typewriter and gives it back to him to illustrate and to bind into an experience booklet. He can later take his collection of experience stories home to read to his family.

Culturally disadvantaged children are often greatly stimulated by having their photograph taken and a story dictated about the photograph. Such photographs and their accompanying stories can help a deprived child develop a positive self-concept, or feeling of personal worth. A positive self-concept is absolutely necessary if a disadvantaged child is to achieve success, for the deprived child often comes to school feeling inadequate and worthless.

The language-experience approach has been used with disadvantaged children in several research studies. An example is the CRAFT Project, sponsored by the City University of New York and the New York City Board of Education. This study was designed to compare the effectiveness of two major approaches to teaching reading to disadvantaged urban Negro children: the skills-centered approach and the language-experience approach. In general, disadvantaged children who used the language-experience approach supplemented by audiovisual materials achieved the most in reading.[5]

Certainly the language-experience approach—with or without the addition of audiovisual materials—can very profitably be used with disadvantaged children in the initial stages of reading instruction; since it helps them to understand that "reading is really talk written down," motivates them to learn to read, and capitalizes on their own experiences. However, a danger in using this approach with disadvantaged children is that they may dictate or write experience stories using incorrect grammar and inappropriate vocabulary. A possible solution to this problem may be

[5] A. J. Harris and Blanche L. Serwer, "Comparing Approaches in First-Grade Teaching with Disadvantaged Children," *The Reading Teacher,* XIX (May 1966).

found in the teacher's transcribing the child's experience story making immediate corrections in usage and vocabulary in a non-threatening way. While working with disadvantaged children, the primary-grade teacher must accept each child and his language as it is at present, but must also lead him to correct usage and vocabulary if he is to make progress in today's complex society.

Another useful approach to primary-grade reading instruction for disadvantaged children is the use of self-directive dramatization and individualized instruction. Lessie Carlton and Robert Moore of Illinois State University have conducted research on the use of self-directive dramatization with culturally disadvantaged children in grades one, two, three, and four. Self-directive dramatization of stories was defined as "the pupil's own original, imaginative, spontaneous interpretation of a character of his own choosing in a story which he selected and read cooperatively with other pupils in his group which was formed for the time being and for one particular story only."[6] This study found that the children who used self-directive dramatizations generally made better gains in reading over a long-term period than children who used a typical basal reader approach. Equally significant was the fact that the children using self-directive dramatization made many favorable changes in their self-concept.[7]

Individualized instruction may profitably be used with disadvantaged children in all subject areas. Individualized instruction is primarily based on Willard Olson's child-development view that children can self-select their materials, can pace their own instruction, and wish to do so.[8] These principles of child development are particularly applied to reading instruction. In an individualized reading plan a child selects his reading material from tradebooks, basal readers, supplementary readers, experience stories, content area books, or children's newspapers or magazines. He then reads the material independently and meets with his teacher individually several times a week to discuss the material and to read part of it aloud. The child and teacher keep a record of the reading, and the teacher diagnoses and remediates the child's word recognition and comprehension deficiencies during this individual reading conference.

Individualized instruction in content fields such as social studies and science can best take place by the use of the unit plan. In this method of curricular organization, a theme is chosen to be studied or a problem is selected to be solved. Each child then reads independently on a particular aspect of the theme or problem at his instructional reading level from content area books or children's reference books.

[6] Lessie Carlton and Robert H. Moore, *Reading, Self-Directive Dramatization and Self-Concept* (Columbus: Merrill, 1968), p. 10.
[7] *Ibid.*
[8] *Reading as a Function of Total Growth of the Child* ("Supplementary Educational Monograph," No. 51, Chicago: University of Chicago, 1940), pp. 233–37.

A Combination Reading Program
for Culturally Disadvantaged
Primary-Grade Children

The language-experience approach can be used as the introductory device for reading instruction since it so effectively capitalizes upon the children's experiences. Undoubtedly the language patterns of culturally disadvantaged children should be modified as transcribed by the teacher if they are grossly incorrect in usage or vocabulary. However, the teacher must rephrase the language tactfully to insure that the deprived child does not feel that his language is being rejected.

The specially prepared readers for the disadvantaged using the basal reader method provide a good way to insure that various word recognition and comprehension skills are presented in a sequential manner. The content of these readers undoubtedly has more appeal for disadvantaged children than does the material found in the middle-income oriented basal readers.

The self-directive dramatization presently has enough positive research evidence to warrant that it be included in a reading program for disadvantaged children. Probably its major strength lies in the value that dramatizing has for deprived children in the development of a positive self-concept. Since the child chooses his own story and character that he wishes to dramatize, he undoubtedly gains a feeling of worth.

The individualized reading plan can effectively reinforce the word recognition and comprehension skills that are learned while using the readers for the disadvantaged. The child reads self-selected stories, and this opportunity provides him with the pleasant reinforcement of his reading skills. The feeling of importance that the disadvantaged child gains by his teacher's undivided attention during the individual reading conference can also be very beneficial.

Opportunities for individualized instruction through the use of the unit plan can be important to disadvantaged children. Opportunities to work independently at their own reading level on a self-selected theme or problem may insure the success that these children so desperately need to achieve.

45 | Basic Principles of Remedial Instruction*

Guy L. Bond
Miles A. Tinker

The complexity of the reading act, the nature of reading difficulties, and the many characteristics of child growth and development that have a bearing on reading success make it clear that no two cases of disability are exactly alike. Four detailed aspects of this general fact have also been shown; no two cases of reading disability result from the same set of circumstances, no two have exactly the same reading patterns, no two cases have the same instructional needs, and no two can be treated in exactly the same manner. Every child is different in many ways from every other child. Because his difficulties in reading stem from a wide variety of causes, the diagnosis of his case involves a study of the child to find out his instructional needs and everything else that may influence a remedial program for him.

The remedial teacher studies the diagnostic findings and then arranges a learning situation that will enable the child henceforth to grow in reading at an accelerated rate. The remedial teacher's problem is to appraise materials and methods in order to select the combination that will best suit a given disabled reader. The many kinds of reading confusions children

*From *Reading Difficulties: Their Diagnosis and Correction,* Second Edition, pp. 241–266, by Guy L. Bond and Miles A. Tinker. Copyright © 1967. Reprinted by permission of Appleton-Century-Crofts, Educational Division, Meredith Corporation.

manifest indicate that no two disabilities will be corrected exactly the same way. Nonetheless, there are some basic principles underlying remedial instruction irrespective of the specific nature of a particular reading disability. There are certain common elements among corrective programs, whether we are treating a comprehension case, a problem of word recognition, or an oral reading limitation.

Among the more important general categories of basic principles underlying treatment of disabled reading are the following:

1. Treatment must be based on an understanding of the child's instructional needs.
2. Remedial programs must be highly individualized.
3. Remedial instruction must be organized instruction.
4. The reading processes must be made meaningful to the learner.
5. Consideration of the child's personal worth is necessary.
6. The reading program must be encouraging to the child.
7. Materials and exercises must be suitable to the child's reading ability and instructional needs.
8. Sound teaching procedures must be employed.
9. A carefully designed follow-up program is necessary.

Treatment Must Be Based on an Understanding of the Child's Instructional Needs

The remedial program must be designed to emphasize those phases of reading growth that will enable the disabled reader to grow rapidly and solidly. The program designed for each child must be based on a diagnosis of his instructional needs. The purpose of the diagnosis is to obtain information about each child that is necessary in order to formulate a remedial program suited to him. Watkins(21) has shown that the child who is in trouble in reading often has an unequal profile showing an unfortunate pattern of reading skills and abilities. Some phases of reading will be well learned while other phases will be developed poorly. Still other phases may have been overemphasized to the point that they restrict the child's development in reading. The diagnosis must ferret out these inconsistencies in the child's attack on reading.

The child having difficulty in reading will show irregular performances. He may have a large sight vocabulary but he is unable to phrase well. He may be high in word recognition but low in comprehension. A reading diagnosis is designed to locate the inconsistencies that preclude rapid and effective growth in reading. The diagnosis is designed to locate essential areas of growth that have been neglected, those that have been faultily learned, or those that have been overemphasized. It is impractical to start a remedial program in reading until the nature of the instruction needed by the disabled reader has been established. Otherwise, the program may stress areas already overemphasized or omit areas needing attention or perhaps underemphasize such areas.

The remedial program must be based on more than an understanding of the child's reading needs. It must also be based on the child's characteristics. The child who is hard of hearing needs a different approach to reading than does his counterpart with normal hearing. The child with poor vision needs marked adjustments in methods and, if his limitation is severe enough, in materials also. The child who is a slow learner needs modified methods and so does the child who is emotionally disturbed.

Inasmuch as each case is different, there can be no "bag of tricks" nor can there be a universal approach which will lead to the solution of disabled readers' problems. Many times, remedial training suited to one child would be detrimental to another. If, for example, a remedial program has been planned to develop more adequate phrasing, the child might well be required to do considerable prepared oral reading in order to help him to read in thought units. This same recommendation would do serious harm to the youngster who is already overvocalizing in his silent reading. It would exaggerate the faulty habit he had acquired and increase his disability. To sum up, every remedial program must be made on the basis of a thorough appraisal of the child's instructional needs, his strengths and weaknesses, and the environment in which correction is to take place.

CLEARLY FORMULATE THE REMEDIAL PROGRAM

After the diagnosis has shown the kind of instruction that is needed, the remedial program should be carefully planned. This requires writing down what is to be done for each case. This must be done because it is too difficult to remember each child, his needs, the level of his attainments, and his limitations with the exactness that is necessary in order to conduct an effective corrective program. The written case report should indicate the nature of the disability and the type of exercises recommended to correct the difficulty. It should identify the level of material that is to be used. The written report should state any physical or sensory characteristics of the child that need to be corrected or for which the program needs to be modified. Any indication of faulty personal adjustment or unfortunate environmental conditions should be included. The child's interests, hobbies, and attitudes should become part of the written record. Most important, it should include a description of the remedial program recommended and the type of material and exercises to be used.

THE REMEDIAL PROGRAM SHOULD BE MODIFIED AS NEEDED

The original plan of remedial work is not to be considered a permanent scheme of instruction. It will need to be modified from time to time as the child progresses in reading. Often a child who is having difficulty in learning changes rapidly in respect to his instructional needs. The better the diagnosis and the more successful the remedial work, the more rapidly will the child's needs change. One disabled reader, for example, may have failed to build analytical word-recognition techniques but is depending on sight vocabulary and context clues as his means of recognizing new words. He would be given remedial work designed to teach him the analytical techniques. After a time, he may develop considerable skill in word study, but he may not make a corresponding gain in rate of reading. His problem would no longer be one of developing word analysis. In fact, emphasis on this phase of the program might become detrimental to his future reading growth. The use of larger word elements and other more rapid word-recognition techniques and further building of sight vocabulary would be advisable. As the problem changes, so must the program of remediation be modified in order to meet the new reading needs of the child.

Inasmuch as the child's instructional needs change rapidly, it is unwise to set him into a remedial program that resembles the production line in a factory. Such a program assumes that once a given child's level of reading performance is identified, all that is needed is to put him through a set of exercises uniform for all children. There is no single method suited to all children even in the developmental reading program. The disabled reader whose needs change rapidly as his limtations are corrected, is in dire need of a program that readily adjusts to every change in his reading pattern. To achieve success, a remedial program must be based upon a continuous diagnosis and it must be modified as the child's instructional needs change.

In some instances, the original program for remediation does not result in improvement. When this occurs, a reevaluation of the diagnosis and perhaps additions to the diagnosis are in order. A somewhat altered approach to instruction may be necessary to bring success.

A VARIETY OF REMEDIAL TECHNIQUES SHOULD BE USED

There is an unfortunate tendency, once a form of remedial instruction has been prescribed, to stick to the use of that specific type of exercise to overcome a known deficiency. Basing a remedial program upon a diagnosis does not imply that a given exercise can be used until the child's reading disability is corrected. There are many ways to develop each of the skills and abilities in reading. An effective remedial program will use a variety of teaching techniques and instructional procedures.

Many sources of help describing teaching techniques are available to the remedial teacher. Professional books on remedial instruction in reading give suggestions for correcting specific types of reading retardation. Russell and Karp(15) have compiled a helpful group of remedial techniques. Manuals and workbooks accompanying basal reading programs are the most fruitful source of teaching techniques. The exercises suggested for teaching the skills and abilities when first introduced in such manuals and workbooks are the sort of things that prove beneficial for remedial programs. If, for example, a fifth-grade child has difficulty with finding root words in affixed words, the teacher can find many and varied exercises in second- and third-grade manuals to teach this skill. The remedial teacher could have the child start with exercises which have simple variant endings on words, such as *walked* or *looking*. As the child improves, the exercises can be increased in difficulty up to those found in fourth- and fifth-grade manuals or workbooks which involve words with prefixes and suffixes, such as *unlikely* or *reworkable*. Teachers' manuals and workbooks accompanying basal readers give exercises and suggested activities that may be used to teach all skills and abilities in reading. The newer basic series of books have lists of these exercises with page references. As she examines the teaching techniques suggested in such materials, the remedial teacher can accumulate a variety of exercises for each of the important types of disabilities. She can keep the program dynamic and interesting to the child by using a variety of teaching techniques and at the same time be sure that the instruction emphasizes the skill development that is needed.

In attempting to use a variety of teaching methods and techniques, care must be taken that the teaching approaches do not confuse the child. The directions given him should be simple and the teaching techniques should not be changed too often. The exercises should be as nearly like the reading act as possible. Artificial or isolated drills should be avoided. The child should not have to spend time learning complicated procedures or directions. Enough variety should be introduced, however, to keep the program stimulating.

An effective and interesting teaching technique should not be used too long nor so often that it loses its value. A fifth-grade child, for example, may be weak in visualizing what is read. For him, the remedial work is planned to emphasize the ability to form sensory impressions and to stimulate the imagination. The teaching techniques used have him read a story and then draw some illustrations for it. This is an effective means of getting this particular child to visualize as he reads. But remember, if he should have to draw pictures of what he reads every day, he may decide that he would rather not read at all. Variety could be introduced by visualizing for different purposes. At one time, pictures for a play television show might be made; at another time, the child might describe how furniture could be arranged for a creative dramatic presentation; at another time, he might read and tell how he thought the scene of a story looked. All of these purposes would require visualization of what is read.

Basing treatment upon an understanding of the child's instructional needs means that the remedial program is planned after a thorough diagnosis has been made. It does not mean that the program becomes fixed or that further study of the child is unnecessary. It is true that if the basic principles of remedial instruction discussed in this chapter are followed, approximately 65 percent of disabled readers will improve even without diagnosis. However, there will remain somewhere around 35 percent of disabled readers who will not get along well. Aside from those children who are described as cases of simple retardation, there is no way of knowing which children will be among the successful and which will be among the 35 percent for whom the remedial work will fail. Whichever children the failures happen to be, they will probably become even more stubborn cases than they were before the remedial instruction started. Those children who did improve without a diagnosis would have improved even more rapidly if the remedial program had been designed to meet their specific needs. Mass training by common methods is unfortunate even if given the label of remedial instruction.

The reason most programs that attempt to correct reading disability meet with some degree of success is because the children are treated individually and many desirable adjustments are made. Even artificial programs, which are basically poor, will demonstrate a modicum of success if they are given by an enthusiastic teacher because they are given to individual children. Well-rounded remedial programs based on careful and continuous diagnosis, using a variety of teaching techniques and taught by an equally enthusiastic teacher, will give far better results.

Remedial Programs Must Be Highly Individualized

The disabled reader is one who has failed to respond to reading programs that are designed to meet the instructional needs and characteristics of the majority of children. The onset of reading disability is usually gradual. The child who becomes a disabled reader gets into a moderate degree of difficulty, misses some instruction, or in some way falls behind or gets confused. The reading curriculum and the class itself go on, while the child is left farther behind. Soon he finds himself hopelessly out of things. He can no longer read well enough to keep up with his group. He may develop an aversion to reading and he is quite likely to develop unfortunate reading habits. All of these things accumulate until it is apparent to the teacher that the child has become a disabled reader. He has not learned the skills and abilities essential to effective reading. Faulty habits and unfortunate modes of reading have become established. He is developing or has already developed an attitude of dislike and antagonism toward reading and his sense of defeat mounts higher and higher.

Such a child's difficulty has been brought about gradually through his failure to progress in the usual fashion. The teacher, confronted with thirty-five other children, at first failed to see the child's need or could not take the time to adjust the instruction to his requirements. The child thus developed an abnormal and unfortunate variation in his reading skills and abilities.

A program designed to treat reading disabilities is based on the assumption that children learn differently and need programs that meet their individual requirements. Such programs must be based on a recognition of a particular child's physical and mental characteristics and must be designed individually to be efficient in overcoming his difficulties.

THE REMEDIAL PROGRAM SHOULD BE IN KEEPING WITH THE CHILD'S CHARACTERISTICS

The expected outcomes of instruction and the methods used in achieving these outcomes will need to conform to the child's characteristics. If the child is lacking in general intelligence, he can neither be expected to reach the ultimate stature in reading of children of greater mental capability nor can he be expected to progress as rapidly. The remedial teacher will be wise to modify the outcomes of the program. The prognosis for rate of gain is usually directly proportional to the general intelligence of the child. In addition to lowering the results she expects, the remedial teacher would be wise to modify the methods of instruction also to meet the slow-learning child's needs. Such children need more concrete experiences, more carefully given directions, and more emphasis on repetition and drill than do children of higher intelligence.

If a child has poor vision or poor hearing, modifications in methods will need to be made. Such limitations make learning to read more difficult but in no way preclude the child from achieving. Deaf children have been taught to read about as effectively as their contemporaries with normal hearing when methods of instruction were adjusted to their needs. Children with marked visual defects have learned to read well, but they are more likely to get into difficulty. The disabled reader with lesser degrees of sensory handicaps can be taught more efficiently if his limitations are known and modifications in methods of instruction are made.

REMEDIAL INSTRUCTION SHOULD BE SPECIFIC, NOT GENERAL

The remedial teacher should focus instruction upon the specific reading needs of the child. The diagnosis has usually indicated that there is something specifically wrong with the pattern of the child's reading performance. One child, for example, may have learned to read with speed but falls short of the accuracy required in certain situations. Such a child should be given material to read that has factual content and he should read it for purposes that demand the exact recall of those facts. Another child may be so over-concerned with detail that he reads extremely slowly, looking for more facts than the author wrote. He becomes so concerned with the detail that he cannot understand the author's overall intent. The teacher, in this latter case, would be specifically endeavoring to make the child less compulsive so that the rate of reading and its outcomes can become compatible with the purposes of this particular reading.

The principle that remedial instruction should be specific and not general means that the remedial teacher should emphasize those phases of reading development that will correct the child's reading limitation. It does not mean that just one type of exercise should be employed nor does it mean that a specific skill or ability should be isolated and receive drill. In the case of a disabled reader who has an insufficient knowledge of the larger visual and structural elements used in word recognition, the teacher would be making an error if he used a method that gave isolated drill on word elements. A more effective procedure would be to have the child read a basic reader at the proper level of difficulty. He would read for the purposes suggested in the manual, but when he encountered a word-recognition problem, the teacher would help him by emphasizing the larger elements in the word. When the exercises given in the manual for developing basic skills and abilities were studied, the remedial teacher would have this child do the ones that gave him experience in using the larger visual and structural parts of the words. The teacher could construct some additional exercises that would provide experiences with the larger elements in words the child already knew so that he could learn to use these in recognizing new words. Types of exercises suggested in manuals of other basic reading series using vocabulary known to the child could also be used in constructing these teacher-made materials.

The workbook exercises accompanying the basic reader should be used. The disabled reader may need to have certain pages selected for him so that he does not have to do all the exercises. This must be done because the child has an uneven profile and he may have emphasized one phase of reading instruction to the detriment of another. The child who needs a greater knowledge of large visual and structural elements may have failed to develop them because he had overemphasized phonetic letter-by-letter sounding in word recognition. Such a child should avoid for the time being the exercises that teach the knowledge of letter sounds.

Children have been given remedial instruction by various procedures at the University of Minnesota Psycho-educational Clinic. Children who were taught by using a regular developmental reading program, modified to emphasize those skills in which a given child needed further training and to minimize those which he had overemphasized, showed far greater gains than did the children who were taught by isolated drill exercises. It is to be concluded that remedial training is best done in nicely controlled reading programs such as are found in basic readers, but with modifications to meet the instructional needs of each child.

REMEDIAL INSTRUCTION SHOULD BE ENERGETIC

Growth in reading presupposes an energetic learner. Of course, the child must learn to read by reading. He must attack the printed page vigorously and often if he is to succeed. A fatigued child cannot be expected to make gains during the remedial period. Therefore, the length of the period for remedial instruction should be such that concentrated work is possible. The disabled reader frequently finds it difficult to attend to reading for any considerable length of time. His lack of attention may be due to a variety of causes. In one case it may be lack of physical stamina, while in another it may be that he is not getting enough sleep at night, or it may be that his emotional reactions to reading sap his vitality. His inattention or lack of vigor may be due to habits of escaping from an unsuccessful and uncomfortable situation. Whatever the cause, most children if properly motivated can apply themselves to the reading situation at least for a short period of time. Obviously, if the lack of attention and vigor result from a condition that can be corrected, the correction should be made. In any case, the length of the remedial reading period should be adjusted so that an energetic attack can be maintained.

Frequently it is necessary to divide the remedial sessions into short periods. The child may work with the remedial teacher for a period of forty-five minutes. At the start of the remedial training, it may be necessary to have him read from a basic reader for only ten minutes for specific purposes and then have him use the results of his reading in some creative activity, such as drawing, constructing, modeling, discussing, or the like. Then the child might work on some skill development exercises which emphasize the training he needs. These exercises might entail rereading the material he read at the first part of the session or they may be word-recognition drill on new words introduced in the basic reader. Finally, the child might be asked to tell about the book he has been reading independently. As he gains in reading growth, the length of concentrated reading time should be increased. Soon the child who has no physical limitation will be reading longer without interruption. When this is so, the use of creative activities can be less frequent. Then the child can read for several days during the remedial periods before he utilizes the results of reading. He will still need to discuss what he has read and do the exercises suited to him as suggested in the manual or as found in the workbook.

Remedial Instruction Must Be
Organized Instruction

Reading instruction in both the developmental and remedial aspects must be well organized. The skills and abilities grow gradually as the child meets more complex applications of each. There is a tendency for remedial teachers to neglect the sequences involved in teaching the child each of the basic areas. In word recognition, remedial work is often erroneously given in one phase before the child has developed the learning that should precede it. The child may, for example, lack ability to break words into syllables so the remedial teacher gives him exercises to develop that skill. A study of the sequence in word-recognition techniques might show that the child had many other learnings to master before he could be expected to be successful in this relatively mature approach to word recognition.

In order that growth in word recognition may develop smoothly, with no undue burden upon the learner who is already in difficulty, a gradual orderly sequence must be maintained. Such organization is necessary so that there will be no omissions in developing the essential skills, so that there will be little chance for overemphasis, and so that new skills are introduced to the child when he has the necessary prerequisites for learning them. In learning to recognize words, the child should first establish the habit of left-to-right orientation before he is allowed to employ any detailed analytical attacks. He should also learn to recognize word wholes when he knows them, rather than to employ analysis; to use the context and initial elements before he is encouraged to attend to variant endings; and to form the habit of viewing the word systematically from start to finish before he is required to visually separate the words into syllables.

The child who is in confusion in reading requires even more systematic instruction than does the child who is learning without difficulty. The remedial teacher must either be completely aware what sequence of learning is desirable in all the areas of reading growth or she must use the basic reading material in which the orderly development of skills has been carefully planned out. The remedial teacher cannot afford to use haphazard approaches. She must follow the sequence and explain carefully each new step in it. Therefore, the most successful remedial teachers find it expedient to use basic reading programs, modified to fit the child's specific needs whatever they may be.

The Reading Processes Must Be
Made Meaningful to the Learner

One reason why the disabled reader is in difficulty is because he does not understand the processes involved in being a good reader. The remedial teacher has the responsibility not only for maintaining orderly sequences of skill development, but also for making the steps involved meaningful to the child. The teacher should not only teach the child to use context clues in word recognition, but also she should let the child see how helpful such an aid to word recognition can be. The teacher should show the child how to organize the material he reads for effective retention. She should, in addition, let the child understand why such an organization is effective. The child should be led to understand the importance of reading certain material carefully with attention to detail, while other material can be read rapidly to understand the general ideas it advances.

If the remedial teacher expects the child to retain a knowledge of word elements, it is important for her to show him how much they will aid him in recognizing new words. For too long, many remedial teachers have felt that if the child is stimulated to read material at the correct level of difficulty he will automatically develop the needed skills. This point of view can be seriously questioned. A more reasonable assumption is that the child should be shown how to go about his reading and how much use he can make of each added reading accomplishment. Suppose a child, for example, has learned by rote to pronounce prefixed words. How much better it would have been to point out to him the prefixes in those words and show him how they change the meaning of the root words.

The remedial teacher will find that making the processes of reading meaningful to the learner helps to solve his reading confusions. Drill on isolated parts of words is not as effective as is a meaningful approach to reading. Modern developmental reading programs are planned to enable the child to develop the needed skills and abilities and to understand the usefulness of each. The remedial program should be concerned even more with making reading processes meaningful to the child. The day has long since passed when it was assumed that if we but interested the child in reading, he would effectively go ahead on his own to develop skills of which he was unaware.

Consideration of the Child's Personal Worth Is Necessary

The disabled reader frequently feels insecure and defeated in school. Any remedial program designed to treat reading disabilities must make the child feel his successes from the start. It must also take into account the child's sense of personal worth. The child who is in serious trouble in reading is often antagonistic toward reading and thoroughly dislikes it. He would like to wake up some morning knowing how to read, but he believes there is something wrong with him that precludes his learning to read. Frequently he thinks that he is mentally incapable of learning or that he has some other defect. Often he has a poor estimate of himself as a person.

Remedial programs should consider the fact that the disabled reader builds a barrier between himself and all reading instruction. One of the first tasks of a remedial teacher is to gain the child's confidence. Resistance to the remedial program will be magnified if the child is classified in any unfortunate way. Whenever the remedial work is to be done by the classroom teacher, the child should be a working member of that class. He should be able to enter into the various activities even though his part in them is meager.

If it is necessary to give a child remedial training in the school reading center, great care must be taken when the work starts. Remedial programs should be considered a privilege and should be entered voluntarily. When the remedial groups are made up, it is strategic to include in them the brightest children who are disabled readers. These children are known to be bright and capable in other areas of the school curriculum and so the other children will see that the program is for able children who are having some specific difficulty. Another reason for selecting the more able children to start with, is that in their instances there is a greater chance for rapid improvement. This will enable the program to get off to a good start and will make it possible to do the most service to the greatest number. Besides, such an approach will place the remedial work in its proper perspective of being special instruction in reading rather than a class designed for the mentally inept.

In many schools, cases are selected for remedial work by sending the four or five poorest readers from each room to the reading center. This is an unfortunate practice. As has been previously explained, the poorest readers in the room are not necessarily the children who will profit from remedial instruction in reading. Many such children are essentially slow learners. They are not disabled readers. Only children who are properly classified as reading disability cases should be sent to the school reading center for remedial instruction. Another tendency is to refer disciplinary and delinquent children to the reading center for individual work or for work in the smaller group. While it is true that many delinquent and disciplinary cases are poor readers, it is unwise to give the remedial teacher too large a number of these children at any one time. The correction of reading disability is a difficult task and if too many kinds of problems are concentrated in any one group, the teacher cannot hope to be successful. Also, the reading center will acquire a reputation as a place for misfits.

In general, it is desirable to inaugurate remedial work with children who have the following characteristics:

1. General intelligence of over an I.Q. of 90 as measured by suitable tests.
2. Children who have asked to be admitted after the work has been discussed with them.
3. Children whose parents have requested such service.

4. Children who are classified as having reading disability as their major problem.
5. Not too great a proportion of children with behavior problems at any one time.

Frequently the disabled reader is emotionally tense or insecure. He has had no real opportunity to gain confidence in himself because most of the school day involves reading. For some time he has been much less effective in school work than his intellectual level would indicate that he should be. Such a child may become submissive or demanding, aggressive or withdrawing, or show his basic insecurity in a variety of ways. He may develop attitudes of indifference, dislike, or rejection. He may resist help, display few interests, and be antagonistic toward reading instruction. Remedial reading programs must overcome these unfortunate attitudes and compensatory modes of behavior. One of the first responsibilities of the remedial teacher is to develop in the child a need for learning to read. The second is to gain the child's confidence to such a degree that he will know a personal interest is being taken in him and that now his reading problem is going to be solved. A direct attack on the reading problem by a businesslike, considerate adult will do much to overcome tensions and faulty attitudes. When a child recognizes that an interest is taken in him and his problem, it will give him the much-needed sense of personal worth and the confidence in himself that he has hitherto lacked.

The Reading Program Must Be Encouraging to the Child

Most disabled readers are discouraged about their failure to learn to read. They frequently think that they cannot learn. This lack of confidence in their ability to learn is detrimental to possible reading growth. The effective learner is a confident and purposeful learner, one who has a desire to learn and finds pleasure in working toward this goal. In order that a child may go ahead rapidly in learning to read, it is necessary for him to know that he can learn and to see that he is progressing satisfactorily.

There are several principles underlying remedial instruction that give the child this sense of confidence he needs. The following principles will help to give the child the necessary encouragement:

1. The teacher must be optimistic.
2. The child needs group as well as individual work.
3. The child's successes should be emphasized.
4. A positive approach should be used in pointing out errors.

5. His growth in reading should be pointed out to the child.
6. Remedial programs should not be substituted for enjoyable activities.
7. Remedial programs must be pleasant and free from undue pressures.

THE TEACHER MUST BE OPTIMISTIC

A teacher who would help a child to overcome a reading disability should be a buoyant, energetic person. She must make the child sense her confidence in him. At times, the problems involved in correcting a complex reading disability may seem to her to entail almost insurmountable teaching problems. Nevertheless, the teacher must approach each disabled reader showing that she knows he will learn to read. Such an attitude is an out growth of a thorough understanding of the instructional needs of the child that is, a sound diagnosis, and of having the remedial program planned well enough in advance so that the general nature of remedial instruction is clearly in mind. In addition, the teacher gains immediate confidence through knowing exactly what is going to be undertaken during each remedial lesson. A well-prepared teacher who knows exactly where each session is going will instill confidence in the child. With this preparation, progress in reading ordinarily takes place.

The teacher may well be optimistic because the vast majority of reading disability cases do show immediate gains from remedial instruction. If the child's reading problem and his characteristics have been carefully appraised and if the program has been carefully formulated, success is almost assured. Of course, the teacher's confidence may sometimes, and from time to time, be shaken. There are periods during the corrective treatment of practically every remedial case when there is little evidence of new growth. But all the same, confidence in the child's ultimate success must be maintained even when things do not appear to be going well. Under some circumstances the remedial program should be restudied and the diagnosis reviewed, but all this need not lessen confidence in the child's ultimate success.

THE CHILD NEEDS GROUP AS WELL AS INDIVIDUAL WORK

The disabled reader needs to share experiences with other children just as much as, or even more than, the child whose growth in reading is normal. Not only should his classroom work be organized so that he can participate in some of the important activities with which the class is concerning itself, but also it is beneficial for the child who is in difficulty to see that there are other children who are having similar difficulties. It is therefore recommended that whenever it is possible to have disabled readers work in groups, this should be undertaken. Much good can be gained by the disabled reader in seeing other children right around him who are in a like difficulty, and who are making progress in overcoming it. It is sometimes assumed that remedial reading instruction is a formal procedure in which the child is separated from other children and drilled until his disability is corrected. Such instruction is most unwise. It is a boost to the child to know that there are other children who are learning to read and who are able to use their newly gained proficiencies in group situations.

The summer program of the University of Minnesota Psycho-educational Clinic provides a good illustration of how both individual and group remedial work can be made available to the child. Of course, in the school reading center or in the typical reading clinic, slight modifications would have to be made. The children who come to the summer reading clinic at the University of Minnesota are, for the most part, extremely disabled readers. The great majority of them would be described as complex or limiting disability cases. The most successful approach that we have been able to devise for these children has been to separate them into groups or classes of about fifteen to twenty children. They work with a classroom teacher for an entire morning. In the classroom work, there is a regular unit of instruction, using topics to be found in readers and selected so as to be at the reading level at which the greatest number in the class can read comfortably. These topics are supplemented by additional reference books in the room. For some of the children, picture books or pictures in books which supply information are used. In addition to the unit the children are reading about, there is group instruction using basal material at the appropriate level for each group within the class. Then for a period of from a half hour to an hour every day, each child is withdrawn from the class, either in small groups of four or five or for individual instruction, whichever is deemed best from the nature of the case. In this situation, the children are given remedial instruction designed to overcome their specific remedial problems. Children in the same major classification of disability form the small groups. Children who do not fit into any groups are handled individually. In a typical school reading center, the remedial reading teacher would not have additional personnel to handle small groups. Therefore the modification recommended for the school reading center would be to have those children who were less seriously retarded or who constituted a very similar type of disability, such as the slow readers, brought together for instruction in relatively large groups. Those children with more complex disabilities could be handled in smaller sections. Such group sessions could be conducted during the morning. Then the remedial teacher would be free in the afternoon to handle smaller groups or work with certain individual children whom he had observed during the morning sessions were in need of additional help.

THE CHILD'S SUCCESSES SHOULD BE EMPHASIZED

In order that the remedial program may be encouraging to the child, his successes rather than his mistakes should be emphasized. Teachers have a tendency to point out errors to children rather than to make them feel that for the most part they are doing particularly well. A child whose errors are continually focused upon may become overwhelmed by a sense of defeat. A wise teacher will start the child in a remedial program that is somewhat easy for him so that his successful performance will be immediately apparent. As he gains confidence, the difficulty of the reading situations may be increased. The teacher should always be quick to recognize when the child has put forth a real effort and has done something well. Many times, particularly at the start, recognition will have to be given for activities related to the reading rather than the reading itself. Gradually the teacher will find increased opportunities to give praise for the actual reading that is well done. At all times it should be remembered that the effectiveness of remedial instruction depends in no small measure upon the child's gain in confidence. This gain in confidence is brought about through successful experiences with reading which in the past had caused the child so much difficulty.

A POSITIVE APPROACH SHOULD BE USED
IN POINTING OUT ERRORS

The emphasis upon success does not mean that errors are to be altogether overlooked. The faulty reading of a child must of course be brought to his attention. Errors in word recognition must be pointed out. Faulty habits in reading which limit his speed must be recognized by him before they can be corrected. Sometimes it is necessary to demand greater exactness in reading on the part of the child. While it is true that the teacher must point out the child's mistakes, she must at all times indicate that the child is improving and that for the most part he is really doing well. If, for example, a child should call the word *house, horse* in the sentence "The dog ran up to the house," the teacher should point out to him that he had the sentence nearly correct, but that in order to be exactly right he should have looked at the center part of the last word a little more carefully. As a matter of fact, the child did recognize most of the words in the sentence. He made an error that indicated that he was using the context well and that his error was a very slight one indeed. The words *house* and *horse* do look much alike.

In a comprehension lesson, the child may give the wrong answer to a question. Instead of saying that the answer is wrong and calling on another child in the group, it would be far better for the teacher to say, "Let's see what the book says about this" and then find out wherein the child made his error. It will frequently be found that he did not understand the meaning of a word or that he failed to notice a key word such as *not,* or that he had not grouped the words into proper thought units. Whatever the cause of his error, it should be located and the child should be shown the correct way to read the passage. The attitude of the teacher should be not one of pointing out errors but one of helping the child learn to read.

GROWTH IN READING SHOULD BE DEMONSTRATED TO THE CHILD

The disabled reader needs to have his growth demonstrated to him. There are many ways in which reading growth can be shown. The diagnostician has isolated the child's needs in this regard and indicated the amount of emphasis that should be given. It will be recalled that the method for demonstrating the progress of the child to him depends upon the nature of the reading problem. If, for example, the child is trying to develop a sight vocabulary, he could make a picture dictionary of the words he was trying to learn. As the dictionary became larger, the child would recognize that he had increased his sight vocabulary. The child who is working on accuracy of comprehension could develop a bar chart (Figure 1) in which he would indicate his level of percent of accuracy on successive periods. If such a child failed to gain over the period of a week, the teacher could simplify the material or ask more general questions so that accuracy would increase. Then as the child gained confidence, the difficulty of the material could be gradually increased again. It is a good plan for the child to go back, from time to time, and reread something that he has read previously. He will discover that material that was difficult

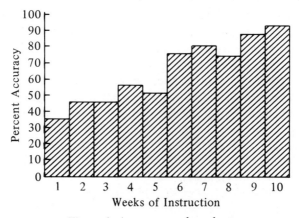

Figure 1. An accuracy bar chart.

for him a short while ago, is now relatively easy for him to read. This will be especially true if the teacher takes time to develop the necessary readiness prior to the reading.

Whatever the nature of the difficulty, it is important for the remedial program to be organized to demonstrate to the child that he is progressing toward his goal of better reading. The child who has been in difficulty for a long time needs whatever encouragement can be given him. He needs not only to be in a comfortable learning situation, but also he needs to see that he is making effective advancement in reading.

REMEDIAL PROGRAMS SHOULD NOT BE SUBSTITUTED FOR ENJOYABLE ACTIVITIES

The remedial teacher must so organize the periods of instruction that children are not required to come for training at a time that competes with other activities of great importance to them. For example, it is a frequent practice to have children come to a clinic for remedial instruction after school. This is a decidedly unfortunate time for a boy who enjoys outdoor sports with his friends, and who finds this the only time that such outdoor games are played in his neighborhood. In scheduling summer reading programs, it is wise to delay their start until a week or so after school is out and the children have found that they have time that they do not know what to do with. Even then the better scheduling time for classes is probably in the morning because the majority of things that the child likes to do, such as going swimming or playing baseball, are done in the afternoon.

The busy classroom teacher frequently finds it difficult to give an individual child attention he needs when the class is in session. She may therefore select recess time or the time in which other children have their hobby clubs, or are in the auditorium viewing a movie, for helping a child with his reading. Such a practice is understandable but is unfortunate for the correction of a reading disability. A better time would be to work with the children needing reeducation while the rest of the children are busily engaged in studying or reading independently. Whatever time is used for giving remedial help, it is important that it does not conflict with activities which are important to the child.

REMEDIAL PROGRAMS MUST BE PLEASANT AND FREE FROM UNDUE PRESSURES

An effective remedial program must be one that is satisfying to the child, makes him feel that he is getting along well, and keeps at a minimum any anxiety which he feels about his reading progress. The teacher's responsibility in encouraging the child to read energetically is indeed great. She should neither unduly hurry the child nor allow him to dawdle; she should be sure the child is working hard and yet avoid putting undue pressure on him. Most children, in fact, practically all children can be expected to work intently in developing reading ability. This is especially true if the reading materials are at the right level, if the child is properly motivated, and if he is reading for purposes that are real to him. There should always be a friendly atmosphere, but an atmosphere that keeps uppermost the point of view that the child is there to learn to read.

Materials and Exercises Must Be Suitable to the Child's Reading Ability and Instructional Needs

The selection of appropriate material for remedial work in reading is one of the most important problems the remedial teacher has to solve. Some teachers feel that the most important element in the problem is that the material should deal with a subject in which the child is interested. Others feel that the level of difficulty of the material is of even greater importance. Still others believe that having the type of material that is compatible with the nature of the remedial instruction is of paramount importance. There can be no doubt that all three of these elements enter into the selection of appropriate material for remedial instruction. Without trying to decide here between them, we may conclude that the more important considerations in selecting material are:

1. The materials must be suitable in level of difficulty.
2. The materials must be suitable in type.
3. The materials must be at the appropriate level of interest and format.
4. The materials must be abundant.

THE MATERIALS MUST BE SUITABLE IN LEVEL OF DIFFICULTY

The child grows in reading by reading, therefore the material that is used for remedial instruction should be of a difficulty level that enables the child to read comfortably and with enjoyment. The diagnostician will have suggested the level of difficulty of the material the child could be expected to read. The remedial teacher must pick out materials at that level to suit the child. The difficulty of material can be judged in many ways. Readability formulas, such as the Lorge formula (10), the formula of Dale-Chall(6), and that of Spache(17) have proven useful in estimating the reading level of materials. Most of the basic readers are carefully graded and indicate the level of reading maturity necessary for their use. In general, of course, books of second-grade level are suitable to the child whose skills are of second-grade maturity. Third-grade books are suitable for the child whose basic skill development is approximately that of a third-grade child. Ungraded books can be estimated by a formula or by using a basic reading series as a difficulty rating scale. The difficulty of an ungraded library book may be judged by comparing it with the various grade levels of a basic reader. For example, a library book can be compared with a third-grade reader. If it is judged to be harder, it may then be compared with a fourth-grade reader, and so forth, until the approximate level of difficulty can be estimated. In making the judgment, the teacher should look at the number of unusual words it contains, the length of its sentences, the number of prepositional phrases, the number of unusual word orders, the complexity of the ideas it includes. In judging level of difficulty, it is important that the remedial teacher remember that the results of standardized survey tests tend to give an overestimation of the skill development of a reading disability case. Therefore, it is usually wise to start remedial instruction with material that is somewhat lower than the child's general reading score as indicated by standardized tests.

The difficulty of the material that is suitable for remedial instruction will vary somewhat with the nature of the child's disability. The teacher should modify the general estimate of level of difficulty according to the outcomes of instruction to be achieved by the use of that material. For example, if the child's major problem is one of developing sight vocabulary, the material should be relatively easy with few new words being introduced. Those that are introduced should be used often in the material. For such a child, a relatively easy level in a basic reading program would be desirable. On the other hand, for the child who is trying to analyze words effectively, a higher concentration of new vocabulary would be desirable. The child could well afford to meet one new word in approximately every 20 running words. This would give him an opportunity to employ the techniques of word analysis that he needs to develop and at the same time it will enable him to maintain the thought of the passage so that context clues can be used as a means of checking the accuracy of his word recognition.

A child who is trying to increase his speed of comprehension should use material that is for him definitely easy. Such material would have few if any word-recognition problems for him. On the other hand, the child who is trying to increase his power of comprehension should use material with which he must tussle, but he must have a reasonable chance of successfully comprehending the material.

THE MATERIALS MUST BE SUITABLE IN TYPE

It is often said that any kind of material that is suitable for teaching reading in the first place is suitable for remedial instruction. While this is true, it is important to recognize that the material must be nicely selected to meet the child's instructional needs. The type of material that is suitable for one kind of disability is not necessarily suitable for another. If the child's major problem is that of increasing his speed of reading, the most suitable material would be short stories whose plots unfold rapidly. The material should not only be easy in regard to reading difficulty, but the nature of the content should be such that the child can read it to gain a general impression or the general significance of the story. If, on the other hand, the child's problem is one in the word-recognition area, a basic reader along with the exercises found in the manuals and the workbooks related to the word-recognition problem would be the most desirable type of reading material to use. If the child's problem is in the comprehension area and it is desired to increase his accuracy in reading, material in science or in social studies that has considerable factual information should be used. In every instance, the material should be at the appropriate level of difficulty, but also in every instance, the material should be of a type that is appropriate to the outcomes of reading expected.

THE MATERIALS MUST BE AT THE APPROPRIATE LEVEL OF INTEREST AND FORMAT

A relatively mature and intelligent 12-year old will usually not find first- and second-grade material interesting, nor will he find the format very attractive. Such a child with second-grade reading ability must nevertheless use material that he can read. The problem facing the remedial teacher in this respect is very great. The second-grade book is designed for a child who is 7 or 8 years of age. The pictures in it are of small children and its print looks large and juvenile. The topics dealt with in the book are appropriate to the 7- or 8-year-old and not to a 12-year-old. Therefore, many books that are used for remedial reading instruction lose some of their value because they lack interest and have the wrong format. In such a case, however, there can be no compromise with the need for using material that is at the suitable level of difficulty. The problem resolves itself, then, into how to find material that is of a suitable level of difficulty and is as appealing as possible to a child of more mature age.

An increasingly large number of books suitable for remedial work are being developed. There are those books that are primarily designed for the less capable reader. They include such useful books as *The Cowboy Sam*

Series(5), *The Deep-Sea Adventure Series*(7), *Everyreader Series*(8), *The Morgan Bay Mysteries*(13), and *Interesting Reading Series*(9).

There has been an increase, happily, in the amount of published material designed to give effective aid in developing the skills of disabled readers who are diagnosed as having specific instructional needs. Such materials as are found in *The Macmillan Reading Spectrum*(11), *Classroom Reading Clinic*(4), and *The S.R.A. Reading Laboratories*(18) are suitable for correcting some of the deficiencies in skills of disabled readers.

Phonetically regular materials and certain word-recognition skill books are useful for children who are found to be unable to progress at a normal pace toward satisfactory proficiency in word recognition. Such series as *Phonetic Reader Series*(14), *Breaking the Sound Barrier*(16), *Eye and Ear Fun*(19), and *Phonics We Use*(12) will prove helpful in this respect when used judiciously.

A new type of material that appears to have merit for use with disabled readers is programmed learning material. An example of reading exercise material of this kind is *Programmed Reading*(20). Other organized learning programs should be forthcoming shortly.

Basic reading programs are being developed that have parallel readers, such as the Regular and Classmate Editions of the *Developmental Reading Series*(2). In this series of readers, there are two editions which are alike in all important respects. They have the same covers, the same titles, pictures, content, and interest level. The difference lies in the fact that the *Classmate Edition* is written with a smaller vocabulary load, shorter paragraphs, simpler sentences, and fewer words per page. The classmate editions are considerably easier in reading difficulty than are the regular editions. The sixth-grade book in the regular edition requires sixth-grade reading ability, whereas the same stories can be read in the classmate edition by children who have only third-grade reading ability.

The workbooks that accompany basic readers are also suitable material. The workbooks look considerably more mature than the basic readers they accompany. The pictures are in black and white. The drill exercises give no indication of the maturity level of the children who are expected to read them. There are many lists of books that are suitable for use in remedial work. Many of these lists indicate the level of reading maturity which is required to read the books and also indicate the maximum age of a child who will enjoy reading the material.

THE MATERIALS MUST BE ABUNDANT

In selecting material for remedial work, the first and most important consideration is that it must be of the proper level of difficulty. The second is that it should be appropriate in type. The third is that it should be interesting in format and meet the interest level of the child. Another consideration in securing materials to be used in remedial reading is that they should be abundant. There should be a wide variety of material meeting many interests and at various levels of difficulty. For any one child, there should be ample material suitable for him to read. There should be material for his remedial instruction and also material for his independent reading. The independent reading for a remedial reading case should be considerably easier than that used in giving him remedial instruction. The material for independent reading needs to be on a wide variety of topics because the children will have a wide variety of interests. The material that the child is to read independently should fulfill an existing interest which the child already has, while the material that is used for instructional purposes must be such that he can be motivated to take an interest in reading.

Sound Teaching Procedures
Must Be Employed

During the entire discussion of principles for treatment of reading difficulties, it has been implied that remedial instruction is the application of sound teaching procedures directed toward the specific needs of the child. Instruction in remedial reading is not unusual in character nor is it necessary to use expensive and artificial equipment. The skills and abilities should be emphasized in actual reading situations free from isolated drill. Sound teaching procedures such as those used for introducing the reading skills and abilities in the first place should be used. The materials best suited to remedial instruction are those that are best for the developmental program.

The difference between remedial instruction and the developmental program is in the extent of individualization and in the study of the child rather than in the uniqueness of the methods or materials it employs. There are certain principles of reading instruction that are sometimes neglected in remedial work. Readiness should be carefully built for every topic and every selection to be read by the disabled reader. This includes the creation of interest in, the development of background for, and the introduction of new words for each selection the child reads. The child who is in difficulty in reading, just as much as other children who are not, should have the purposes for reading well understood before the reading is done. He should also use the results of his reading in a creative enterprise of one sort or another. If, for example, he has read a selection about flood control to find what techniques are used, it would be important for him to make a diagram of a river bed illustrating what he had learned, just as it would be for children in the developmental reading program. Seeing that children use the results of their reading is a good procedure for all children. It becomes an essential practice, though an often neglected one, for children who are in difficulty in reading. The form of use to which the results of reading are put may be a discussion, a picture drawn, a chart made, a map planned, or any one of many such enterprises. The relative amount of time devoted to these things should be small, however, and above all, the creative work should be the child's own.

Consideration must be given to the learning environment of the child both in and out of school. Whether the remedial work is done in the classroom, the school reading center, or the clinic, only a small segment of the child's reading is done during the corrective lessons. If the remedial program is to be successful, the rest of the child's reading day must be adjusted to his needs and reading capabilities. The effective work of the remedial periods can be destroyed if unfortunate demands or pressures are placed upon the child either in school or at home. As has been stated earlier, both the classroom teacher and the parents will be willing to cooperate if they are given an understanding of the child's reading problem. The parents are often endeavoring to help the child with his reading, and this is as it should be, but the remedial teacher should consult with them so that their work will be of the greatest benefit to the child. Bond and Wagner(3) show many ways in which parents can help a child to grow in reading.

The remedial teacher will find it helpful to keep a cumulative account of the child's progress. The record should include the books read; the type of exercises used, and the success of each; any charts used to show the child his progress; and the results of periodic tests. In this connection, any indications of fields of interests and anecdotal accounts of the child's reactions to the remedial program will be a help. By studying this record, the teacher can compare periods of rapid growth with the type of exercises used and books read at those times. A study of past records will recall to the teacher those approaches that were successful with other similar cases. The teacher can assemble a file of such folders, arranged according to the specific problem involved.

A Carefully Designed Follow-up
Program Is Necessary

When the child has made progress sufficiently to permit his release from the concentrated remedial program, he should gradually be put into situations where he must rely to an increasing extent on his own resources. All such children should be carefully followed up by the classroom teacher.

For many, continued reinforcements by means of further remedial help are most important. In a study of the long-term effects of remedial reading instruction, Balow(1) found that continued remedial training, amounting to long-term treatment rather than a short-course program, is desirable. He concludes that concentrated remedial work gives remarkable results, but that "severe reading disability is probably best considered a relatively chronic illness needing long-term treatment rather than the short course typically organized in current programs."

Many of the children with less severe reading difficulties may be able to make the adjustment into regular classroom work. Even these children may become discouraged again if their work does not go well after they finish remedial instruction. Any indications of loss of interest or of confusions in learning should get immediate attention by the classroom teacher during the readjustment period.

Summary

Although the remedial work for each disabled reader must be different in certain respects, there are some common elements among the corrective programs. The remedial program must be designed to emphasize the child's instructional needs as shown by the diagnosis, and therefore there can be no universal approach in all cases. The remedial program for each reading case must be carefully planned and what is to be done should be written down. It will be necessary to modify the program from time to time in order to keep abreast of the child's changing instructional needs. Even though the program is well planned to give emphasis on overcoming a specific disability, a variety of remedial techniques should be used. The remedial teacher will find manuals and workbooks that accompany basal reading programs the most fruitful source of teaching techniques.

Remedial reading programs must be highly individualized and they must be designed in keeping with the child's instructional needs and characteristics. It is necessary to modify the approaches to reading in order to adjust to such limitations as poor hearing or poor vision. Remedial instruction should not drill upon one specific skill or ability in isolation, but should provide new experience in whatever skills are needed in connection with purposeful reading. The length of remedial sessions should be so planned that the child will not become fatigued or inattentive.

Reading instruction for the disabled reader must be well organized in order that skills and abilities may be developed smoothly with no undue burden for the child, with little chance for overemphasis, and with no omissions of essential learnings. The teacher should not only maintain an orderly sequence of skill development, but also should make the steps involved meaningful to the child.

The remedial reading program must be encouraging to the child since much of his trouble arose because he had lost confidence in his ability to learn. The teacher should be optimistic; the child's successes should be emphasized; and his progress should be demonstrated to him. Materials must be suitable to the child's reading abilities and instructional needs; they should be suitable in level of difficulty and type of content; they should be as nearly as possible appropriate in level of interest; and they should look "mature" to the child. The materials used for remedial instruction must be of such difficulty that the child can read them and of such maturity that he will be motivated to read them. There can be no compromise with the difficulty level of the material because the child will not be interested in reading material he cannot read, no matter how attractive the subject matter. In all remedial work, sound teaching procedures should be used and artificial devices and isolated drill should be avoided.

SELECTED READINGS

Blair, G. M., *Diagnostic and remedial teaching,* rev. ed. New York: Macmillan, 1956, Chap. 4.

Bond, G. L., and Wagner, E. B., *Child growth in reading.* Chicago: Lyons & Carnahan, 1955, Chap. 11.

Bond, G. L., and Wagner, E. B., *Teaching the child to read,* 4th ed. New York: Macmillan, 1966, Chap. 16.

Brueckner, L. J., and Bond, G. L., *Diagnosis and treatment of learning difficulties.* New York: Appleton-Century-Crofts, 1955, Chap. 5.

Durrell, Donald D., *Improving reading instruction.* New York: Harcourt, Brace & World, 1956, Chap. 14.

Gates, Arthur I., *The improvement of reading,* 3rd ed. New York: Macmillan, 1947, Chap. 5.

Harris, Albert J., *How to increase reading ability,* 4th ed. New York: Longmans, 1961, Chap. 11.

Kottmeyer, William, *Teacher's guide for remedial reading.* St Louis: Webster, 1959.

Tinker, Miles A., and McCullough, C. M., *Teaching elementary reading,* 2nd ed. New York: Appleton-Century-Crofts, 1962, Chap. 12.

REFERENCES

1. Balow, B. "The Long-Term Effect of Remedial Reading Instruction," *The Reading Teacher,* Volume 18, (April, 1965), pp. 581–586.
2. Bond, G. L., and M. C. Cuddy. *The Developmental Reading Series,* (Regular and Classmate Editions.) Chicago: Lyons & Carnahan, 1962.
3. Bond, G. L., and E. B. Wagner. *Child Growth in Reading.* Chicago: Lyons & Carnahan, 1955.

4. *Classroom Reading Clinic.*
5. *The Cowboy Sam Series.* Chicago: Beckley-Cardy, 1951.
6. Dale, Edgar, and Jeanne Chall. "Formula for Predicting Readability," *Educational Research Bulletin, 27.* Ohio State University, Columbus. January–February, 1948, pp. 11–20 and 37–45.
7. *The Deep-Sea Adventure Series.* San Francisco: Harr Wagner, 1959.
8. *Everyreader Series.* St. Louis: Webster, 1962.
9. *Interesting Reading Series.* Chicago: Follett, 1961.
10. Lorge, Irving. "Predicting Readability," *Teachers College Record,* 45, (March, 1944), pp. 404–419.
11. *The Macmillan Reading Spectrum.* New York: Macmillan, 1964.
12. Meighen, Mary, and Marjorie Pratt. *Phonics We Use.* Chicago: Lyons & Carnahan, 1948.
13. *The Morgan Bay Mysteries.* San Francisco: Harr Wagner, 1962.
14. *Phonetic Reader Series.* Cambridge, Massachusetts: Educators Publishing Service, 1962.
15. Russell, D. H., and E. E. Karp. *Reading Aids through the Grades, Revised Edition.* New York: Bureau of Publications, Teachers College, Columbia versity, 1951.
16. Sister Mary Caroline. *Breaking the Sound Barrier.* New York: Macmillan, 1960.
17. Spache, George. "A New Readability Formula for Primary-Grade Reading," *Elementary School Journal,* 52 (March, 1953), pp. 410–413.
18. *SRA Reading Laboratories.* Chicago: Science Research Associates, 1961.
19. Stone, C. R. *Eye and Ear Fun.* St. Louis: Webster, 1943.
20. Sullivan Associates. *The Programmed Reading Series.* New York: McGraw-Hill, 1963.
21. Watkins, M. *A Comparison of the Reading Proficiencies of Normal-Progress and Reading Disability Cases of the Same I.Q. and Reading Level.* Unpublished PH.D. thesis, University of Minnesota, Minneapolis, 1953.

Index